MOTO-CROSS
THE GOLDEN ERA

Paul Stephens

MOTO-CROSS
THE GOLDEN ERA

DEDICATION
To Cecil and Roy Lane, who introduced me to the motorcycle.

First published in 1998 by Osprey Publishing, Michelin House, 81 Fulham Road, London SW3 6RB

© Text Paul Stephens

Editor: Shaun Barrington
Design: the Black spot

All rights reserved. Apart from any fair dealing for the purpose of private study, research, criticism or review, as permitted under the Copyright, Design and Patents Act, 1988, no part of this publication may be reproduced, stored in a retrieval system or transmitted in any form or by any means, electronic, electrical, chemical, mechanical, optical, photocopying, recording or otherwise, without prior written permission. All enquiries should be addressed to the publisher.

Jacket photographs:
Front **Don Rickman, British 500cc Grand Prix, 1966. Photograph by Nick Nicholls.**
Front flap **1963 Hants Grand National at Matcham's Park, Ringwood. BSA factory trio Arthur Lampkin (42) John Burton (43) on his red-painted Gold Star, and eventual winner Jeff Smith (41). Photograph by Gordon Francis.**
Back of jacket, clockwise from top left **Arthur Lampkin, 1966 500cc British GP, Farleigh Castle. As a reminder that moto-cross didn't disappear at the end of the 1960s, as this book may imply! – and to whet the appetite for Volume 2 – John Banks, 1975, 500cc CCM and Vic Eastwood at Newbury in 1977. Jeff Smith at Halstead in June 1968. (All pictures Nick Nicholls). John Harris at Winchester Club's BBC Grandstand scramble, Morestead Down, 1964. Photograph by Gordon Francis.**

Half title page **Thirsty work: Dave Curtis takes a well earned drink after winning the Britsh 500cc Grand Prix in 1961.**

Title page **Alan Clough hustles his DOT through a right-hand bend during the Brian Stonebridge Memorial Scramble at Hawkstone Park in March 1960.**

Right **Swedish Powerhouse. The mighty Bill Nilsson glides the mighty Husqvarna to an emphatic victory in the British 500cc Grand Prix at Hawkstone Park in 1960; the year he won the world title for a second time.**

For a free catalogue of all books published by Osprey, please write to:

The Marketing Manager, Osprey Publishing Ltd, P. O. Box 140, Wellingborough, Northants NN8 4ZA

FOREWORD
by Jeff Smith

I find a certain amount of satisfaction from the title of this book. While it was 1950 before I rode in my first scramble, the years cover the most successful period of my career and it's comforting to know that it was The Golden Era.

Until 1955 my major interest was in trials. Looking back it's clear that trials provided the perfect training ground for anyone who wanted to learn about the vagaries of off-road surfaces. I learned quickly, and at no great risk to my well-being, what happened on wet or dry surfaces, cambered climbs, in ruts or stream crossings, and so on. Things happen slowly in trials. The worst punishment you could expect would be to pick up your fallen bike. A similar error on a 400lb (177Kg) scrambler could be dramatic and painful.

By 1955, two points became crystal clear to me. Firstly, in trials we were professional riders at the mercy of amateur observers. Often there were strange discrepancies between the marks we thought we had lost and those recorded. The second, that in scrambling—or moto-cross as it became more widely known—there was rarely any doubt where one finished or why. I liked the finality of the result in moto-cross, and the thrill of racing. The pay was also better. The stimulation of stalking another competitor seemed to satisfy some primeval urge; let's call it the hunter instinct. Beyond that was the beauty of the process. There is a poetry to travelling fast and accurately on two wheels over rough ground.

Once I had turned to moto-cross, I became more engrossed by its challenge. I had served a five-year apprenticeship at BSA, so I enjoyed the mechanical side and the preparation of motorcycles. Eventually I was able to move from mere preparation to new concepts in harness with BSA's most successful competitions manager, Brian Martin. He was a friend and guiding-light throughout my career and, 30 years later, Brian and I remain good friends.

Something else became obvious as I added the years. If I was to put into action the vision I had of how to win races, a training regime would be necessary. So I began to train very hard. Each weekday, when not travelling, I trained for 45 minutes during the lunch break. I ran for three or four miles, did endurance work and lifted weights. In this I was helped by an Olympic Silver Medal steeplechaser, Maurice Herriott, who worked at BSA. The training paid handsome dividends and extended my useful racing life well past my 30th birthday, allowing me to take advantage of the experience I had accumulated and improving machinery.

My race theory was simple. The logical approach to moto-cross was to win races at the slowest possible speed. This would conserve the machine and my energy. This method is the opposite to the one adopted by most riders. The general tendency has been to race hard from the start to the chequered flag. But this plan is fraught with many dangers. The machine may become damaged or the rider tire, and so make some calamitous mistake. The perfect race would be one in which you follow the rider who will finish second and pass him on the final lap.

What were those golden years like? A network of motorways had yet to be developed throughout Europe, and our journeys in a Dormobile van, with a maximum downhill speed of 70mph, were tortuous and hard. The bikes for every grand prix went separately by truck, so the van was crowded with humanity—Brian Stonebridge, John Draper, Phil Nex, Geoff Ward—with me as the junior member of the team, doing the driving. When it was time to let someone else take over the controls, we had

worked out a system of changing drivers without stopping or even slowing. Looking back on how dangerous it was, it's amazing the whole BSA team wasn't wiped out during one of these manoeuvres.

We ate like kings on a Sunday night after a grand prix, when the business was done and the tension over. We sat alongside our fellow competitors from Sweden, Holland, France, Italy and Belgium. We joked in that curious paddock tongue which uses words from many languages. But we all understood. The talk may have centred on the day's racing, or the route to the next event. Whatever, it was good humoured and friendly. There was very little carping or whining in those carefree days. How tremendously enjoyable it all was.

Racing against heroes, riders I had read about, and occasionally beating them, gave me a great buzz. Names which leap off the pages of this book – August Mingels, Victor Leloup, Bill Nilsson, John Draper, Les Archer – I learned much from them all, for I had ample opportunity to follow and observe. Slowly they left the stage to be replaced by men more my own age: Dave Curtis, Rene Baeten, Sten Lundin, Rolf Tibblin, the Rickman brothers. After them came a younger group again: Arthur Lampkin, Dave Bickers, Paul Friedrichs, Joel Robert, John Banks and Vic Eastwood. All great competitors. All part of the golden tapestry.

Great fun though racing is, the best part is winning. To have been a member of such wonderful Moto-Cross des Nations teams is more satisfying now than it was then. In some years I rode in 50 or more events, racing so frequently there was little time to savour success, before it was down to the business of preparing for the next grand prix. The size of the crowds for some World Championship rounds in those years has never been surpassed. How encouraging it was to have 40,000 partisan enthusiasts willing you on at Hawkstone Park. The largest audiences of all were for the BBC's Grandstand series. Throughout Britain people knew of our exploits, and even today folk recall certain events from the televised tournament.

What great days they were. I have thoroughly enjoyed Paul Stephens' book and, as you can tell from my musings, it has touched a nostalgic nerve. The wealth of information, the photographs and the narrative has given me endless pleasure, as it will for countless other fans of The Golden Era.

Jeff Smith
Wausau, Wisconsin
United States of America

Left **Jeff Smith hurtles over a muddy hilltop at Cassel, in northern France, during the 1960 Moto-Cross des Nations, when Great Britain won by virtue of being the only team to qualify for the final.**

INTRODUCTION

MOTO-CROSS, THE GOLDEN ERA has been in my head for much longer than I care to remember. At first I thought it might be worthwhile to write a history of The British Moto-Cross Grand Prix. After all this race meeting was the high point of the domestic season. It was a commemoration of everything best about the sport in Britain and was an important shop window for the home motorcycle industry; and yet had never been properly documented. When I considered all the reasons why a record of this single contest should be committed to print, it left any number of questions unanswered. Why just the British Grand Prix? Why not write about the trade-supported events which led to a national championship, the growth of moto-cross as a pan-European sport, the movement which gave rise to the establishment of the World Championships, and the influence of television on moto-cross in the United Kingdom?

This led me back to my childhood, or at least my youth, when nearly all organised sport was played on Saturdays. Moto-cross, or scrambling as it was then known, was different from most other activities because it conducted itself almost exclusively on Sundays. Not that this indicated any heathen tendency. While it is not any purpose of this book to consider the religious convictions of moto-cross devotees, it is a fair bet that if any of them believed in reincarnation, then a return to earth would be to relive that cherished 25-year period from the end of the Second World War to 1970. Now what a seductive idea that is; for it was in every sense a golden era.

The memory needs stretching almost to breaking point to recall the mid-1950s when

Typical weekend scene, when moto-cross was at the height of its popularity. Chris Horsfield (6) leads the field on his CZ from Alan Clough (Greeves, 20), Dave Bickers (CZ, 1), Bryan Wade (Greeves, 27), and Bryan Goss (Greeves, 2) in a BBC Grandstand Trophy 250cc race at Leighton, Frome, in 1966. Television was to make household names of them all.

Murray Walker is flanked by Geoff Ward (left) and Dave Curtis before the Brian Stonebridge Scramble at Hawkstone Park in 1960. Curtis was the eventual winner. The irrepressible Murray Walker, who made his name as a radio and television commentator, was a keen competitor and competent enough to win a Gold Medal in the International Six Days Trial in 1949. His love of motorcycle sport is perhaps not well known, associated as he is for all time with F1 cars. But his father Graham starred for Norton in innumerable trials, sprints and hillclimbs, and the Isle of Man TT; which is why Murray kindly wrote the foreword to *Norton: A History* (Osprey, 1992).

there were more than 20 motorcycle manufacturers in England exporting throughout the world; 10 of them—including names like BSA, Triumph, Royal Enfield, Velocette, James and Francis-Barnett—were located in the midlands. Some 15 British constructors of sidecars exhibited at the International Cycle & Motorcycle Show at Earls Court in 1955. It was a golden era for the makers of motorcycles and accessories, as well as those who rode them in competition. Even the foreign stars—like police forces across the globe—bought British in those days.

With many of the manufacturers offering bikes designed specifically for use in trials and scrambles, it was perhaps no wonder that those sports evolved in the way they did. As interest in them grew, so too did the number of enthusiasts who took part. In no time Britain had uncovered a group of riders capable of competing on equal terms with any in the developed world. In a glittering epoch, which endured until the home industry itself went into meltdown, Great Britain won the Moto-Cross des Nations 15 times in 21 years. John Draper, Les Archer and Dave Bickers were European champions. Jeff Smith was twice world 500cc champion.

The title winners, along with Brian Stonebridge, Arthur Lampkin, Geoff Ward, Dave Curtis the Rickman brothers, John Banks, John Burton and Vic Eastwood, comprised the Crown Jewels of British moto-cross. And there was a galaxy of minor stars like Alan Clough, Malcolm Davis, Phil Nex, Brian Martin, David Tye, Chris Horsfield, Dave Nicoll and Jerry Scott who twinkled away in this glamorous period. Not to mention those like Fred Rist, Bill Nicholson, Harold Lines, Hugh Viney and Basil Hall, among the many who had arrived at the firmament's edge like meteors, and blazed a trail for others to follow.

For a quarter of a century the sport throughout Britain enjoyed exceptional popularity. Attendances at centre scrambles could often be numbered well into the thousands; tens of thousands if two or three of the big names were riding.

The trade-supported events drew very big crowds; at the British Grand Prix they were even bigger. This enthusiasm led to the inauguration of a vibrant British Championship and

Above **Harold Lines leads the Belgian Grand Prix on his Ariel, at Namur in 1949, with Auguste Mingels (FN, 28), André Milhoux (BSA, 15), and Nic Jansen (Saroléa, 1) in closest pursuit.**

the inevitable evolution of both European and World Championships.

Until I began my research, no one had attempted to draw all these strands together to complete an account of the sport's development, together with a complementary record of results. The very early years was almost uncharted territory, and surprisingly little survives which can be relied upon. Though thanks to the help I received from so many, almost everything which could has come under my scrutiny. So the results section at the rear of the book is as accurate as can be, given the indifferent quality of some source material.

The story of those summers, when motocross blossomed into a meaningful activity out of fairly undistinguished beginnings, is not unlike those charting other forms of motor and motorcycle sport. Because it involved so much British success – for the makers of motorcycles as well as the riders – it is an intoxicating tale for Brits such as myself (Though I hope simply the inclusion of so many marvellous makes provides interest to an international audience).

The story is all the more compelling for having a melancholy, largely unforeseen ending. Preserving illusions of supremacy is a game the British have played for generations. While British riders and machines were supreme, the illusion took a firm hold.

That domination couldn't last of course, nor was it to. During the time it did, there were no misgivings. For this was The Golden Era of Moto-Cross.

Paul Stephens
Bishop Monkton, North Yorkshire
Autumn 1998

Left **Sweden's Lars Gustafsson hurries his Monark around the packed enclosures of Hawkstone Park in 1958, to become the first overseas rider to win the British 500cc Grand Prix.**

ACKNOWLEDGEMENTS

No author, however knowledgeable about a subject, can write a book such as this without the very considerable help of others. In the first place one needs an understanding publisher and the encouragement of an enthusiastic editor. I am fortunate in having both. Nicholas Collins was my first editor at Osprey, before handing on to Shaun Barrington. Without Shaun's patience and understanding, my project would not have reached print.

I use the word 'project', for that has what it has been. During the early days when I began the research, I was grateful for the help I received from Norman Vanhouse, who provided me with masses of information and results from the immediate post-war period. Ralph Venables read the opening chapters and he imparted some sound advice. So, too, did the late Brian Woolley, associate editor of The Classic Motor Cycle, who led me round the EMAP archives when they were located at Peterborough. Once they were moved to a smart new home at Kettering, Richard Rosenthal – the EMAP archivist – and his assistant Jan Branaghan, were enormously helpful.

As the book began to take shape, I was grateful for the hours spent by those riders who were interested in contributing towards a pictorial history of moto-cross. Whether by letter, on the telephone, or during interview, I have every reason to be thankful for the reminiscences of Les Archer, John Draper, Dave Curtis, Geoff Ward, Don and Derek Rickman, Dave Bickers, John Banks, Harold Lines, Eric Cheney, John Avery, Rolf Tibblin, Joel Robert, and Vic Eastwood, who all gave freely of their time. As did Jeff Smith – whose foreword is a most welcome reminder of The Golden Era – and whose contribution to those glorious days will never be forgotten.

The bulk of the photographs were provided by Bill Cole, Malcolm Carling, Mick Walker, Cecil Bailey, Gordon Francis and Nick Nicholls – who also offered much help and useful information, especially about the 1950s – while I received valuable assistance and support from Bob Light, Rob Carrick, Tom Sawyers, Volker Zogel, Phil Hingston, Richard Wirix, Bob Miles, Robin Strickland, Phil Perryman, the late Denis Parkinson, and John Bussell, among many others who sent me old press reports, photographs, programmes and volunteered to lend a hand.

Chantal Geoffroy and Danielle Rasmo were painstaking in their search for results in the depths of the records department at the FIM in Geneva. Brian Newbury loaned the programmes from the British Grand Prix, and George Clempson the programme from the Brian Stonebridge Memorial Scramble. I am in debt to them all. As I am to Helen Cooper who processed the results section at the rear of the book and to Shona Walker who waded through my handwritten manuscript covering the years between 1952 and 1967. Without Shona's help in particular, this book might never have been started.

PHOTOGRAPH ACKNOWLEDGEMENTS

Nick Nicholls: 1, 2, 4, 7, 9, 11, 57, 58, 60, 61, 63, 64, 66, 67, 69 bottom, 73, 74, 75, 76, 77, 81, 82, 84, 85, 86, 87, 88, 89, 90, 92, 93, 95, 96, 97, 98, 99, 102, 103, 104, 105, 111, 113, 116 bottom, 121, 122, 123, 124, 125, 126 top, 128, 129, 130, 136, 137, 138, 140, 142 top left, 143 top right, 144, 145, 146, 154, 155, 156, 157, 159, 160, 161, 162, 163, 164, 165, 166, 167, 168, 169, 171, 172 top, 173, 175, 176 top, 177, 179, 182, 183,185.

EMAP Archives: 31, 32, 44, 51, 52, 116 top, 172 bottom, 174.

Gordon Francis: 7, 8, 50, 68, 69 top, 70 top, 72, 80, 91, 94, 108, 109 below, 110 top, 112 below, 114, 115 top, 117, 119, 132 top.

Bill Cole: 12, 13, 14, 15 top, 16, 17, 18, 19, 21, 22, 23, 24, 26, 27, 28, 29, 35, 37, 40, 46 top, 62 right.

Malcolm Carling: 101, 110 below, 132 below, 133, 134, 142 centre, 150, 153, 180.

Harold Lines: 10, 15 bottom, 16 top, 20.

Cecil Bailey: 78 top, 79, 106 below, 107, 115 bottom, 143 top left, 148, 151, 184.

Mick Walker Archives: 36, 38, 41, 48, 49, 54, 55, 70 below, 71, 78 below, 100, 106 above, 109 above, 112 top, 126 below, 131, 141, 152, 158, 176 below, 178.

1945-51

FRED RIST and BILL NICHOLSON dominate the major domestic events for BSA, as the sport struggles back to its feet after the war years. Nicholson, Rist and Bob Ray win the first Moto-Cross des Nations, held at Duinrell, Holland. Geoff Ward wins the inaugural British Championship for AJS. Brian Stonebridge, John Draper, Les Archer and John Avery are fully established.

No two riders wore the colours of the Birmingham Small Arms company with greater distinction in the months following the end of the Second World War, than Fred Rist and Bill Nicholson. While BSA did not rely solely on Rist and Nicholson for their competition successes in this period, had they staged a parade of riders who had won important trials and races on BSA machinery, Rist and Nicholson would have been marching at its head.

In the years since the first authentic scramble was organised by the Camberley & District Motor Club in 1924, the motorcycle manufacturers, eager for the publicity which flowed from competition achievements, concentrated on road racing and trials. In the pre-war days—and, beyond question, for some while after the cessation of hostilities—the most prized victories were those demanding stamina to acquire them. For stamina equated with reliability. What engineering sophistication or subtlety built into motorcycles of that era or, for that matter what passed for style, was third, fourth and fifth to strength and reliability.

To demonstrate that their product possessed these essential qualities, any motorcycle manufacturer proud of the badge on the petrol tank, was obliged to show the consumer that their machinery was able to pass the stiffest examination. This meant succeeding in the long-distance classics such as the Scottish Six Days Trial or the International Six Days Trial. Next in importance was the Scott Trial, a gruelling event decided on time

and observation, run across the rough moorland of north Yorkshire. It was in this daunting endurance test where Fred Rist first came to prominence.

Reared in the foothills of those windswept heaths, on his parents' poultry farm at Stokesley, near Middlesborough, Rist became the quintessential all-rounder. Born in 1916, Rist was 22 when he entered his first motorcycle competition—the 1938 ISDT, held that year in Wales—while he was a serving soldier in the Second Battalion Royal Tank Corps. Rist was one of 13 British riders, from a multi-national entry of 200 who won a Gold Medal. The other 21 who did so were foreign competitors. Two months later, Rist made the second best performance on observation in the Scott, in which he finished third overall, despite his B25 350cc BSA throwing its chain on three occasions.

Well before the onset of war, Bert Perrigo, who had joined BSA in 1926—and won innumerable trials for the factory as well as six ISDT Gold Medals, before becoming competitions manager in a career which ran until 1968 for the Birmingham concern—recognised the need for new blood. In Rist, Perrigo had discovered a star. Had it not been for the outbreak of war, Rist would have undoubtably shone for so much longer. Even with a six-year break, he did much to ensure that BSA were always ahead of their rivals in the contest to be regarded as the maker of the best-built and most successful off-road motorcycles.

While it is only possible to speculate what Fred Rist may have accomplished, but for the interruption of war to his burgeoning reputation, Rist was soon joined at BSA by the Belfast-born, Bill Nicholson, who went on to achieve even greater things than Rist. What a pair they made.

It is as true of motorcycle racing and trials as it is of other sports, that exceptional talent almost always announces itself early. And yet Rist and Nicholson were each in their twenties before they began competing, and almost 30 before they were able to make their indelible marks on motorcycling's sporting landscape. Nicholson, born a year after Rist, did not sit on a motorcycle until 1939, when he first met the

road racer and Tourist Trophy winner Artie Bell.

Motorcycling had experienced almost continuous growth in popularity during the inter-war years, which led to the formation of many new clubs and a boom in sporting competitions. This gave rise to a classification of events into those for which only members in the same club, or centre, affiliated to the Auto-Cycle Union, would be eligible. The largest events were granted a national permit, and were open to all holders of a valid ACU competitions licence. It was these which the motorcycle manufacturers employed for publicity. Realising it was only practicable to give their backing to so many national contests, the manufacturers agreed among themselves which they would nominate as trade-supported events.

By 1947 there were 15 trade-supported national trials, though never anything like that number of scrambles. Eventually only four or five enjoyed endorsement from the factories, and these glamour scrambles formed the core of what was to become the British Moto-Cross Championship. In 1946 only two received trade support; the Cotswold in June and the Lancashire Grand National in November.

The Stroud Valley Motor Club's Cotswold Scramble was one of the great events in the

Below, left **Eddie Bessant (Matchless, 10), who was the runner-up, and Bill Nicholson (BSA, 32) relax in the winners enclosure after the Junior race of the Cotswold Scramble in 1947. Nicholson completed a Senior-Junior double over the Nympsfield course that season, as he had the previous year, and was to do so again in 1949. Right, in braces, is Cyril Halliburn of BSA who had every reason to smile.**

Left **A rare shot of Bill Nicholson putting a foot down, as a youthful John Draper gives chase over the Experts' Grand National course at Berrow Hill Farm, Feckenham, near Droitwich, in 1948.**

Above **Geoff Duke, riding a 500cc Norton, tackles a steep incline at Ashgrove, near Cheltenham. Better known for his achievements as a road racer, Duke—with a hat-trick of victories in the Senior TT, and six world titles – was an accomplished scrambler and could count a fourth place in the final of the 1948 Moto-Cross des Nations as his best off-road finish. Though he also took third place in the Senior race at the Sunbeam Point-to-Point that spring, and was regularly in the silverware at the Lancashire Grand National.**

Right **John Avery in the 1948 Cotswold Scramble riding his B21 BSA 250cc trials bike. Bill Nicholson lifted the Stroud Cup that season. But Avery went on to win the Lightweight race at Nympsfield classic two years later, and again in 1953 and 1954.**

British calendar. First run in 1934, it was eight years younger than the Lancashire Grand National, and though a true test for bike and rider it did not hold quite the same terrors as those remarkable endurance examinations over Holcombe Moor.

Nicholson dominated the Cotswold, winning the Junior and Senior races on his McCandless-sprung 350cc BSA, almost as he pleased. In the Junior he was comfortably ahead of Jack Williams' Norton, with the BSA of Ray Scovell in third place. In the Senior, Rist pushed Nicholson hard until he was slowed by a deflating rear tyre. Though unable to catch Nicholson, Rist still had sufficient in hand to keep Scovell at bay.

No one was capable of keeping Fred Rist at bay in the Lancashire Grand National. Holcombe Moor was not available after the war until 1948, so a new course was used at Close Barn Farm, between Rochdale and Bury, which incorporated many of the dreads of Holcombe. But Rist was immune to them and he was an easy winner from Williams, with Bob Foster third on his AJS. Nicholson was fifth.

Bill Nicholson completed his campaign by winning the Scott, to leave no one in any doubt that he and Fred Rist had been the men to beat in 1946. It would be much the same the year after.

INTERNATIONAL ORGANISATION

By the time the 1947 season got underway, 18 months had passed since the war had ended. Even so there had not been time for motorcycle sport to regather itself completely. Bear in mind, there was no manifesto for moto-cross in Europe. Unlike Speedway, which grew up in the United States in the 1920s, there were no promoters, any more than there was a proper structure. The sport relied exclusively on unpaid volunteers for the core of its disparate organisation and, until 1951, there would be no British Championship. There was a number of major events which the factories and the leading riders concentrated on and, by the end of the summer, there was the prospect of some meaningful international competition.

Before this mouthwatering opportunity could be realised, Fred Rist and Bill Nicholson set about the new season with all the relish they had ended the previous one. The Ringwood Motor Cycle & Light Car Club had established their Avon Castle track between the wars and the Hampshire Grand National

was to become one of the biggest events of the era. On Good Friday 1947 Fred Rist treated a bumper crowd to a fine exhibition of riding. He easily won the Junior Race – then for machines with a capacity of 250cc – beating Les Archer's Velocette into second place. In the eight-lap Senior Final, Jack Stocker's Ariel made the early running, but Rist eventually prevailed, with Stocker second and the BSA of Ray Scovell third. Thereafter, Rist had to play second fiddle to Nicholson, who won almost everything. This included the other big south-coast event, the trade-supported Sunbeam Point-to-Point making a welcome first appearance on the fixture list, where he won the Junior from Rist, the Senior from Stocker.

Left **Basil Hall (left), Harold Lines (centre), and Geoff Duke, wearing his wartime battle dress, after an international event at Eupen, Belgium, in 1949.**

Below left **Harold Lines, in his Union Jack vest, surrounded by well-wishers after an international meeting at Montreuil, near Paris, in 1949. Belgium's Victor Leloup – with the laurel wreath on the handlebars of his FN – is almost engulfed by those wishing to get in on the action.**

Right **Harold Lines** negotiates a safe landing for his Ariel during the 1949 Moto-Cross des Nations at Brands Hatch. Lines was runner-up to Belgium's Nic Jansen in the second 12-lap heat, but turned the tables on the Saroléa rider in the 15-lap final, to help Great Britain to victory in the coveted team contest.

Below **Fred Rist** brings his 250cc BSA to earth with a thump in the Lightweight race at the 1949 Cotswold Scramble, in which he finished second to Hugh Viney's AJS.

In the Cotswold, Nicholson was the master of both the Junior and Senior races, just as he had been the previous year. But on a blissfully sunny afternoon at Nympsfield there were sure signs of the emergence of crop of talented riders, some of whom – like the trials specialist Hugh Viney, and John Avery – would go on to be scrambles stars in their own right. Rist had a troublesome day, finishing ninth in the Junior, unplaced in the Senior, and with a sheared engine-sprocket key in the lightweight. Nicholson completed the year by taking the Lancashire Grand National, Rist the runner-up, and adding a second successive Scott Trial victory to his growing list of accomplishments.

While these individual triumphs were sufficient to ensure that Bill Nicholson's name would be gold leafed on any honours board erected to venerate the greats of the sport Nicholson, along with Rist and Bob Ray, made history by becoming the first winners of the international team contest, the Moto-Cross des Nations.

The Dutch Federation – Koninklijke Nederlandse Motorrijders Vereniging, to give the organisers their full name, or KNMV for short – decided it would be a good idea to have a competition for teams from interested countries, and this was held for the first time at Duinrell, a heavily-wooded estate on the outskirts of The Hague, the administrative capital of Holland. Only three nations: the host country, Belgium and Great Britain accepted an invitation to compete.

The method of running the event was unusual and untried, though exact enough to produce a clear winner. There were two separate races, each over eight laps of the two-mile circuit, and team members and reserves took part in both. Each rider's times for the two heats were added together and a total for each team was produced by taking the three best aggregate times. The Great Britain A team comprised Nicholson, Rist, and Ray Scovell all riding 500cc BSAs, with Jack Stocker and Bob Ray both on 497cc Ariels. The fastest three combined times produced by this quintet were those posted by Nicholson, Rist and Ray, who beat the Belgium B team by just nine seconds.

Quite apart from the significance of the entry of the competition into the history books, it was a sure sign that moto-cross was beginning to grow up. Very soon it would be able to take its place alongside the other popular forms of motorcycle sport which had predated it.

Having led the British team to triumph in the first Moto-Cross des Nations, Bill Nicholson was on the point of repeating that performance in the second running of the international team contest, when the gearbox of his BSA cried enough; allowing Nic Jansen to head the field home in the final. Still very much at the development stage, it would have been little short of a miracle if the Moto-Cross des Nations had already become the examining forum for the world's elite. But within the space of a year, if there were any doubts that the competition had the capacity to take hold of the public's imagination, they were dispelled at La Fraineuse, near Spa, where some 30,000 turned up to see Belgium capitalize on Nicholson's misfortune.

To some extent it was the story of Nicholson's year. He began by winning the Junior and Senior races at a controversial Sunbeam Point-to-Point, which was marred by the organisers alleged failure to make clear to competitors which fuels would be allowed. These were the

Below left **Norman Vanhouse (Ariel, 36) and Basil Hall (Matchless, 45)** survive a coming together at a watersplash during the 1949 Cotswold. Ariel won the Manufacturers' team prize in the Senior, while Hall was runner-up to BSA's Bill Nicholson.

Below **Basil Hall takes his Matchless to victory in the Experts' Grand National at Feckenham in 1949 – the year before the event was first run at Rollswood Farm – where Hall again triumphed.**

days of petrol rationing, so most riders had their engines tuned to run on dope. Although petrol coupons were supplied with the final instructions, some competitors arrived at Weaver's Down with their engines unsuitably prepared to run on commercial fuel. Not that this misunderstanding had any effect on Nicholson, who won the 12-lap Junior from Bert Gaymer's Triumph and the Matchless of Basil Hall. In the Senior, the Ulsterman was equally emphatic, finishing well ahead of the Triumph ridden by Jim Alves and Geoff Duke's Norton.

The popularity of moto-cross had by now attracted the attention of the broadcast media and for the Cotswold, Graham Walker and Charles Markham provided commentary for BBC Radio. Those expecting Nicholson to repeat his Junior-Senior double victories of the two previous years were to be disappointed. Nicholson won the Lightweight race so did not return home completely empty-handed, but Fred Rist won the Junior from John Draper with Nicholson suffering a slipping clutch and finishing third. In the Senior, Nicholson was the early leader, but his gearbox failed allowing Basil Hall, riding a Matchless, his only win in the event. Bob Foster was third on an AJS.

Hall went on to win the Lancashire Grand National, which had returned to Holcombe Moor after an absence of 10 years. Jim Alves' Triumph was second, and Geoff Duke third, riding a Norton.

Within a couple of years the remarkable Duke would exchange his moto-cross bike for a road racing machine, and win his first Tourist Trophy Senior on the Isle of Man, where he became something of a legend. Duke attributed some of the successes he achieved as a road racer – which included six world titles – to his early years in trials and moto-cross, where he learnt to control a powerful motorcycle on slippery surfaces. Though before then Duke, and 11 other British riders, had an appointment to keep in the beautiful Ardennes, close to the West German border.

The regulations for the second Moto-Cross des Nations were approved at the FICM's spring congress in Brussels. These included a provision for teams of up to 12 riders to compete in two heats, the quickest three from each heat going through to a final; plus the fastest remaining riders to make up the maximum number of 30 in the final. After the triangular competition in Holland in 1947, six teams would compete in Belgium; the original three, plus Sweden, Luxembourg and France.

The first heat was a Belgian tour de force, as Nic Jansen led André Milhoux and Marcel Spiroux across the line, after Basil Hall had fallen when leading. In the second race, Nicholson trailed Marcel Meunier's Triumph to the flag, with Hugh Viney's AJS fourth and the Triumph of Jim Alves fifth.

In the final, Belgium's Marcel Cox was the pace setter until Jansen and Nicholson squeezed past. With Duke, Hall and Viney in the top six, Great Britain were still in with a chance of repeating their victory in Holland. But once Nicholson pulled out, Belgium went on to win; the combined time of their best three rid-

Above **John Avery enjoys a little mud-plugging on his trusty 250cc BSA during the Gotherington Gallop Scramble, Cheltenham, in 1950.**

ers being three minutes and 10 seconds better than the aggregate recorded by the leading three Britons.

BASIL HALL'S RISE TO STARDOM

Where the early post-war seasons lacked substance and shape, by 1949 the summer had both. Sure there were still no titles to chase, but the big events were getting bigger and, while the earliest seasons had been dominated by two riders, there was now the opportunity to relish the possible emergence of exciting new talent. By the end of the year there was confirmation it had arrived.

Foremost among those who had advanced far enough to render themselves serious challengers for major honours, were Basil Hall and Harold Lines. Much had been made of Hall's sudden rise to stardom after his Lancashire Grand National and Cotswold Senior triumphs. But Nicholson was still the man to beat, as the BSA rider demonstrated unequivocally with his third Junior-Senior double in the Cotswold. Even though Hall had drawn first blood in the new season's trade-supported events, by beating Nicholson into second place in the Senior race at the Sunbeam Point-to-Point.

Neither Hall nor Lines bore any resemblance to Nicholson in either appearance or

19

demeanour. Nicholson, often irascible, and with little by way of a sense of humour, was a loner. There has been any number of riders with a belief in the sanctity of skill, but few who could cement their talent with the application and determination to ensure them the consistent success Nicholson achieved. All in the sport were aware of Nicholson's skills and his will to win. But he had an extra dimension. The strength of his personality lay in his dedication and attention to detail. He had an aura about him. At times it appeared to be an armour of invincibility.

With Nicholson now 32, Hall and Lines, both 28, had youth on their side. Hall, a tall, fair-haired farmer's son, from Markyate in Hertfordshire, was popular, reliable and courteous, with an unmistakable integrity. Apart from his successes in Britain, Hall won five international events from seven starts in France that summer, and was hailed as the new French champion. Lines, too, made his reputation in mainland Europe. Living in Sussex, close to the Channel ports, Lines preferred the lifestyle in France and Belgium, where the prize money was much better than in England. Apart from occasional appearances in events close to his home, like the Sunbeam, Lines was never seen at the major English meetings. So by the time the biggest moment of his career was reached, very few enthusiasts in England were fully aware of Lines' talents. An omission Lines was soon to redress.

Great Britain's first opportunity at staging the Moto-Cross des Nations was the scene for a second victory. The venue was Brands Hatch, where a crowd of 25,000 saw the home team defeat Belgium in the final, led to victory by Lines on his Ariel, with Bob Manns fourth, riding a Triumph, and Ray Scovell's BSA fifth.

Only four countries sent teams. France and Luxembourg being unable to call on sufficient quality manpower. Hall had been second to Lines until the closing laps, when his Matchless developed a misfire. Nicholson, who was destined never to collect another winner's medal in the team tournament, was troubled by gear-box difficulties and a leg injury. As Nicholson's star was beginning to fade – though there were three more Scott Trial victories to savour – the two celestial lights burning above the names of Harold Lines and Basil Hall were never more vivid.

RECORD ATTENDANCES

By 1950 the major events like the Sunbeam Point-to-Point, Lancashire Grand National, Cotswold, and Hampshire Grand National, had

Below **The Great Britain team line up at Namur before the 1951 Moto-Cross des Nations, where they were beaten by Belgium. Pictured (left to right) are: Brian Stonebridge, Phil Nex, Eric Cheney, Geoff Ward, Les Archer, Ted Ogden, Jack Stocker, Jim Alves, Bill Nicholson, John Avery, Harold Lines, John Draper and team manager Harold Taylor.**

been joined by the Ipswich club's Shrubland Park Scramble and the Experts' Grand National; the latter two also enjoying trade support. In fact the Shrubland Park had been an open event for two years – Bill Nicholson winning the Senior on both occasions – though the Experts was so called for the first time this season, once the Redditch club had relocated their popular event to Rollswood Farm, near Alcester. More silverware and more prestige, revealed more new names to test the skills of the engravers. Two of the newcomers, Brian Stonebridge and Geoff Ward, were marked out for greatness.

Stonebridge might have won the Experts' had his Matchless not run out of brakes. Basil Hall, having exchanged his Matchless for a BSA, did win it after a meteoric charge through the field. Eric Cheney was the surprise winner of the Senior race at the Sunbeam and the Hants GN, where Ward's AJS took the Junior. Though Stonebridge announced himself at the Sunbeam by taking the Junior. Nicholson, keen to prove that the competitive fires which had sustained his memorable career for so long had not yet been extinguished, won the Cotswold Senior, Stonebridge was runner-up in the Junior to Basil Hall.

There was more colour, closer finishes and unpredicted outcomes to the major events in Britain and they were drawing bigger crowds. Even at the relatively inaccessible Holcombe Moor, there was a record attendance to see Brian Stonebridge sweep to victory in the Lancashire Grand National. Stonebridge had almost a minute in hand over John Avery's BSA and the Triumph of Jim Alves, who were separated by a mere second after almost 80 minutes of racing.

Before this first significant victory of Stone-

Below **John Avery urging every ounce of effort from his BSA at the 1951 Cotswold. But John Draper took the major honours at Nympsfield that year with a Senior-Junior double.**

Right **Brian Stonebridge takes his Matchless through a watersplash ahead of Geoff Ward's AJS during the 1951 Cotswold. Stonebridge was runner-up in Senior and Junior.**

bridge's illustrious career, he had finished third behind Bill Nicholson in the Junior at Shrubland Park and runner-up in the Senior; both races having been won by Basil Hall. Avery won the lightweight category – as he had done at the Cotswold – and he and Ward were in the silverware in the other classes. So it was no surprise to see their names on the team sheet for the Moto-Cross des Nations, along with those of 17-year-old Graham Beamish, and Stonebridge.

With so much talent available, it was no surprise either that Great Britain proved too strong for the other four nations who entered teams. The Swedish track at Skillingaryd, was not unlike some English circuits and proved much to the liking of the holders, who ran out easy winners with an advantage of almost five minutes over runners-up Sweden. Hall, Avery and Nicholson dominated the first 12-lap heat, while Harold Lines and Stonebridge did similarly in the second. The 17-lap final was a rout. John Draper won from Hall, with Lines fourth, Ward fifth, Nicholson sixth and Stonebridge eighth.

At home, if not in Europe, it was the last season when, apart from the Moto-Cross des Nations, there were no formal competitions and riders had only the prestige and pleasure from succeeding in the trade-supported events.

BIRTH OF THE BRITISH CHAMPIONSHIP

Geoff Ward was born in Maidenhead in 1929 and, by the outbreak of the Second World War 10 years later, his personal circumstances looked as bleak as the nation's. His father had disappeared and his mother died, leaving Ward effectively parentless with the unappealing prospect of life in an orphanage; for a few years at least. A schoolfriend, Robert Neville, alarmed at Ward's plight, persuaded his mother Lucy to give Geoff a home. So Ward moved in with William Neville's family above their

butcher's shop in Slough. When war was over, Robert asked his father to loan him and Geoff enough money to buy 20 ex-WD motorcycles. They were sold at a handsome profit, casting Ward on a business career which has made him one of the wealthiest independent motor retailers in the west of England, to where he and his wife Rita moved in 1966.

Geoff Ward was a big man for a moto-cross rider – just short of six foot (1.8m) and 224 lbs (101Kg) – broad and jovial, and he will forever be associated with AJS, for whom he rode once he went to work as a salesman for Harold

Left **Jim Alves making a splash with his Triumph in the 1951 Cotswold. Alves was the first winner of the British Trials Championship, which was inaugurated in 1950.**

Below **The effortless style of Brian Stonebridge is captured beautifully in this shot taken by Bill Cole.**

Below **The wide open spaces in the hills above Stroud suited John Draper. Geoff Ward (AJS, 12) never got any closer to his BSA rival in the 1951 Cotswold. Though Ward had the satisfaction of becoming the inaugural winner of the British Moto-Cross Championship, which first saw the light of day in the same year. Ward went on to lift the title three times. Draper never won it.**

Taylor's motorcycle business in Balham, south west London. Ward was quickly signed up by Jock West and Hugh Viney, and was soon winning for the Plumstead Road concern.

While Harold Taylor was Ward's mentor, AJS were providing the engines and Taylor's foreman Jim Pocock was looking after machine preparation, there were few more productive relationships in British moto-cross. By the summer's end of 1951, Ward had repaid their confidence in him with the British title.

The first months of the British Championship were as tentative as any experienced by those at the centre of events in the post-war years. The Auto-Cycle Union had introduced a championship for trials riders in 1950, which Jim Alves won. So the following year they launched a moto-cross competition, which was known as the ACU Scramble Drivers' Star. There were 12 nominated rounds, which included the Lancashire, Hampshire and Cumberland Grand Nationals, the Sunbeam Point-to-Point, Shrubland and Cotswold, though for some unexplained reason, not the Experts' Grand National. A rider's eight best scores would count, always assuming he could understand the method of scoring, which appeared as if it had been designed by a crossword-puzzle contributor for his own amusement. But the system was the same for the trials competition, and stayed in place until the ACU adopted the more familiar method used in the European Championship.

The unnecessarily complicated arrangement awarded the winner a point for every 10 entries – fractions were discounted – up to a maximum of 10 points. Where there were finals for 350cc and 500cc machines, both would count for points. So it followed that it was much better to win an event with a big entry than a small

one. This is probably why most of the leading riders avoided the Birmingham Grand National which was the first round of the embryonic tournament. It was no help either that it was staged in January, or the Halesowen course had been snow covered in the days leading to the event.

Rex Young, riding a Norton, was the unlikely winner of what turned out to be a farce in a mud bath. Don Evans was second on his Ariel and Les Archer – who was to complete the season as championship runner-up to Ward – was third riding his Norton. All, including Bill Nicholson, John Draper and Brian Martin, who sank without trace in the glutinous conditions, were glad to see the back of the Birmingham Grand National.

Archer was in the points again at the Hants Grand National, on a wet and windswept Good Friday, winning the Senior, while Ward took the Junior. Then, in the space of eight days, Ward opened up a 12-point gap on Archer by winning both races at Hawkstone Park, before repeating the treatment at the Sunbeam with a Junior-Senior double. Draper was the toast of Nympsfield, by annexing both Junior and Senior at the Cotswold.

But Draper's major triumph that summer was victory in the Scottish Six Days Trial, and he only scored two more points in the moto-cross competition. Though beaten by Brian Stonebridge and Les Archer in the Lancashire Grand National Ward, who was third, had accumulated sufficient points to repel Archer's challenge, and he was champion.

BELGIUM WINS THE MOTO-CROSS DES NATIONS

The fifth Moto-Cross des Nations was held at Namur, which was to become to Belgian enthusiasts what Hawkstone Park was to their British counterparts.

Over the years there have been many British successes at the Citadelle; there have been plenty of disappointments as well. In 1951, there was a justifiable expectation that Great Britain could continue where they left off in Sweden, the previous summer.

There was no hint of what was to follow when BSA's John Draper won the first seven-lap heat, with five seconds in hand over Belgium's Nic Jansen, riding a Saroléa. Bill Nicholson wasn't yet finished with moto-cross, and he had warmed up for the team tournament which he always enjoyed, by winning the Senior race at the Gloucester Grand National. Though now concentrating on trialling, Nicholson – who won the ACU Trials Star that year – was fourth in the opening heat, one place up on Harold Lines' Ariel, and three on the Matchless of Brian Stonebridge. in the second heat, newcomer Phil Nex, who had been drafted in to replace the injured Basil Hall, was the leading Briton. Nex brought his BSA home in second place behind the Saroléa of Belgium's Marcel Meunier. Les Archer was third riding the factory-supported Norton.

Even without the formidable Auguste Mingels, who had crashed into a tree during the first heat, the Belgian line-up for the 11-lap final looked as if they would take all the beating in front of 30,000 of their home supporters. So it proved.

Stonebridge, Ward and Draper all had their moments in a compelling race. However, the Belgian trio of Victor Leloup riding an FN, and the Saroléas of Jansen and Meunier, finished ahead of the three Britons with a combined advantage of more than four minutes. Nicholson was well off the pace, finishing eight minutes adrift of Leloup in 10th place.

It was his last ride for Great Britain, and a considerable personal disappointment for Nicholson, who was an inspiration to to the younger riders.

1952

BRIAN STONEBRIDGE is victorious at the first British 500cc Grand Prix, and helps the host country win the Moto-Cross des Nations at Brands Hatch. John Avery is national champion.

Brian Stonebridge surely had other things on his mind than the historical impact of his country's belated entry into the European Championship, when he became the first winner of the British Moto-Cross Grand Prix in September 1952. Stonebridge, 23, was the tall, lean son of a Cambridgeshire farmer and had been competing for only two years when the Matchless Factory signed him for their team. He soon justified their confidence by winning the 1950 Experts' and Lancashire Grand Nationals, as well as collecting a gold medal in the International Six Days Trial. The following season Stonebridge finished third in the inaugural British 500cc Championship – or ACU Scramble Drivers' Star as it was then called – behind Les Archer and first winner, Geoff Ward.

'Strawberry', as Brian was popularly known to his contemporaries, possessed an effortless riding style combined with extraordinary mechanical ingenuity, in an era when technical know-how was prized second only to riding ability. Immediately recognizable by virtue of his height and the riding gear of his early days – invariably featuring an army battle-dress

tunic or flak jacket – his languorous approach concealed a formidable competitiveness which made him a difficult adversary.

Few British riders of the time had any extensive experience of international competition, though Stonebridge could be counted among those fortunate enough to have tasted the spirit of European rivalry in post-war meetings staged by a French businessman, Roland Poirier, on behalf of the Amicale Motocycliste de la Seine. These races, at the chalk pits of Montreuil near Paris, were attended by vast crowds of up to 80,000, paid generous prize money and were the forebears of modern international moto-cross.

THE EUROPEAN CHAMPIONSHIP

Basil Hall, who was a member of Britain's triumphant team in the 1950 Moto-Cross des Nations, encouraged Stonebridge – whom he considered his protégé – to ride at Montreuil and elsewhere on the continent to widen his experience and sharpen his competitive edge. By the time a formalized European tournament had been decided upon, Stonebridge had honed it razor sharp.

The governing body of World motorcycle sport, the FIM – *Fédération Internationale Motocycliste* – were hugely encouraged by the success of their international team contest, the Moto-Cross des Nations, first run in 1947. At the autumn meeting of the FIM in Paris in 1951 it was agreed to run an inter country tournament for individual riders to be known as the European Moto-Cross Championship. Britain supported the idea of this competition to be run on similar lines to the road racing championships, with identical scoring values. Eight points would be awarded to the winner, six for the runner-up, four for third; then three, two, one for fourth, fifth and sixth places.

The tournament had a confusing inauguration as the Secretary-General of the FIM was

Opposite **Although John Draper's greatest triumphs were secured with a BSA saddle underneath him, he occasionally rode something else. At Birdlip, Draper takes wing on a Norton.**

Above **When it was needed most, Brian Stonebridge could add substance to style. On Saturday 13 September 1952 he took his Matchless to victory in the first British Moto-Cross Grand Prix.**

Above **Victor Leloup – shod as always in Wellington boots – passes Les Archer's fallen Norton in the British 500cc Grand Prix. Belgian Leloup finished fourth on his FN and, in 1952, became the first winner of the six-nation European Championship.**

under the impression that the Belgian Federation had been deputed to finalise the rules, the new championship being Belgian in conception. The misunderstanding delayed the publication of an appendix and with the first of the events so close, Monsieur Lenfranc, the Belgian delegate, pressed for the competition to be abandoned for 1952. However, as all the preparations for the opening meeting at Imola, Italy had been successfully completed, all the other countries concerned voted for the regulations to be produced immediately and a start to be made in 1952, as originally planned. Six rounds were scheduled; the best four scores of each rider to count, at ties in France, Sweden, Luxembourg, Belgium, Britain and Italy.

The muddling start to the European Motocross Championship was soon forgotten as Belgium's Auguste Mingels won at Imola on a British-made Matchless, in front of a crowd of over 20,000, in bright sunny weather. There were two eight-lap heats and a 14-lap final over a rough, dusty course measuring two miles, on that epochal Sunday, 1 June 1952.

Basil Hall took the first heat on his works BSA with Belgium's Victor Leloup, who only had vision in one eye, second on an FN. Harold Lines riding an Ariel, despite sustaining a cut face, finished fifth. The best performance by a Briton in the second heat was by John Avery, who rode to third place on a BSA. Only Hall of the British contingent shone in the final, making it to fourth behind the trio of Belgians: Mingels, Marcel Cox on a second Matchless and Leloup.

AVERY TO THE FORE

The European Moto-Cross Championship had been born and was apparently in bouncing good health. Unfortunately, the same could not be said for British livestock, which was plagued by an outbreak of foot and mouth disease causing the postponement of the second round, which should have been run in conjunction with the Cotswold Scramble at Nympsfield, in the west of England on Saturday 28 June, a month after the Italian opener. So instead of travelling to Gloucestershire, the title contenders had to wait until 3 August for the series to resume in Belgium. Luxembourg came next – both rounds providing victories for the FN-mounted Leloup – before a first British success could be claimed in the fourth tie at Saxtorp, Sweden on Sunday 24 August.

It had taken four seasons for John Avery to attract the attention of the BSA factory, after an impressive run of five performances in the major British events with his privately-entered 1939 B21 250cc BSA. The machine had mostly seen service as a trials mount before its conversion ten years later to scrambles trim, with some home tuning and a pair of telescopic forks. He promptly won the 250cc race at the national Shrubland Park scramble, which he repeated the following season to add to class victories in the Cotswold – beating the redoubtable BSA works rider Fred Rist in the process – and Experts' Grand National. Now armed with a 500cc Gold Star, Avery finished runner-up to Brian Stonebridge in the Lancashire Grand National, and his outstanding form deservedly earned him selection to the British team for the 1950 Moto-Cross des Nations, at Skillingaryd, Sweden. Although Avery finished second to Basil Hall in the first heat, the best three scorers in the 17-lap final, who lifted the trophy for the third time for Britain, were Hall and John Draper on works BSAs and Harold Lines' Ariel. But Avery had made his mark. From Oxford, Avery always turned out with immaculate bikes and riding gear to match. He thrived on difficult courses and, extrovert by nature, loved to throw himself higher and further through the air than other riders.

The legendary Bert Perrigo in his final three years as competitions' manager of BSA, before he was succeeded by Dennis Hardwicke, recognised the need to strengthen his team with fresh talent. He began by recruiting Basil Hall from Matchless in 1950, to support Fred Rist, Bill Nicholson and John Draper. Avery followed two years later and he rewarded the Small Heath concern with the 500cc British title in his first season as a fully-fledged factory entrant and, in the same summer, became the first British rider to win a round of the European Moto-Cross Championship.

CHANGING FORTUNES

The latter triumph was achieved in some style, as Avery won the first 12-lap heat at Saxtorp and series leader Leloup the second. In the 20-lap final Leloup led for six laps until Avery forced his way to the front to win by a distance, with the Belgian third. Two weeks later in the French Grand Prix at Montreuil, Leloup on the ungainly FN, with rubber-sprung forks and plunger rear suspension, gained his revenge with a third victory and clinched the title. Avery was third at the chalk pits classic, and with 12 points moved to third place in the standings behind Leloup, – with an unassailable 28, – and Mingels with 20.

There was therefore an understandable air of anti-climax as the curtain was raised for the final scene in the opening act of the fledgling tournament. Not that this in any way inhibited the ambitions of the home riders who were keen to augment Avery's triumph with success of their own. For them, Europe was soon to have no frontiers.

The Cotswold Scramble, first run in 1934, was one of a handful of trade-supported events which formed the core of the British

Left **The programme for the first British 500cc Grand Prix, which was combined with famous Cotswold Scramble, at its first running in 1952. The Cotswold was first run in 1934.**

Championship. During the second half of the 1950s, the 500cc race became the personal property of Dave Curtis who won it five times in succession for Matchless, seven in all. For many years it assumed a special relevance, being the last big event before the British GP. The famous old course, almost two and a half miles long, with watersplashes, rocky patches and a covering of mud on parts of the grassland circuit in the hills above Stroud, provided as stern a test as had been devised for riders and machines of that era.

It was unfamiliar territory for the newly-crowned Leloup, whose solitary attempt to add a fourth win to his earlier achievements went unrewarded.

The champion alone made the trip from the Continent to meet the Britons on their own ground, and thus the international character of the event was considerably adulterated. The list of non-starters was a major let down for a large crowd, and we can only speculate at what might have been the outcome of the first British Moto-Cross Grand Prix had it been the second leg of the series instead of the sixth.

Such trifles were of no concern to the depleted field of 19 who came to the line for the single 10-lap race. Geoff Ward was the early leader on a factory AJS with Stonebridge's Matchless and Phil Nex on a BSA close astern. Leloup was fourth, with Derek Rickman fifth riding a BSA, just ahead of the American Bud Ekins on a works-replica Matchless.

Les Archer fell at the start, retiring his Norton, while the BSAs of John Avery and Bill Nicholson suffered a loose front mudguard and a sticking throttle respectively, to bring about their demise.

Stonebridge sneaked past Ward on lap four and both of them led Nex by six seconds; the three pulling away from the pursuing group led by Rickman. With only a bike's length separating the leading pair at half distance it was still an open race; but then Ward fell. Nex inherited second place as Ward's recovery was spoiled when his clutch failed, leaving Stonebridge in command, 32 seconds in front.

The crowd's attention was subsequently centred on an absorbing contest for fifth between Ekins and Bill Barugh on a diminutive 197cc DOT, which went the American's way in an exciting finish by just half a length.

To some extent this made up for some of the crowd's earlier disappointments. But there was no disappointment for Stonebridge. He had made history.

BRIAN STONEBRIDGE's second British Grand Prix triumph. Geoff Ward takes the domestic championship and partners John Draper and Les Archer to another British success in the Moto-Cross des Nations.

The abiding fame and immense popularity which Brian Stonebridge eventually achieved as a Greeves rider, was some considerable way off as he prepared to try and repeat his Nympsfield triumph for Matchless at Brands Hatch. Although the stylish Stonebridge by now had the measure of most of his contemporaries, dominant performances were only intermittent, and he had not quite become a rider of all the talents. Nonetheless his star was assuredly in the ascendant and the omens looked good.

The choice of Brands Hatch as the venue for the British GP most certainly suited Stonebridge who had not only been a member of the winning team there in the 1952 Moto-Cross des Nations, but had also taken the individual award. Stonebridge headed the 15-lap race, with a 40-second advantage over Belgium's Auguste Mingels, while Geoff Ward and Phil Nex occupied third and fourth places, to seal Britain's fourth win in the international team just in six years.

Throughout its history the British GP has, for the most part, been run in early July. In the first seasons, home riders prepared for the big event by competing in the domestic championship. An early guide to form could be gauged from the results of the Hants Grand National and industry-supported Sunbeam Point-to-Point and Cotswold Scrambles.

Geoff Ward, who won the first British championship in 1951, took the Senior race at the 1953 Gloucestershire classic, with John Draper second, ahead of Les Archer's Norton; Stonebridge was fifth. In the Junior race for 350cc machines, Ward and Stonebridge fought a tremendous duel until the Matchless expired with mechanical problems. At the Sunbeam, Stonebridge was the emphatic winner of both Junior and Senior; the larger class from Archer and Dave Curtis. Ward had fallen after a mid-air collision with Stonebridge, during a thrilling dispute for the

Left **Auguste Mingels of Belgium was the second winner of the European Championship. Mingels**—pictured here on a Matchless winning the Italian round at Imola—also rode an FN during that season.

31

Right **Reigning European champion Victor Leloup crests a hill on the way to third place in the Swiss Grand Prix at Geneva, where the seven-nation 1953 tournament opened. Leloup was third on his trusty FN, behind Auguste Mingels and winner Basil Hall.**

leadership, but was thankfully uninjured.

In addition to British form, there was also the Europe Factor. Within a few months of Victor Leloup's accession to the European moto-cross crown, the FIM announced an extension to their nascent championship. For 1953 the number of qualifying rounds had been extended by two to eight. As well as the six countries who had formed the initial tournament, Switzerland and Holland had successfully applied to host the opening counters of the enlarged competition. Strangely, there was no commensurate increase in the number of contributory scores; once more, it would only be a rider's four best performances which mattered.

But Britain was slow to catch the mood of innovation, which was principally fuelled by a plentiful supply of continental zeal, as moto-cross was offered up on a broader stage. There was at first little more enthusiasm for the new tournament than British soccer clubs could muster for the European Cup. However, just as Manchester United led the way in association football, so BSA of the British motorcycle makers were first to do so in moto-cross. The other manufacturers eventually followed once they saw the opportunities to display their wares in a serious, summer-long competition throughout the Continent, rather than just once a year in the Moto-Cross des Nations.

Their laggardly, low budget change of heart was in part induced by the pioneering spirit fostered by Harold Lines, Basil Hall, Eric Cheney, Les Archer, and others who were crossing the English Channel with increasing regularity. Of greater significance was the frequency with which they returned in triumph having taken on and beaten the best of the foreign riders on their home tracks, albeit in non-championship international races.

Motor Cycling's reporter was perhaps being unusually prescient in describing the 1953 British Grand Prix as counting towards the 'coveted' European championship. If coveted the embryonic competition was, then the Belgians were its most eager seekers.

There was early season encouragement for Les Archer who took overall victory in a three race meeting at Montreuil in April, with Graham Beamish on a BSA and Eric Cheney's Ariel both in the prize money. The celebrations were prolonged to the end of the month when Basil Hall won the Swiss GP at Geneva, which got the European series under way. Hall's BSA team-mate Phil Nex was seventh. As Hall and Nex had each finished second in their respective heats and Hall led the final from start to finish this was a heartening result, especially with the Sunbeam Point-to-Point being run on the same day. The unfortunate clash of dates meant that few British competitors travelled to Switzerland; most – including the peripatetic Archer – preferring to make the shorter journey to Hampshire.

BRITISH ADVANCES IN EUROPE

Hall's early advantage evaporated in the Dutch tie, three weeks later, where British representation was up to four. Hall being accompanied by Nex, Stonebridge and Geoff Ward on a lone AJS. The 10-lap heats were run on the Saturday and in the first, Stonebridge won from Hall, the Britons being narrowly ahead of Leloup and Auguste Mingels. Ward was third in the second heat, almost a minute and a half behind the Matchlesses of Belgian Marcel Cox and Dutchman Frans Baudoin. Only Ward of the British quartet was in the points in Sunday's final, which Mingels won from Baudoin and Leloup, with the English rider fourth.

It was much the same story a fortnight later in the French GP at Charbonnieres near Lyons. Mingels won, Leloup was runner-up and third was Henri Frantz of France on another FN. Les Archer was the best Briton in fourth on his trusty Norton as Nex went out with gearbox problems and Hall's chain broke.

The somewhat torpid, diffident European approach by the English motorcycle makers was of no immediate concern to the home riders at Brands Hatch in 1953, where British drivers in a variety of formulae were in later years to score numerous triumphs in World and European motor racing. Jim Clark's victory at the Kentish circuit for Lotus in the 1964 Formula One GP and Nigel Mansell's win in the European Grand Prix of 1986 for Williams, being perhaps the most memorable. In between when, Derek Minter became 'King of Brands' and three of the circuit's best-known hazards were named after motor cycle racing's greats: John Surtees, Mike Hailwood and Minter himself.

Looking back on this improbable scene it is unlikely Brian Stonebridge was imbued with anything more pragmatic than the desire to add a second British moto-cross GP win to his growing tally of accomplishments. For Auguste Mingels and Victor Leloup there was substantially more at stake : the European crown.

The two Belgians were members of their national team, beaten – though far from disgraced – by Great Britain in the Moto-Cross des Nations at Brands Hatch the previous year. However, in the intervening 11 months, the reputation and authority of both had grown enormously. The broad Mingels, with his high forehead and neatly cropped hair, was in sight of his target. The maximum possible score was 32, and with three wins and a second, Mingels, who started the season on a Matchless but switched to FN for the closing rounds, was on 30. Although there were four rounds to go, Leloup, whose best score had been as runner-up in France, trailed his compatriot by 13 points and needed to win all four of the remaining ties if he was to retain his title.

Brands was *en fête* as Leloup made ready to sustain his defence in front of a sizeable crowd on a hot sunny day, only made bearable for the riders by a light breeze. Over land which was first used for motor sport when motorcycle grass track racing was staged there in the 1930s, a roughly rectangular circuit was laid out, being about 1.75 miles in length.

To the delight of those enthusiasts who had crossed the Channel, Leloup led the field away in the first of two 10-lap heats; qualification for the 15-lap final was restricted to the top 10 in each heat. But within a lap there was drama as

Leloup's place in the final was jeopardized by a front wheel puncture. As Geoff Ward took over at the front on the factory AJS, Les Archer was forced to pit his Norton to retrieve a piece of stocking fabric which had been sucked into his carburettor. Archer rejoined the race a lap in arrears, but soon caught and passed the limping Leloup, who could only be sure of making the final when Sweden's Gunnar Eriksson suffered a collapsed front wheel on his Saroléa on the penultimate lap.

STONEBRIDGE IN THE ASCENDANT

The second heat was less eventful, though Molinari crashed his Gilera into retirement as Monty Banks headed the field on his BSA. Stonebridge soon supplanted him and, after some spirited resistance from Mingels, won almost as he liked with Bob Manns second on an AJS and the veteran Banks third. The youthful Lars Gustafsson of Sweden, who was to make such an impact in later British GPs, was forced out when his BSA expired on the seventh lap.

Heavy rain in the days prior to the event, followed by strong sunshine, had made the track rutted and bumpy, placing a premium on mechanical reliability. The failure rate of cycle parts was unusually high; unacceptably so for David Tye and John Draper, who had insufficient time to repair their BSAs before the final. So Tye and Draper – with a broken frame – were missing as only 18 riders came to the line for 15 decisive laps.

Although choking dust and machine failure played their part in the outcome, these were no impediments to Stonebridge's brilliant progress. The privately-entered, but potent Ariel of Harold Lines and Les Archer's Norton collided at the start and though Archer was briefly able to continue, within a lap he toured in holding his rear brake pedal in his hand. Mingels and Leloup gave chase to the flying Matchless with Banks, Basil Hall and Dave Curtis in close pursuit on a trio of BSAs, with Ward's AJS sounding ominously off-song.

After five laps Stonebridge had opened up a

10-second gap on the Belgian duo, with Hall an undisputed fourth, but the pace, dust and bone-hard terrain began to take its toll. By two third's distance Mingels came in with his front wheel looking a badly tangled piece of knitting and Leloup soon joined him with a spent motor, having been lapped by the leader. Ward, despite his problems, had inherited third, as reigning British 500cc champion Avery, with rear brake troubles which required two stops, was vainly trying to retain sixth. Don Rickman had almost unobtrusively worked his BSA to fourth ahead of the exhausted Banks. At the flag, Stonebridge

A wonderfully evocative picture of a well wrapped-up Les Archer taken during the British Grand Prix at Brands Hatch. Archer had an unhappy day, and pulled his Norton out of the 15-lap final with a broken brake pedal.

was 27 seconds ahead of Hall – who had ridden superbly – with Ward a minute and a half further back in third as the race, which had lost much of its early interest, came to a processional close. What remained of Stonebridge's adolescence after his triumph in the Cotswolds a year earlier was gone. Brian Stonebridge had become a man. As a motocross rider, he was now the man to beat.

However, beating Mingels, even for Stonebridge, was another matter. The Belgian 'man mountain' only needed two more points with another win, to improve upon his second place in Switzerland and therefore secure a maximum. It was ultimately not required of him, for Les Archer won in Luxembourg and Baeten took the Belgian and Swedish rounds to finish second. Leloup, ostensibly Mingels' only realistic challenger, subsided to third place. Leloup was unable to record a victory in an otherwise remarkably consistent campaign, so Mingels was annointed European champion with a comfortable 11 point margin of victory. Belgium had to wait another 38 years to achieve a second clean sweep of gold, silver and bronze FIM medals, by when Sweden had achieved it three times. Only Italy in the 1997 125cc Championship have repeated the feat.

35

1954

The birth of Hawkstone Park, where PHIL NEX leads home four English riders in the British Grand Prix. A Moto-Cross des Nations hat-trick, as Geoff Ward's AJS spearheads victory together with the BSA of Brian Stonebridge and Dave Curtis' Matchless. Ward retains his national title.

Right **Brian Stonebridge is introduced to the latest model BSA Gold Star by Bill Nicholson. Stonebridge, seated on the bike while on a visit to the Armoury Road works, had previously ridden a Matchless, but switched to BSA for the 1954 season.**

When the Auto-Cycle Union settled on Hawkstone Park as the venue for the third British Moto-cross Grand Prix they could hardly have been aware of the profound effect the decision was to have in shaping the future of British moto-cross. Brands Hatch the year before was perhaps not seen as an overwhelming success, but it did have the double advantage of being close to London and accessible to the Continent. Additionally, spectator facilities at the Kent track were frequently being improved to accommodate crowds growing in size as the popularity of most forms of motor sport continued to rise. However, the ACU's choice of the Shropshire circuit was completely vindicated as all attendance records there were broken. An estimated 35,000 were packed around the verdant, hillside track – the tickets sold out at 33,000 – and the foundations were laid at Hawkstone Park, which in a few short years was to become, and has subsequently remained, the spiritual home of British moto-cross. Brands Hatch was only very infrequently used again as an international off-road arena, as when the Moto-Cross des Nations was staged there in 1957, and the Trophée des Nations in 1966.

Despite its rural location, with difficulties and frustrations in discharging big crowds into narrow lanes, the Hawkstone circuit has hardly altered in 40 years and consequently has lost little of its original appeal. It was first used for motoring competition as a hill climb in the 1930s and events were staged there by the Crewe & Nantwich Light Car Club. After World War Two the Salop Motor Club began to develop it for moto-cross. Infused by their immortal secretary Cuth Bate, the Salop club were ambitious, clearly realized the potential of Hawkstone and worked tirelessly to make it the premier circuit in England. Their enterprise gained early reward in July 1954 when the first of 21 grands prix in the 500cc category to be held there in the history of first the European, then the World championships, was without doubt the biggest day in British moto-cross so far. By happy coincidence it was quite the most triumphant day in what was to be the tragically foreshortened life of Phil Nex.

Hopeful as Nex was, if a poll had been taken among all the competitors, his chances would not have rated higher than those of the leading Belgians or the British sextet of Avery, Ward, Stonebridge, Curtis, Draper and Archer, who had already accomplished much more than Nex at home and overseas. It was not that Nex was underrated by his contemporaries or had significantly underachieved, but for the most

36

part he had been outshone by the dominant English six.

Philip Alan Nex was born at Bexhill-on-Sea in 1928 and moved west along the Sussex coast to Fareham in Hampshire where his mother became housekeeper to the Bishop of Portsmouth, which later gave rise to Philip's nickname: 'The Bishop'. On leaving school he became apprenticed as a coppersmith in a Portsmouth boat building yard. His early interest in motorcycles was encouraged by Bob Evans whose two sons, Rob and Fred, were keen on competition; Fred going on to become a proficient trials rider. Initially, Nex – like the Evans family – rode Ariels and had his first taste of championship success when he finished second to Ray Scovell's BSA in 1950. Cheney, better known as a close friend of Les Archer and then as a tuner and builder of moto-cross machines, travelled extensively to the Continent with Nex until 1960, where they competed in the enjoyable round of relatively lucrative non-championship events.

'Phil was a very natural rider', reflected

Below **David Tye making somewhat stately progress in the Sunbeam Point-toPoint on his BSA. Tye was much underrated and, in the British 500cc Grand Prix in 1954 he finished third, riding a 350cc BSA. Tye completed the season in third place in the British Championship, having been runner-up to Geoff Ward the previous year.**

Right **Phil Nex, winner of the first British Grand Prix held at Hawkstone Park.**

Cheney. 'He was very particular about his appearance and the preparation of his bikes, which was in every respect first class. He was always very fair, but if he made a move on the circuit, he carried it out. If anything, his self-belief betrayed him and though he was invariably near the top, with a little more confidence he could have achieved so much more. I must say I thought he was at his best on wet and slippery grass, where delicate control is so important.'

There may have been some wet grass to negotiate when Nex took second place in the first British GP, but there was none to trouble him at Hawkstone, nor had there been at any of the three successive Hants Grand Nationals he won from 1952. Like the best thoroughbred race horses, Nex could act on any going. By 1954 he was at his peak. In addition to his Hants GN win, he was triumphant at a dramatic Cotswold a week before the British GP, when he took full advantage as Geoff

Ward's AJS snapped its primary chain in mid-race and Jeff Smith dropped his BSA in sight of the flag. Smith recovered to claim second from John Draper, with Curtis's Matchless and the Norton of Les Archer, heading home a trio of BSAs ridden by Don Rickman, David Tye and Brian Martin. Before the year was out, Nex was runner-up to Geoff Ward in the British 500cc Championship, leading a phalanx of BSA Gold Star riders who filled the next six places. The Gods were smiling on Phil Nex.

In the early part of the season they had looked down just as favourably on Victor Leloup and Auguste Mingels in the third European series. The championship format was unchanged from 1953, with the same eight countries participating, though the calendar was in a different sequence. Mingels and Leloup made it an FN one-two in the first tie in Switzerland with Stonebridge, Hall and Nex on their BSAs, in third, fourth and fifth. There was a six week gap before the next round in Italy,

Right Dave Curtis at the Experts' Grand National, where he finished out of the top three, having earlier won the 10-lap 500cc race riding a Matchless.

Opposite, below Brian Martin, who was to oversee many BSA triumphs as team manager, helps Phil Nex (on the right) to adjust the chain of his BSA.

where Mingels consolidated his position at the head of the table with another win, though Stonebridge this time relegated Leloup to third, with Avery fourth and Harold Lines annexing the last point, with sixth place for Ariel.

Hall crashed badly, dislocating a shoulder which helped hasten his retirement the following year. Basil Hall had a string of successes in domestic events but then broke his right leg in Sweden a year after he had partnered John Draper and Harold Lines to an outstanding triumph at Skillingaryd, Sweden in the 1950 Moto-Cross des Nations.

The ever-popular and courteous Hall was never to score another championship point. At a national meeting in Belgium, he again broke his right leg when it became trapped between the kick-start and footrest and consequently retired on medical advice.

Jeff Smith, who began his career as a trials rider with Norton, was originally called to BSA's colours when Bill Nicholson announced his intention to leave Small Heath and develop sports cars for Jaguar. In his first full season for BSA, Smith had won the ACU Trial Drivers' Star in 1953, at the tender age of 19. Now, covering for the wounded Hall, Smith announced his entry into European championship moto-cross with outright victory in the Dutch GP; it was to be the first of many.

Leloup was second and as Mingels had no-scored in Holland, the compatriots were tied on 16 points apiece when they travelled to England. Stonebridge was the leading Briton, with 10 points.

Hawkstone Park was like no other British circuit. Set out in wood roughs at almost a mile and a half to the lap, its most formidable feature was an extraordinary hill section, about 400 metres in length, ascending to a gradient of one in two at the summit. A fearsome descent including two hairpins followed, and the Salop club – who had done their homework well – were anxious to give their big track a big international debut. There was a strong continental flavour as the riders paraded prior to the start and were introduced to the club's patron and the landowner, Brigadier Sir Alexander Stanier, Bart, DSO, MC. The flags of the nations fluttered aloft as a band of the St John Ambulance Brigade played the national anthems of the competing riders, representing Belgium, France, Sweden, Australia and Great Britain. To enhance the spirit of patriotism all competitors were required to wear bibs which bore their national flag.

In advance of the preliminaries, there were invitation races for machines up to 500cc and to a maximum of 1000cc; each comprising two four-lap heats and with a six- and eight-lap final respectively. Jeff Smith's father would not allow his son to take part in the grand prix itself, declaring it too dangerous. Apocryphal or not, Smith junior gilded the story by winning his heat in each section and stormed to victory in both finals on a 350cc BSA, providing an appreciative crowd with a foretaste of his mastery at the daunting Shropshire circuit, where eventually he became nigh unbeatable.

The grand prix was scheduled for 15 laps – there were no heats – and after Smith's explosive entry into early Hawkstone folklore, fireworks were anticipated from both leading Belgians and the top Britons from among the 23 starters. The crowd's expectations were soon to be realized.

SALOP INNOVATIONS

Another innovative feature introduced by the Salop club was the use of red and green lights, as well as elastic tape, at a clutch start. At the second attempt the field were led away by Geoff Ward's AJS with the colourful Mingels in a voluminous blue riding suit billowing over his FN, narrowly ahead of Sweden's Bill Nilsson, Brian Stonebridge and Phil Nex – all on BSAs – having the advantage over Les Archer's Norton, with Nic Jansen's Saroléa and Dave Curtis sandwiched between the BSAs of John Draper and John Avery. Victor Leloup on the second FN was out of contention, neither the circuit nor the conditions to his liking.

Les Archer's father, Les senior – who became famous as a road racer with New Imperial and Velocette – provided commentary over the public address system as his son came past in fifth place on the second lap, with Mingels having wrested the lead from

Ward; the Anglo-Belgium duo now seven seconds ahead of Stonebridge and Nex.

There was no let-up at the front as Mingels and Ward kept the crowd on their toes, such was the ferocity and pace of their duel. They crossed the line side by side at the end of the third lap, Mingels led up the hill, but Ward passed him again at the top and the Englishman held on to his narrow lead until he crashed, sustaining a shoulder injury, on the sixth lap. As Mingels relaxed, seeking to catch his breath no doubt, Stonebridge and Nex closed on the Belgian maestro, quickly narrowing the gap to two seconds. At two third's distance the course of the race was twice changed dramatically within the length of a lap. Mingels made a sudden exit when carburation problems halted his FN, which raised the prospect of a Stonebridge hat trick until the 1952 and 1953 winner pulled in at the end of the llth lap no longer able to hold on with a worsening thumb injury, so handing the race to Nex.

With four laps remaining, Nex had almost a minute's cushion over Curtis who was coming under pressure from David Tye on a 350cc BSA, with Archer in a lonely fourth after Nilsson had fallen and retired, in advance of a rear wheel puncture which signalled Draper's retirement. There was no more drama as an eventful grand prix drew to a close with Phil Nex the deserved, if unexpected, winner by a 58 second margin.

Nex was thoughtful, even a mite clever; he rode well within his capabilities, and was respected by his fellow competitors; few of whom, if any, really knew him. There was little unconfined joy in his camp after victory, he took it philosophically much as he might have accepted defeat, as long as he had ridden as well as he could. After his first and only grand prix triumph, he and his travelling mechanic Tony Street packed up and headed back to Hampshire, returning the bikes to Tom Sawyers who built and prepared them between meetings. But Phil Nex was more than a loner who had difficulty in communicating with those beyond his tight circle of family and friends. There was something distressingly darker about his occasional brooding introspection. We shall never know how Nex was affected by a racing accident which left his friend Rob Evans paralysed, or the hovercraft disaster in which Tony Street lost his life. In 1965 Nex emigrated to Australia, returning in 1970 to pick up the threads once more in Fareham. On the eve of a second tour to the Antipodes, the inadequate adhesive which bound Nex's self-control broke loose. In a bloodied frenzy, Nex died by his own hand having first murdered his wife and child. Sadly, Phil Nex will always be remembered more for the violent manner in which he ended his life, rather than for his brilliant successes at Hawkstone Park.

Mingels will be remembered for the tenacity which enabled him to keep possession of the title, winning again in Luxembourg to come once more within two points of a maximum score of 32. Baeten won in front of his home crowd for the second successive year and triumphed in France, but if he was to dispossess his compatriot he needed a win in Sweden. Bill Nilsson denied him, and with Mingels second and John Avery third the chance of an upset was lost. Mingels remained on the throne.

Geoff Ward had every reason to remember 1954. Hawkstone Park proved to be his nemesis. Not for the only time would it be the venue where it appeared as if he was on target to win the British Grand Prix, only for the big prize to evade him. He didn't hate the Shropshire circuit in the way Sten Lundin was to. But the AJS maestro was no more fortunate there than the Swedish rider, who went on to win the World 500cc Championship twice in a glittering career which saw him finish in the top three for eight successive seasons.

Ward's disappointment was in no small measure mollified by his performances elsewhere. His third British title brought him much pleasure, as did his part in another triumph in Britain's colours at the Moto-Cross des Nations, held at Norg in Holland. Having been a member of the winning team in the two previous years, Ward became the only competitor to take the rostrum who had ridden in all three events, which enabled Great Britain to complete the first hat-trick in the team contest.

JOHN DRAPER is European Champion. Jeff Smith turns in the best individual performance at the Moto-Cross des Nations, but Sweden lift the team prize. Smith wins British Grand Prix, Scottish Six Days Trial, Pinhard Prize and the first of his nine home championships.

1955

A disorientated racegoer attempting to find the hidden east entrance to the Cheltenham racecourse off the Winchcombe road might instead stumble into one of the nearby lanes where John Draper lives. The race fan could be forgiven if he mistook the genial little man advising on the correct approach to the famous Gold Cup venue to be a retired National Hunt rider. Indeed, 30 years after he withdrew from serious motorcycle sport, there is a striking similarity between John Draper under his habitual flat cap and champion jockey Pat Eddery. Draper might be a shade fuller in the face, but carries little more weight than he did when he joined the BSA team in 1948.

George John Draper was born in the shadow of Cleeve Hill in 1929, just a gallop away from Cheltenham's famous fences and grandstands and has lived there all his life. But horses held no interest for young Draper, a farmer's son; motorcycles were his passion. His father Harold encouraged the Cheltenham Home Guard and other local clubs to run events on his land at Lower Hill Farm which stimulated John's early involvement and led to his first trial on a 250cc Rudge. With paternal support this was replaced by a 350cc AJS which Draper campaigned until Bob Foster persuaded Bill Nicholson to come down to the Cotswolds and take a look at Harold Draper's boy who showed much early promise. Foster was a great motorcycle racer whose exploits on New Imperial, Levis, Velocette and AJS – particularly in the TT – stamped him with greatness. He used to buy produce from the family farm, and quickly recognized John Draper's natural ability. Foster's appreciation was soon endorsed by Nicholson and a 350cc BSA was rapidly transferred to Draper's hands, putting him on the road to stardom.

John Draper's early successes were mostly in trials, beginning with the best newcomer award in the notorious time and observation classic, the Scott, which he went on to win in 1952. Second place in the Junior race at the Cotswold Scramble behind team-mate Fred Rist, was improved upon the following spring when he won a sparkling victory in the 350cc class at the Sunbeam Point-to-Point. Draper's big breakthrough came in 1950, when at the end of the season he won the individual award at the Moto-Cross des Nations in Sweden as Britain scored a second successive triumph in the renowned team contest.

DRAPER TAKES OFF

Draper's reputation was gaining momentum at home and overseas. In 1951 he won the Junior and Senior races at the Cotswold in scintillating style and with equal command brought BSA their first solo win in the Scottish Six Days; the only major trial the Small Heath factory had not previously won. To add greater authority to his credentials as an all-rounder – as if any more were needed – he took a BSA scrambler to Cadwell Park, shod with road racing tyres, and qualified for the TT. In his only serious attempt at this branch of the sport, he won third place in the Junior Clubman's TT on a Norton and was third in the Senior Clubman's on a Triumph. Draper never went tarmac racing again after an accident on a road section during the International Six Days Trial taking place in Italy, which almost cost him his life and left him requiring surgery to remove a blood clot, which ultimately led to the mandatory use of crash helmets in the competition. Draper's bright start for BSA had also netted him third place in the 1950 British trials cham-

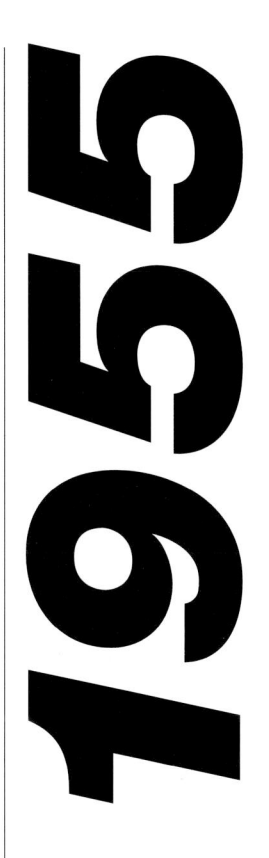

Above **Moto-Cross could often be a muddy business in the 1950s. Geoff Ward (350cc AJS, 32) and David Tye (350cc BSA) slither through the clag in the Junior race at the 1955 Cotswold.**

pionship and fourth in the 1951 national scrambles competition. Not until 1959 was he able to improve on the latter result. Understandably, it came as a considerable surprise to all connected with the sport – especially those at BSA – when he switched to Norton at the end of 1951.

DON'T LOOK BACK IN ANGER...

More than 40 years later, Draper still cannot reconcile himself to the decision. 'I don't know why I did it really,' confessed Draper. 'But I do know it was a disaster. Norton were only properly interested in road racing and I was delighted when Bert Perrigo welcomed me back to BSA in 1953.'

The effect was immediate and Draper collected a second winner's medal in the Moto-Cross des Nations, helping the British team to victory once more in Sweden, this time alongside Les Archer and Geoff Ward..

At a little above 5ft 3in (1.60 m) tall, wiry and with an impish grin there was not very much of John Draper. But distilled into Draper's lean frame was a tigerish determination, allied to uncanny balance and high-proof ability which deceived and unnerved some of the big men who sought to better him. One of the biggest was Geoff Ward, who for a brief spell in 1956 was Draper's team mate. 'Just when you thought you had him beaten he would have another go at you and slip by when you were least expecting it,' recalls Ward. 'In the wet, he was the best I ever saw; even better than Phil Nex. What really used to get me though – especially in the rain and wind – was his cheeky laughter as he passed you and made off into the distance.'

By 1955, then aged 26, John Draper was the finished article; he was the complete all-rounder. There were two factors which perhaps prevented him becoming the finest of his generation. With a little more good fortune he might have won considerably more. For instance, he came perilously close to winning three more Scottish Six Day trials, and was twice runner-up. While in moto-cross he most certainly claimed his share of the honours, if at times he may have sold himself a little short for want of a touch more of the killer instinct. There was a third influence over which Draper had little control and this was the rapid emergence of Jeff Smith, who was ultimately to outshine Draper and everyone else of his era. Nevertheless, 1955 was John Draper's *annus mirabilis*, despite its unpropitious beginnings.

BUSINESS AS USUAL

Hawkstone Park was now on the British championship agenda as well as entertaining the grand prix, and the 12-round series opened in Shropshire before a crowd of 18,000 with Jeff Smith leading home Brian Stonebridge and Geoff Ward. Five days later Don and Derek Rickman cleaned up at Good Friday's Hants Grand National for Royal Enfield and Draper was pointless until he tailed Smith across the line in the Cumberland Grand National. He picked up a couple more points in the Sunbeam – which Ward won – before the eight-tie-trek around Europe began, with the Swiss opener in Geneva. The same eight countries who hosted rounds in the two previous years, furnished the 1955 venues and the same country – Belgium – who provided the first victor of the new campaign; but this time it was Leloup rather than the champion Mingels who took the spoils. René Klym of France on a BSA was second over a minute in arrears of Leloup but two minutes ahead of another Belgian, René Baeten, riding a Matchless. Brian Stonebridge, who had left Matchless at the end of 1953, made a good start to his second campaign for BSA with fourth place, while Ward in sixth took the last point. There was none for Draper who was seventh, or Smith and Nex, both of whom were eliminated with engine troubles.

The French and Italian rounds came next. At Vesoul near the Swiss border, Les Archer beat off a furious challenge from Victor Leloup and Sweden's Bill Nilsson, riding a BSA, to move into second place in the standings, behind Auguste Mingels who did not compete, as he needed time to recover from a knee injury. Archer's reputation in France was given additional impetus by this triumph and he went on to win another three French Grands Prix to set a record which, though subsequently matched by Rolf Tibblin of Sweden and Belgium's André Malherbe, to this day remains unbeaten. The other five British starters – Jeff Smith, Phil Nex, Brian Stonebridge, Eric Cheney and Dave Curtis – all retired. There was better luck for Stonebridge, Nex and Smith in the Italian tie, which was won for BSA by the Swede, Sten Lundin. Stonebridge was second, Smith fifth and Nex sixth.

After Italy it was back to domestic matters and the 16th running of the Cotswold, the only significant event in the month before the British GP. Jeff Smith looked as if he would win both the major races but in each he was thwarted. In the eight-lap Junior, for machines up to 350cc, Smith led until beyond half distance, having dealt with Geoff Ward's initial claims, but as Smith's engine developed a misfire, this allowed team-mate David Tye to take the flag from Dave Curtis's Matchless. In the 500cc Senior race Smith was keen to make amends, soon drawing away from Curtis, Les Archer and Draper. At half way Draper was halted with a broken chain, but towards the end of an absorbing contest Curtis went ahead when Smith faltered over a particularly wet and mud-covered section of the course. Thus began Dave Curtis's long domination of the Cotswold, which was only interrupted when Smith triumphed in the Senior in 1960.

So to Hawkstone for the grand prix, which for the first time enjoyed sponsorship from the now defunct *Daily Herald*. There was an air of expectancy at the Shropshire track which torrential morning rain failed to dampen, as the 35,000 attendance mark was topped by a crowd confident of another home win, despite the fact that Leloup headed the leader-board. Sten Lundin and Brian Stonebridge were tied

Below **Reigning British champion Geoff Ward blasts his AJS out of a crater on his way to victory in the Senior race of the Sunbeam Point-to Point, held in 1955 at Golding Barn, near Shoreham-by-sea.**

in second place with nine points apiece – three fewer than Leloup – while Archer was next with eight, Jean Somja of Belgium was fifth with seven points and René Baeten, René Klym and Nilsson had six each. Smith and Phil Nex completed the list of 10 scorers with two points and one.

During the winter a considerable amount of work had been carried out on the circuit in order to extend the lap distance and add a second sandpit. True to their innovative spirit, the Salop club introduced a two-heat system to decide the grand prix, each race being of 10 laps with the lowest aggregate score deciding the winner and ties broken by reference to elapsed time. One point was awarded to the winner of each race, two for second and so on. Although this scoring system has never been universally adopted, the two-race format – rather than two heats and a final – became obligatory four years after new scoring values were inaugurated in 1969.

By the time racing began, the skies had cleared and much of the surface water on parts of the track had drained away through the soft ground, but the hill was a glistening sandstone stairway which the Belgian and French riders in particular found difficult to climb. But for Smith and John Draper with their trialling expertise, the obstacle held no terrors. While the Salop club were working at their circuit changes, Jeff Smith was polishing up his autumn trials act and celebrating his 20th birthday by winning the first of his two Scotts. A few weeks before his Hawkstone grand prix debut, he won the Scottish Six Days and was clearly in prime form

Geoff Ward got the drop on everyone in heat one, as the 25 starters raced into the first tunnel of trees with Smith, John Avery, Baeten

and Bill Nilsson close astern. As the race settled into a pattern Brian Stonebridge had worked his BSA up to second replacing Ward's ailing AJS but was quietly being pulled back by Draper. However, there was no hauling in Smith, once he had displaced Ward at the front to win by 30 seconds from Draper, who had eventually squeezed past Stonebridge on lap seven. The Continental and Scandinavian competitors had been routed, with Nilsson the highest non-Briton in 10th place, the only one of their number to look at all comfortable in the tricky conditions.

SMITH IN FRONT

The second heat shaped much like the first, though this time it was the precocious Smith who seized the initiative from Draper and Ward. When it was clear this trio – barring accidents or mechanical failure – would not be caught, main interest centred on the race for fourth place between René Baeten, Stonebridge, Archer and Basil Hall, now riding Ariel. Archer narrowly prevailed with Stonebridge and Hall in his wake as Baeten went to ground after a fearful crash had left the Belgian dazed and the frame of his Matchless broken. While Major-General E D Fanshawe was presenting the newly-minted *Daily Herald* silver Challenge Trophy to the triumphant Smith, Baeten completed the lap on foot to cheers almost as loud as those reserved for the winner.

Jeff Smith's victory was remarkable not only for the manner in which it was achieved – riding as *The Motor Cycle*'s reporter put it, 'without notably extending himself' – but it was all the more noteworthy when one considers that Smith was still three month's short of his 21st birthday. For Draper there was the cheer of a hard-earned second place, behind an opponent who had outridden everybody, his first championship points of the season and ultimately the biggest consolation prize of all: the European title.

For the only time in the admittedly brief history of the European tournament, a British rider headed the standings. Brian Stonebridge was a point up on Leloup who had 12, but in the four remaining rounds, Stonebridge would collect only another three for his fourth place in Belgium.

Le Circuit de la Citadelle is the most famous moto-cross venue in the world and the Belgian GP, first held there in 1949, had until 1955 always been won by a home rider.

With the start and finish in a vast amphitheatre, the track winds around the ruins of a Norman fortress high above the delightful city of Namur, where the Sambre and Meuse rivers meet.

Throughout its history it has provided the backdrop to the best attended and most atmospheric grand prix of the year, with the possible exception of the British GP, whether at Hawkstone or Farleigh Castle.

Emboldened by his Hawkstone performance, Draper went to Namur suffused with optimism to record what he regards as the foremost victory of his distinguished career. 'Whenever I pulled on a Union Jack for a grand prix or the Moto-Cross des Nations, it made me 10mph faster,' admitted the proud but modest Draper. 'The Belgians were the tops then and to beat them on their own ground, in front of their own people, was a marvellous feeling.'

In Sweden in the penultimate round, Draper did the same to Bill Nilsson who was second, for the third time in the season, and had acquired 18 points to Draper's 22. Everything now hinged on the final episode in Holland. If Nilsson won, Draper needed only four points for third. This would have tied the scores at 26 each, but Draper would have been declared the winner with two wins to Nilsson's one. Fourth place for Draper was sufficient to give him a one point advantage should the Swede take second.

In the end, one point settled it. In an hour-long final, though badly boxed in at the start, Draper worked his way from 11th to sixth with some inspired riding. Nilsson could do no better than third, coming in almost a minute after his countryman Sten Lundin.

The Union Jack vest had done the trick. Whatever else John Draper achieved, he was now European champion, his place in the hall of fame assured.

1956

LES ARCHER wins British Grand Prix and is European Champion. Jeff Smith, John Draper and Geoff Ward are mighty in victory as Great Britain defeat Sweden at Namur in the Moto-Cross des Nations.

Few other seasons were dominated by a quartet of British riders as was the summer of 1956 when Les Archer, John Draper, Jeff Smith and Geoff Ward held sway in the major domestic and Continental events. Between them they won almost everything worth winning, to irradiate another chapter in a golden era for Britain which stretched from the end of the Second World War to 1970.

With their resources buttressed by the proceeds from a succession of big gates and well aware of the problems some of the overseas riders had experienced with their circuit, the Salop club introduced several changes to Hawkstone Park when they unveiled the track in April, in advance of the opening British Championship round. The club went so far as to convene a press conference to announce the alterations and Bertie Goodman, the sales director of Velocette, provided two machines; one for Alan Bell who enjoyed the factory's support, the other for Geoff Duke. Although he was famed as a road racer, Duke had been a member of the British team who were runners-up to Belgium in the 1948 Moto-Cross des Nations at La Fraineuse, near Spa. The

Right **Geoff Ward forsook AJS for BSA in 1956. Ward appeared at the British Grand Prix on a machine sporting leading-link forks as pioneered by Charlie Salt in the TT. The experiment was a failure and Ward was unclassified.**

Opposite **The long and the short and the tall. Brian Stonebridge (left) and Geoff Ward (right) almost dwarf John Draper at Hawkstone Park.**

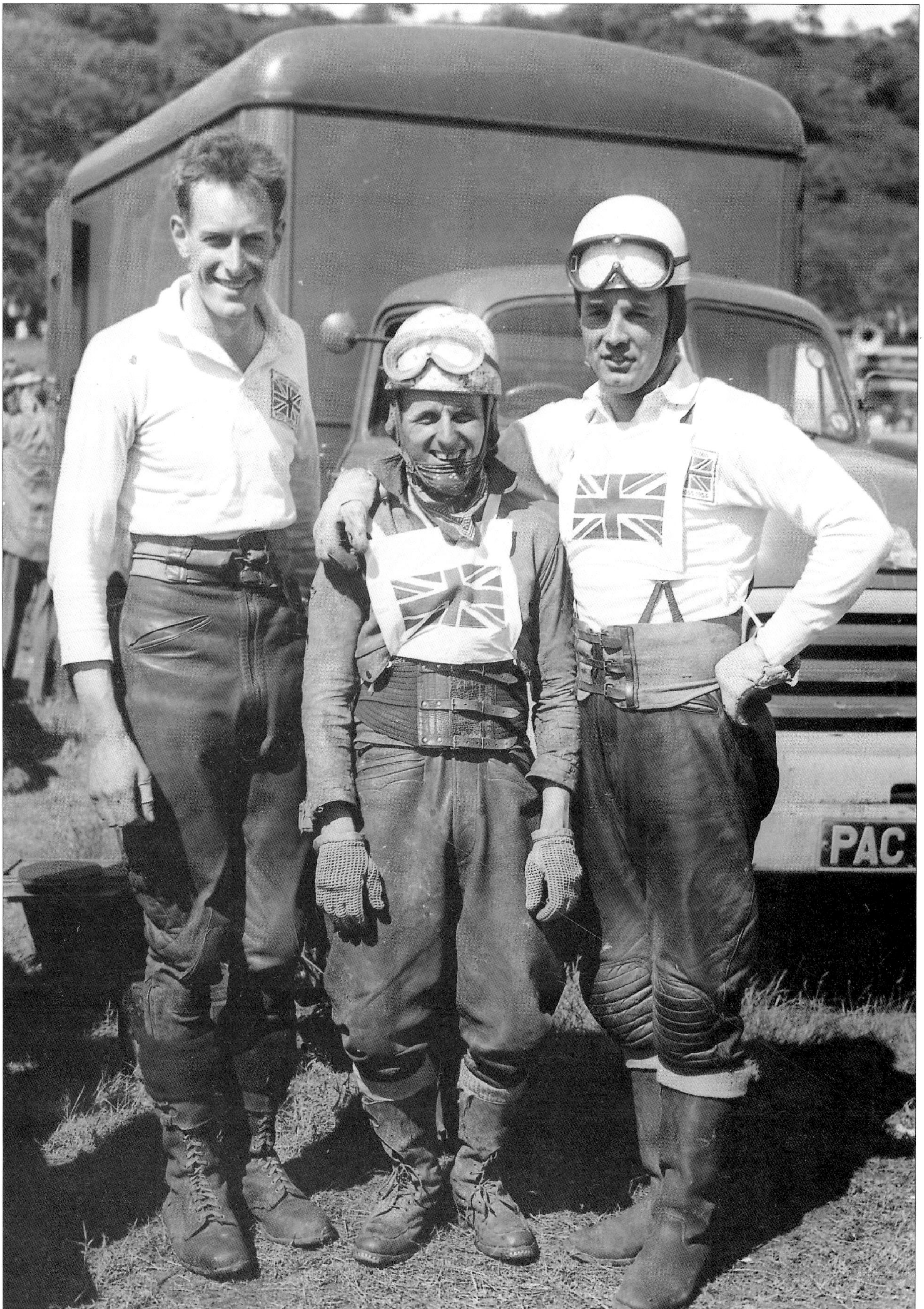
PAC

Right **Les Archer on the Norton which carried him to victory in the 1956 European Championship.**

Opposte, below **Geoff Ward at the top of Hawkstone Park's infamous hill during the 1956 British Grand Prix. Although Ward three times won the British Championship, and appeared in the winning Great Britain team on four occasions in the Moto-Cross des Nations, the British GP was his unlucky event. Like John Draper, Ward was destined never to win it and his two best finishes were third in 1953 and sixth in 1955; each time riding an AJS.**

previous year Duke had competed successfully in the Scott trial on a BSA where he was spotted by Artie Bell who suggested he be taken on by Norton to develop their 500T trials model. Even though Duke's inclusive skills were to lead him to stardom by another route, he, in a small way, contributed to the development of England's foremost moto-cross venue and thus to the advancement of the British Grand Prix.

Duke had never seen Hawkstone before, but he experienced no difficulty in completing several fastish laps over the circuit which had been amended at the top of the hill and re-routed to eliminate the very bumpy finishing straight. Cuth Bate and Harold Johnson – the clerk of the course and father of another secretary of the Salop club, the late Tony Johnson – were suitably impressed by the relative ease with which Duke and Bell had negotiated the revised track, which was conceived with closer racing and better spectator enjoyment in mind.

No one enjoyed the first day of the new season better than Jeff Smith. The BSA factory rider had garnished his first British GP triumph a year previously by winning the ACU Scramble Drivers' Star, so preventing Geoff Ward notching a hat trick in the premier national tournament. With 12,000 spectators thronging the Hawkstone fencing, Smith began the defence of his title in typically assertive fashion. Dave Curtis had won the Junior race, but Smith beat the Matchless rider in the Senior and went on to collect the Salop Cup awarded to the winner of the championship final, with Brian Stonebridge and John

Avery - both on BSAs - second and third, after Curtis's chain had snapped. It was the beginning of an almost cloudless period for Smith in a campaign when there were four more of the big nationals before the home grand prix; three of them won by the champion.

VYING FOR SUPREMACY

In an unusually, if not uniquely, concentrated period of pre-Hawkstone grand prix championship activity, Jeff Smith raced into what proved to be a winning lead by defeating Archer in a thrilling Sunbeam Point-to-Point Senior race, after Ward had expired with a burnt-out clutch on his BSA. Smith took the lead on the 18th of 20 laps; he and Archer had lapped the rest of the field on the Sunbeam's new course at Tottington Mount. The Experts' Grand National at Rollswood Farm, the Lancashire Grand National and the Cotswold were still to come, before Hawkstone would be re-visited for the European championship counter.

The Experts' was a mud bath which Smith won in a BSA one-two-three from David Tye and Brian Stonebridge. Archer and Ward failed to come to terms with the appalling conditions and were unplaced. The Lancashire classic had, like the Sunbeam moved house, and was now domiciled at Cuerden Park, near Preston, having forsaken its original abode at the infamous Holcombe Moor. The Junior race went to Ward from Stonebridge and Tye; but in the points-counting Senior, Smith came out top in a nail-biting finish, a couple of feet in front of Curtis with Brian Martin a lonely third.

The Matchless man got his revenge in the Cotswold to record his second successive triumph at Nympsfield after Smith had crashed. Draper – who won the Junior – was second and Stonebridge third. Smith was now well on his way to his second British crown in a competition he came rightly to regard as second only to the World championship. In his native league table he could be judged alongside his fellow Britons. No rider has won it more often.

Above **Phil Nex heads for the line in a British Championship event at Hawkstone Park on his BSA. Nex loved the Shropshire circuit.**

Meanwhile in Europe, the fifth championship was taking shape; the first four rounds of which had been sandwiched between the Sunbeam and the Experts, beginning traditionally with the Swiss tie at Stade de Champel, near Geneva, which was known as *Le bout du Monde* – the End of the World. Responding promptly to the growing popularity of motocross throughout Europe and Scandinavia, the FIM added Denmark to the list of qualifying countries and this was the final round in the enlarged, nine-part competition, concluded at Randers in early September. There was no increase in scoring values and again, only a rider's four best scores would count.

Geoff Ward now on a BSA, began well enough for his new employers, leading the Swiss GP from start to finish. Auguste Mingels was second and Brian Stonebridge third. Draper, who had made the long overnight trek to Geneva, having competed in the Scottish Six Days Trial, was second to Ward for most of the final, when he fell with two laps to go, remounted and finished out of the points in seventh. A week later in the Dutch round at Schijndel, Les Archer looked the likely winner after Ward had succumbed to a carburettor malady. But on a day when retirements came thick and fast, Jan Clynk delighted the home crowd with victory on his BSA. Draper, who had been 17th on the opening lap, produced another remarkable ride to finish second.

The double champion Mingels had recorded the first grand prix hat-trick in European motocross by winning the Italian round in each of the years 1952–1954. But there was to be no fourth Italian triumph for the Belgian master as his knee injury was by now restricting his effectiveness. Like Ward, Mingels had peaked by 1956 and neither was to win another grand prix, despite several near misses. It was difficult not to be impressed by Mingels, who travelled to events in a drop-head Cadillac, with his bikes on a trailer. Ward thought the Belgian to be the best rider of his era. 'He was very hard on the track, but wonderfully

Leslie R Archer was the son of Leslie J Archer who was a widely experienced road racer and, with his father Jim, ran a garage business in the town selling Norton motorcycles. Archer Jnr was not exactly brought into the world with a silver spoon in his mouth, but his father had the wherewithal to send his son to public school and young Les attended Churcher's College, Petersfield. Archer was raised in an atmosphere of racing bikes and his grandfather Jim forged the careers of his son and grandson. When Les Junior, still a pupil at Churcher's, turned out for his first race in a North Hants MCC event in 1946, Ralph Venables, the well-known motorcycling journalist, commented: 'A pity the lad will never be a great rider like his dad'.

A FAMILY AFFAIR

On leaving school Les served a commission in the Royal Army Service Corps until 1952 and during his army leave he tried his hand at circuit racing winning, as his father had in 1933, the Hutchinson 100. Ron Hankins had introduced Les to moto-cross and once Archer decided to take the sport seriously, thereafter acted as his mechanic. Les started with a 250cc Velocette which Hankins built, before Jim Archer used his influence with Gilbert Smith, the managing director of Norton Motors Ltd, who obliged with factory bikes and parts. The first Norton was a 500T pushrod-engined machine, followed by an experimental Manx, with a modified featherbed frame, which when they emerged from the Archers' workshops, proved superior to the factory models. In no time Les Archer established himself, securing his first big win in the 1951 Hants Grand National which he followed by taking the 250cc class at the Experts' GN on the Velocette, and triumphing later in the year at the Shrubland Park trade-supported event near Ipswich, on the 500cc test-bed Norton. After the Shrubland victory, a jig was made to produce four more moto-cross bikes, which lasted Archer for the remainder of his career. Norton cancelled their own moto-cross programme, though continued to supply Archer with components until he eventually retired in 1967.

companionable off it,' was Ward's generous appraisal of Mingels. 'For sheer riding ability he was the greatest.'

The young Swedish tyro Bill Nilsson won in Italy on a BSA; the only grand prix of the year when there was no Briton in the top six. Mingels, a great favourite with the Italians as well as British supporters, claimed two points for fifth, while Belgium's Jansen was runner-up. The French GP fell to Archer – as it had the year before, and did 12 months later, to complete the second grand prix hat-trick – so on the eve of the British GP the table was at an interesting stage. Ward and Jansen were tied at the top with 12 points apiece, tailed by no fewer than six riders on eight. Archer and Draper were the two Britons alongside Nilsson, Lundin, Mingels and the Dutchman Clynk. The only other British competitor in contention was Stonebridge, with four points.

Les Archer was from a substantially different social background to most of his competitor contemporaries. Born in Aldershot in 1929,

Right **The Norton engine which powered Les Archer to the European title in 1956.**

Opposite, below **Immaculate rider with bike to match. Les Archer, a study in concentration as he goes about his work on the factory-engined Norton.**

Had Les Archer been as successful in a mainstream sport as he was in moto-cross he would in all probability have been gracing the advertising hoardings alongside Denis Compton, endorsing a branded grooming product or some other consumer necessity. Slightly Latin looks with a shock of dark brown hair gave him the demeanour of a matinée idol. Six foot tall with a military bearing which was allied to natural charm Archer was, like his machines, always immaculately turned out. He soon learned there was more prize money to be earned across the Channel than there ever was or would be in England and, his Norton commitments excepted, preferred to race in Europe. He loved France, its people and the French circuits and they loved and were good to Archer. In June 1954, on the same day as Jeff Smith won the Dutch GP, Les was in France winning a non-championship international at Chateauneuf where the rewards were greater. A month earlier he had won at Niort, Ferte-Bernard, Tarare, Valentigney and Avesnes as big-money continental events proliferated. For Archer and others – like his friend, neighbour and sometime fellow-Norton rider Eric Cheney, who often travelled with him – top riders could earn upwards of £100 in appearance guarantees and as much again from the prize fund. At 1998 values this would mean more than £2,000 per event. It was not just the appeal of rural France which attracted Archer, or the fact it was more accessible to him than the most northerly British tracks; though Les Archer was no mere mercenary.

THE SPOILS OF COMPETITION

One of Archer's greatest memories was taking his grandfather Jim abroad for the first time and beating Auguste Mingels in a terrific scrap for the 1953 Luxembourg GP. Although they finished almost side-by-side, Archer gained the verdict to clinch the first of his ten grands prix victories. Mingels was genuine and warm in his congratulation of the 24-year-old Englishman, for whom it was an understandably emotional moment.

'It would be quite wrong to think I went racing only for the money,' is Archer's disavowal. 'Personal ambition, the thrill of competition and the satisfaction of a job well done has nothing to do with the finance essential to running a full-time racing stable with two mechanics. Grands prix and the Moto-Cross des Nations were notorious for the lack of financial reward, though if you won, it helped to improve your rating – and thereby, appearance money prospects – in other international events.'

Although Les could never be accused of being slavish in his commitment to the British series, he still won enough points to place himself third in the 1952 competition and equal sixth the year after, in company with Brian Stonebridge. Nevertheless, Archer had little appetite for the windswept Cumbrian or rain-ruined Lancashire events which were important in the championship mixture. Northern fans rarely saw that famous helmet adorned so effulgently with its big letter A. When Archer ventured into latitudes above those which cut across Birmingham – Britain's motorcycle city – it was to Hawkstone Park, where he left his unforgettable impression in July 1956. Les Archer never made a more profitable and successful journey north.

The decision to move the grand prix to a Saturday was to provide a disappointment as only two or three thousand more than had attended the home championship meeting in April were there to salute a fifth British victory. Clouds of dust had marred Friday's practice, but heavy overnight rain returned the circuit to perfect condition for the two 10-lap heats which comprised the grand prix, sponsored this time by the News Chronicle and Daily Dispatch. Ward dearly wanted a win to erase the memory of his 1954 battle with Mingels, which had ended with the Briton regaining consciousness in the first aid tent. Brian Martin, Stonebridge and Ward's BSAs all sported leading-link front forks as pioneered by Charlie Salt in the TT, but none of this trio was in the leading group chasing the early leader Jean Rombauts of Belgium on a conventionally sprung BSA.

Archer had made a better start and he was soon ahead of the Belgian. By mid-race Curtis and Smith were struggling with bent controls after minor falls and everyone else was then straining to keep Archer within a respectable distance as the Norton rider pulled effortlessly away to win from Ward and the improving Draper, who had seen off Sten Lundin's BSA after a grim struggle. Nic Jansen had ridden sensibly to claim fifth place ahead of Stonebridge, but Mingels had retired with magneto trouble and Jan Clynk took an early turn for the paddock with a sticking throttle slide. Rombaut's fine ride had also ended.

UNEXPECTED HITCHES

During the interval, BSA decided to change their experimental forks, which had not come up to expectations, for regular telescopics. Ward was soon to wish things had been left as they were. He and Archer headed the pack into the trees at the back of the circuit to get the second heat under way, with the exuberant Rombauts in third place. But after another lap, Ward toured in with his front forks jammed on full compression. To be classified, a finish was required in each heat, so another British GP had slipped through Ward's hands.

There were no slips from Archer, Smith or Jansen as the Norton ace glided unspectacularly to victory with 38 seconds in hand over Smith's BSA. Jansen had the satisfaction of leaving Hawkstone tied at the top of the table with Archer on 16 points. Draper was third with 14 and the downcast Ward remained fourth, without adding to his score.

A month later, Archer repeated Draper's feat by winning in Belgium, though not at Namur which was to host the Moto-Cross des Nations. Instead the Belgian GP was held at the sandy Keiheuvel track, near Mol where Archer outdistanced the other 16 runners in his eight-lap heat. Fortified by Jansen's retirement, Archer was absolute master of the 12-lap final, winning with ease from Lundin, Ward and Mingels.

Without a victory in the series, Draper – who was absent in Belgium with gallstone trouble – needed to win the three remaining rounds if he was to retain his title. His return to the fray at Ettelbruck was brave and typically Draper. Jansen, like Ward, required an improbable sequence of three successive victories to unseat Archer, but the Belgian's father died the week before the Luxembourg tie and he was a non-starter. In a gruelling 18-lap, 70-minute race, Ward looked as if he might triumph until he punctured. Draper then took charge to win by over a minute from Archer, with Stonebridge third.

The penultimate round in Sweden settled it. Nilsson, who had unexpectedly missed Hawkstone, won at Saxtorp after Draper fell twice while leading. In torrential rain Archer also came to grief when he collided with Gunnar Johansson's BSA, but recovered to collect three points for fourth place. Draper's tribulations meant that Archer could not be caught. Archer celebrated in Denmark by recording his fourth victory. He had achieved a matchless double in quite brilliant fashion. Draper had to be content with second place in the final table and Ward equal fourth with Nilsson. To complete a marvellous year of almost overwhelming British superiority, Jeff Smith, Geoff Ward and John Draper triumphed in the Moto-Cross des Nations, with Smith winning the individual award for the second year running to add to another British title.

Sweden, having recorded their first win in the competition the previous season – at Randers, amid Denmark's northern lakes and fjords – where Bill Nilsson, Lars Gustafsson and Sten Lundin won by virtue of being the only team to complete the course, were clear favourites to repeat that success.

David Tye had been drafted into the British team as a replacement for Phil Nex, who had sustained a broken leg while competing in a non-championship international in France. But Tye only had a 350cc BSA at his disposal, and the lack of engine power eventually told against him. Even so he finished eighth in the first seven-lap heat, which was won by Les Archer who had a five-seconds advantage over Nilsson. Ward won the second heat, with Lundin sandwiched between Smith and Draper.

Ward and Draper had the unique distinction of appearing in four victorious Moto-Cross des Nations' teams without ever winning their home grand prix. Although still a comparatively young man, Ward was never so effective as he had been in 1956 and before. He left BSA at the end of the season returning to his old love AJS, before trying his hand with a Norton. Draper and Archer soldiered on, winning two and three grands prix respectively, before declining ambition and Father Time eventually overhauled them. Needless to say, the memory of their contributions to moto-cross and the British Grand Prix will always be treasured. From Smith, the baby of the quartet, there was a treasure chest of memories still to come.

1957

Britons eclipsed in maiden World Championship by Sweden's BILL NILSSON. Suez crisis causes cancellation of British series. Though there is sufficient fuel for Jeff Smith to win again at Hawkstone and for Great Britain to triumph once more at Brands Hatch where Belgium are runners-up.

As the tents and the stands which had outlined the Citadelle circuit at Namur for the 1956 Moto-cross des Nations were being packed away, the agenda for the following season was being set by delegates from competing nations. Vic Anstice, Edward Damadian and Harold Taylor were Britain's representatives and they gave their support to a number of proposals which were to be submitted to the FIM at their Autumn Congress in Paris. Mostly these recommendations dealt with organisational minutiae, covering start-line procedures, clothing requirements and changes to the qualifying regulations of the increasingly popular team contest in which Britain was so successful. But the most important motion of all concerned the European Championship, which it was suggested be upgraded to world status, bringing the tournament into line with the road racing competitions.

In October 1956, as the storm clouds were gathering over Suez, the FIM ratified the seminal proposition, and the World 500cc Championship was instituted. Additionally, there would be a competition limited to machines of up to 250cc for the medal of the CSI; though a full-blooded tournament for a European Championship, to be known as *Le Coupe d'Europe* didn't come to life until 1958.

Sten Lundin hated Hawkstone Park and never mastered the demands of the Shropshire track. But he was gifted enough to finish in the top three of the World 500cc Championship for eight successive seasons and win the title twice.

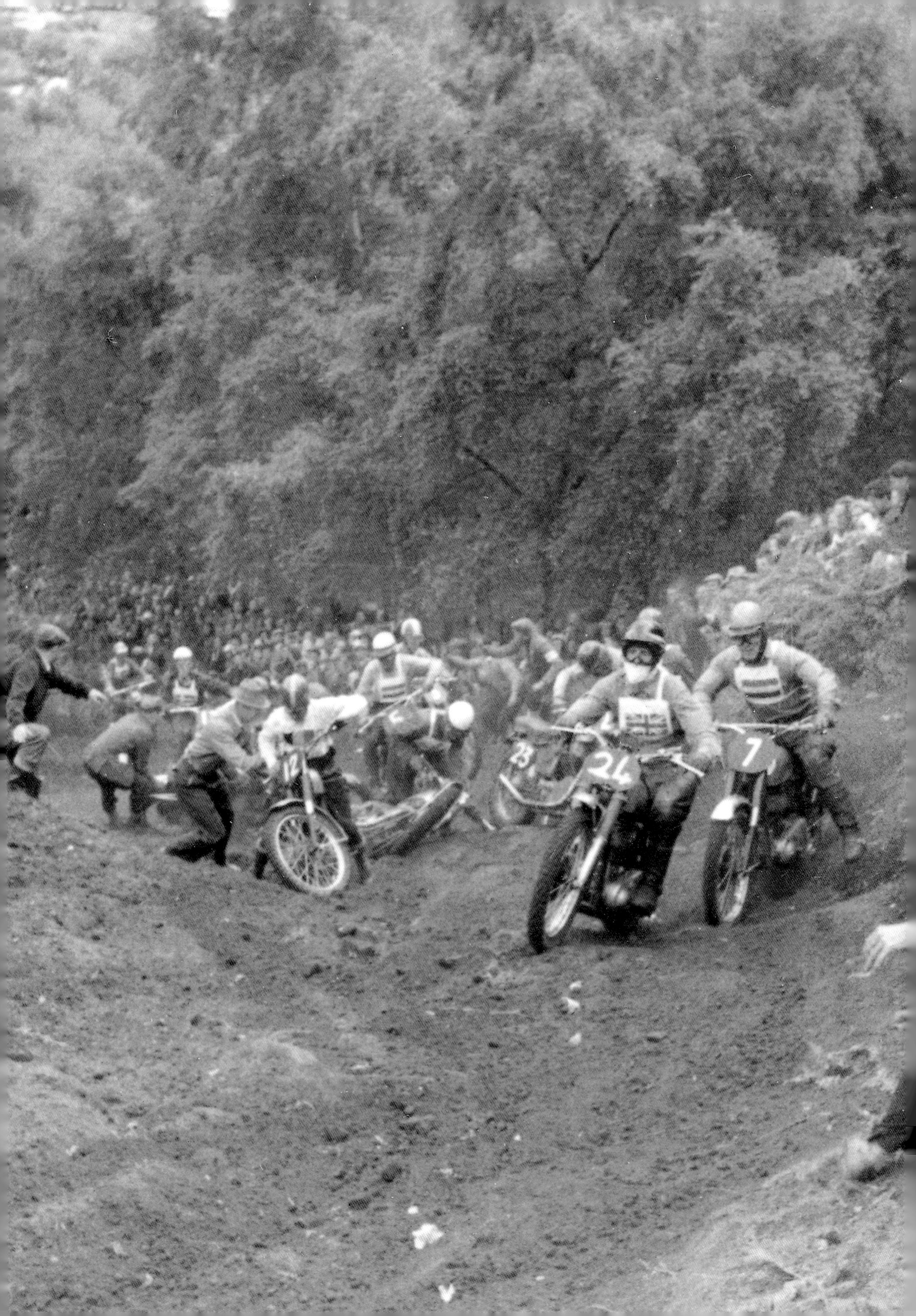
12
24
7

Within a month, the immediate future of all motorsport in Britain was plunged into uncertainty as the Suez crisis broke, bringing with it the prospect of petrol rationing. The ACU's response was unequivocal: there would be no Scramble Drivers' Star in 1957. Fortunately, the critical point in the Middle East emergency had been reached before the British GP, which was again scheduled for Hawkstone as the fifth leg of the newly titled, nine-part series. Sensibly the number of scores to count was increased from four to five. Although the domestic tournament had been aborted there was no threat so far as the overseas competitions were concerned, nor eventually was there to the fourth grand prix scheduled for the delightful Shropshire countryside.

FOREIGN CONSIDERATIONS

In spite of the constraints imposed by the need for fuel conservation, British moto-cross was admittedly less well attended but, for the most part, organised as if the problems in Egypt were of no great concern and would have little lasting effect. Most of the English glamour events which had made up the previous six years' championships were contested by the top riders even though there were no points at stake. The focus of attention was now directed understandably towards a competition, globally by name with – notionally, at least – all the media, sales and promotional opportunities this presented for the export-conscious motorcycle makers.

Early season form was mixed with half a dozen riders picking over the silverware in the three majors. The Rickman brothers shared the honours over Easter at the Hants GN; Derek beating Don in the Senior, only for the positions to be replaced in the Junior. The April Hawkstone meeting saw Jeff Smith come out on top in the 500cc race, ahead of John Draper and Brian Martin. But in the unlimited capacity race for the Salop Cup, Draper won, having been hounded by Brian Stonebridge who had switched during the close season from BSA to Greeves and had earlier in the day won the 250cc race on his new lightweight

Opposite **The stairway of hell. Hawkstone Park's infamous hill was the undoing of many. Eric Cheney (BSA, 24), Albert Dirks (BSA, 12), and Jean Rombauts (BSA, 23) endeavour to come to terms with its complexities.**

European Champions. A talented trials rider, John Draper (left) was one of Britain's most accomplished all-rounders. In 1951 he became the first BSA rider to win the Scottish Six Days Trial and he followed this up by winning the arduous Scott Trial 18 months later.

Les Archer (right) had a career record of 10 grand prix victories and won the European 500cc title in 1956, the season after Draper.

charge. Stonebridge's second change of manufacturer and his remarkable Hawkstone debut, was the launching pad for the Essex two-stroke invalid carriage manufacturer, to herald another glittering episode in British moto-cross history.

At the Cumberland Grand National there was an unpredicted outcome as a newcomer, Arthur Lampkin, won both the Junior and the Senior races. Lampkin, born in Woolwich in 1938, lived most of his life in Yorkshire and was the eldest of three brothers in what was to become a remarkable dynasty of motorcycle sportsmen. Arthur was rewarded for a brilliant 1956 Scottish Six Days' ride – a trial he won outright in 1963 – with a works BSA after Stonebridge and John Avery had left the team. A winner of the coveted Pinhard Prize at 18, he won his first British Championship at 19, the Scott Trial on three occasions – he also made fastest time in four Scotts – and represented his country in the Moto-Cross des Nations, though was never fortunate enough to collect a winners medal. Although he had many outstanding rides on larger capacity machines, Arthur Lampkin – blunt and down to earth – will best be remembered for his contributions in the 250cc class, especially on the C15 BSA in the mid-1960s.

The underrated Nic Jansen had accumulated only three second places in four seasons of European competition, but became the first winner of a World Championship round by heading two of his compatriots across the line in the Swiss GP at Geneva, watched by 25,000 spectators. August Mingels – now on Saroléa – followed Jansen's Matchless home, Rene Baeten was third on his FN and Sten Lundin, who had gone more than a year without a grand prix win, was fourth. Les Archer was fifth and Geoff Ward, on a borrowed Norton, sixth. It was the only World Championship point Geoff scored. Archer took his customary win in France, where John Draper was the only other English scorer with a point for sixth. In the remaining two rounds which preceded Hawkstone, Bill Nilsson took a firm grip on the championship, which ultimately nobody was able to shake free.

Nilsson was one of Sweden's most accomplished moto-crossers. Of his countrymen only Rolf Tibblin and Sten Lundin won more grands prix. But in all other respects, Nilsson's name deserves to be bracketed alongside his native contemporaries. Fearless and uncompromising, Nilsson was a plumber by trade, fair-haired and stockily built. He once declared after a clash with a rival that: 'Moto-cross isn't ping-pong, it is a tough sport for men.'

In the paddock he was the butt of innumerable porcine jokes by virtue of his toothy, pug-like features. Some British riders unkindly called him 'Billy the Pig'. But Nilsson was inured to the name-calling, was affable and well respected by friend and foe alike for his tenacity, skill and unrestrained will to win. Like most other Swedish riders of the time, Nilsson had commenced his career on a BSA, but for 1957 the Birmingham factory had slashed their competitions department commitments and Nilsson was obliged to look elsewhere for something competitive to ride. The unverified story then in currency was that Hugh Viney left a road race 7R AJS at the back door of the Plumstead Road racing workshop for Nilsson to use as he pleased. In fact, the Swedish importer Olle Nygren gave Nilsson a 1956 7R which, with help from Jack Williams and some Norton bits, Bill turned into a beautifully hand-crafted race winner which he named a Crescent, when the AJS factory parsimoniously withdrew their direct support.

Nilsson, then 24, had no-scored in Switzerland, was runner-up to Archer in France and then won his home grand prix for the second successive season; triumphing in the sandy wilderness at Saxtorp when Lundin and Archer were to be forced out with wheel troubles. At Imola a week later, Nilsson beat Jeff Smith in a last-lap dash to the line to take his second Italian GP. As the halfway point in the series was approached, the Swede led on 24 points with Baeten his nearest challenger nine adrift on the FN. British hopes rested with Smith and Archer on ten each – two fewer than Mingels – with Draper on seven. In the run up to Hawkstone, Smith won the Lancashire GN from Dave Curtis and Don Rickman, but in the Cotswold, contested in sub-tropical heat, the Matchless supremo prolonged the Nympsfield

Heavyweight rider, lightweight bike. Brian Stonebridge and Greeves. An unforgettable combination, pictured on their way to victory in the 250cc race at the trade-supported Shrubland Park national in 1957.

Above **The Man Mountain. Belgium's Auguste Mingels. European Champion in 1953 and 1954. The only rider to win the title twice.**

Right **Brian Martin aviates his BSA to fourth place in the trade-supported Cotswold. It was a good year for Martin, who was a member of the winning Great Britain team in the 1957 Moto-Cross des Nations.**

legend with a third triumph, when Smith once again fell with victory in sight.

During the 1950s organizers of the big events were threatened by legal action from the Lord's Day Observance Society, who protested strongly that clubs were breaking the law by charging the public. Administrators eventually circumvented this by hiking up their car park prices and allowing free entry, or allowing admission by programme only, for which they demanded a cover price equal to the cost of an admittance ticket. Once the threats and the protests had eventually receded, nearly all racing was staged on Sundays. In 1956 the Salop club prudently chose Saturday for the grand prix and their caution attracted a commensurately small turn-out. For 1957 the grand prix was returned to a Sunday and the size of the crowd doubled to some 36,000. Under cloudy skies with the constant threat of rain, they were treated to a stimulating afternoon's sport in the invitation races as well as two 10-lap heats of the grand prix, which once more was sponsored by the *Daily Herald*.

For the second time in as many days Jeff Smith was obliged to observe the ceremony of a formal occasion as he joined the parade of riders from six competing nations, before giving his honeymoon a joyous send-off. Twenty four hours earlier Jeff had married Irene, the elder of John Draper's two sisters.

TROUBLE ON THE HILL

Just as he had in 1954, and in the second heat in 1956, Geoff Ward made the early running. Les Archer, Dave Curtis and Bill Nilsson were next as the leading group bounded up the hill, with Smith shadowing the Swede, when Ward dropped the AJS near the summit. Smith managed to avoid Nilsson; but few of the other riders did, as bedlam broke out and the stony slope was a seething mass of fallen riders and bikes. What went through Smith's mind is not difficult to judge. He was soon beyond the hapless Ward, who tumbled on the descent, while Curtis and Archer were quick to discover that they were unable to contain the BSA rider, who was pressing home his advantage with all the resolution he could call upon. Nilsson's recovery was brilliant as he began the unenviable task of working his way up from 20th place. By the penultimate lap, Nilsson had Broer Dirks' BSA in sight, but fourth was as high as the champion-elect could go before time ran out.

SWEDISH SUCCESS

It was to do so again in the second race, which Ward initially led, with Nilsson at his shoulder. Archer and Smith were third and fourth, until a momentary lapse by the Norton star enabled Smith to reverse the positions. Though again, the hill was Nilsson's undoing. As the Swedish rider and Ward were disputing the lead on the stretch beyond the apex, Nilsson fell, leaving Ward temporarily in command. But Archer and Smith were closing fast as Nilsson contemplated a second retrieval action. Once it had begun – from 14th position – Ward faded, leaving Smith and Archer to resolve their dispute for the leadership. There was never much doubt it would be settled in Smith's favour once he got his nose in front of the Norton. Nilsson was unable to display the powers of recovery which had electrified the first race, but he nonetheless worked his way to seventh behind fellow Swede, Lars Gustafsson. This was good enough to ensure fifth overall for Nilsson, to keep his championship ambitions simmering as Smith's came to the boil, just six points off the lead. The first full day of married life had been particularly sweet for Jeffrey Vincent Smith.

Almost before the ink had dried on the Smith's marriage certificate, Nilsson had taken another decisive step towards realizing his principal ambition of becoming world champion. Despite Jeff's victory at Hawkstone, Nilsson saw René Baeten as the most formidable obstacle along the title path. In Lichtenvoorde's deep sand, the Belgian led the Dutch round until the closing stages, when Nilsson forged ahead of him. Smith could only manage fifth and, though the Briton remained second in the table, Nilsson now had a 12-point advantage. For Smith or Baeten to deny Nilsson, either of them would have to win all three of the remaining grands prix. Baeten came closest by taking second place behind Sten Lundin's Monark at Namur but, when the championship season closed at Naestved, near Copenhagen, Baeten's win in the Danish GP was little more then a consolation prize; Nilsson was safe.

Jeff's disappointment at only finishing fourth in the maiden World Championship was to some extent assuaged in the Moto-Cross des Nations. At Brands Hatch, before a vast crowd of 47,000, Smith collected his third successive award for the best individual performance, as Great Britain swept to victory for the eighth time. Although, like Les Archer, Geoff Ward was forced to miss the team contest through injury, the autumn of the AJS rider's career must have looked a little rosier as he won the Experts' and Shrubland Park Grand Nationals. But there was nothing to compare with the bloom of Nilsson's spirits, when he was garlanded as the first world champion.

Left **The brooding Phil Nex. Deep and introspective, Nex took his own life in 1970.**

1958

DAVE CURTIS wins British title. Lars Gustaffson becomes the first overseas rider to win the British Grand Prix. Sweden take the Moto-Cross des Nations on home soil. Belgium's René Baeten is World Champion. First year of *Le Coupe d'Europe* for 250cc machines.

Lars Gustafsson was a notable member of a group of riders from Sweden who first challenged the early ascendancy of Belgian and British riders in world moto-cross, though his achievements were almost invariably overshadowed by the superior talents of fellow Swedes Bill Nilsson, Sten Lundin and Rolf Tiblin. While this great trinity were winning six world 500cc titles – two each – and also amassed seven FIM silver medals for championship second places and five bronzes for third, Gustafsson was an inveterate supporting role player in company with Ray Sigvardsson, Ove Lundell and Gunnar Johansson. But, just

64

as an unknown *domestique* in the *Tour de France* cycle race might have a day when he is thrust into the limelight, Lars Gustafsson had three – two of them in 1958 – to adorn an otherwise unmemorable career; certainly so far as the big prizes were concerned. If this assessment seems a little hard, Gustafsson was nonetheless sufficiently talented to make three important entries in the record book and will everlastingly be remembered as the first overseas rider to win the British Grand Prix. He is also one of only three riders whose sole grand prix victory which counted towards the World 500cc Championship was the British. The other two to claim the mark are both English: Dave Curtis in 1961 and Don Rickman in 1966. Phil Nex did so in 1954 when the British GP was a European Championship tie.

Lars Gustafsson came to notice in 1955 – his first full year of individual international participation – after he had finished tenth in the European Championship with fifth place in each of the rounds where he scored: Luxembourg, Holland and Sweden. Flushed with this meritorious, if unspectacular start in his debut season, Gustafsson was a joyful member of the first Swedish team to win the Moto-Cross des Nations when he, Bill Nilsson and Sten Lundin triumphed in Denmark in late August. Theirs was the only team to finish intact. It was just reward for Gustafsson, who was the highest placed home rider when Sweden staged the team contest at Skillingaryd in 1953, but whose trio could only finish third behind Belgium and winners, Great Britain. In the two years after his team win in 1955, Gustafsson's only results of note were a fifth at Hawkstone in the 1956 British GP which was followed by a fourth place at Namur in the final of the Moto-Cross des Nations, where Sweden were runners-up to Great Britain. Gustafsson's team mates that day were Lundin and Johansson. 1957 was even thinner for Gustafsson whose only championship points were gained in Luxembourg where he was fourth. In the Moto-Cross des Nations, although Sweden were third, it was Sigvardsson, Lundell and Johansson on the podium. Gustafsson, though he had qualified with seventh place in his heat, was edged out in the final as the anticipated Swedish domination failed to materialize. Until the close of the 1957 season Gustafsson had always ridden a BSA, but with Small Heath competition components difficult to obtain – except maybe in Britain – Lars, encouraged by what he saw of the Monark in Ove Lundell's care, decided to change marques. Lars Gustafsson was not the only Swedish competitor whose career took a turn for the better once he ceased trading with Armoury Road.

As Gustafsson was adapting his technique to the characteristics of his new mount, Bill Nilsson and René Baeten were renewing their

Below left **René Baeten, twice runner-up in the European 500cc Championship and second to Bill Nilsson in the first World 500cc championship in 1957. Baeten gained his reward the year after when he turned the tables on the Swedish rider and took the title by a margin of eight points.**

Right **Lars Gustafsson urges his Monark to victory at Hawkstone Park. Gustafsson was the first overseas rider to win the British 500cc Moto-Cross Grand Prix.**

Below **The gifted René Baeten. World Champion in 1958, Baeten was to lose his life two years later, while racing at Stekene in his native Belgium.**

rivalry in the world championship which had been extended by one, to ten rounds, with the last minute inclusion of Austria. The grassy Sittendorf track near Vienna provided Hubert Scaillet with victory on an FN; the Belgian having snatched the lead from Nilsson near the end of a closely contested race. Britain's Peter Taft was third on a privately entered BSA. In the Danish and Swiss ties that followed, Baeten and Nilsson stamped their signatures on the series as each sought control. The title holder – riding the 7R-engined Crescent, but no longer with the support of AJS – won at Naestved, with Baeten second, after a lengthy battle that also involved two other Swedes: Sten Lundin on a Monark and the Crescent-BSA of Gunnar Johnasson. Baeten turned the tables the following Sunday, winning an absolute thriller at Stade de Champel with Nilsson relegated to second over the final 50 metres and Scaillet third. John Draper improved on his first appearance of the year – a fourth in Switzerland – by taking the French at Cassel; a circuit which became legendary after the 1960 Moto-Cross des Nations. By securing the Italian round at Imola, Lundin made it five different winners for the first five rounds of a rigorously striven championship. Hawkstone, hospitable as ever, and with a reputation for setting trends rather than bucking them, would produce the sixth. Despite the fact that the series had reached the halfway point before Hawkstone, it was not easy to judge how competitive the best Britons would be at their own grand prix, because none of them had contested all five of the championship rounds. Dave Curtis, who had been second to Jeff Smith in the 1956 Scramble Drivers' Star, had only taken his Matchless abroad twice, collecting a solitary point in France. Curtis's decision to concentrate on the ACU series was to have its reward as the Bicester farmer went on to win his only Star, in what was a fairly lean season for Smith and BSA. Geoff Ward had ventured across the Channel just once and the improving Rickman brothers were untested against foreign opposition. Only Smith, Draper and Les Archer had contested three or more grands prix.

DOMESTIC CHANGES

At home the removal men had been called in once more to shift the Sunbeam Point-to-Point; this time to Oxenbourne Farm, in the Meon Valley, near Petersfield. They also returned the event to its traditional April date, it having been run the previous year in September. Jeff Smith looked as if he would win the Senior, but he fell after leading for 18 of the 20 laps, allowing Don Rickman – who just got the better of Curtis after a race-long struggle – to win, with Smith redeeming himself for third. Derek Rickman, who had won his second Hants Grand National Senior earlier in the month, was fourth. In conditions quite out of character with the usually sun-blessed Cotswold, Dave Curtis was master of the mud, slithering expertly to win his fourth Senior and second Junior races. Sliding home in Curtis's wake were Ron Langston's Ariel in the big class and the Greeves of Dave Bickers in the Junior; Bickers having beforehand won the 250cc race from Don Rickman's DOT.

With four of the first five rounds in the World Championship having been completed before May was out, the long gap in international competition between the French tie and Hawkstone on Sunday 6 July, was broken only by the Italian GP. With the leader board topped by overseas' riders, Ward and Archer absent through injury and Smith struggling to find his best form, the portents for another British victory were unfavourable. Nilsson led the table with 26 points, six more than Baeten, with Scaillet third on 19. Draper and Lundin were tied on 12, and Smith was next with ten. On a windless, sultry afternoon under a hazy sun, the Ferodo Works Silver Band entertained the 57,841 enthusiasts who had packed into Hawkstone's enclosures, most of whom were expecting Nilsson or Baeten to win. How wrong they were.

Don Rickman was the early pacesetter in the first 12-lap heat with Gustafsson and Gunnar Johansson shadowing the leader and Dutchman Broer Dirks fourth, riding a BSA. From a mediocre start Nilsson pushed hard to get up to fifth place by half distance, when Smith went missing with a broken primary chain. Sten Lundin soon followed. Rickman kept his lead until the seventh lap, when Gustafsson slipped past. The Briton fought back, but Gustafsson held Rickman at bay to win by a mere two seconds, as Nilsson eventually surged to third.

There were two false starts before the second race was allowed to continue and, once it did, Gustafsson was again dictating the pace, heading Baeten and the champion past the control tower and up the hill. Brian Martin and Don Rickman were next, followed by a posse of British riders which

Left **Dave Curtis won the British Championship in 1958. The Oxfordshire farmer brought his Matchless home six points ahead of Don Rickman, who was a further two up on Jeff Smith. Curtis's victory prevented Smith scoring a hat-trick. A feat the BSA rider had to wait until 1963 to achieve.**

Below **Ove Lundell flies his Monark to victory in the second heat of the Moto-Cross des Nations at Knutstorp. Bill Nilsson, Lars Gustafsson and Lundell secured Sweden's second victory in the team contest, their first on home soil, with Great Britain five minutes in arrears, France third.**

included Smith, Draper and Curtis. But Gustafsson was unable to hold off Baeten for long, and was soon in Rickman's clutches. Meanwhile Curtis and Nilsson crashed, allowing Draper into the picture after Smith had moved up to third when Rickman – with badly blistered hands – was forced to yield in the contest for second. This was safely in Gustafsson's grasp as he finished 6$_{1/2}$ seconds behind Baeten to conclude an attritional grand prix, in which only six riders completed both heats to be classified as points' scorers. Gustafsson's win provided no more than a footnote in moto-cross history, but it had sounded a keynote for growing Swedish predominance. The underdog had triumphed. Lars Gustafsson, whose fresh, Nordic features unwaveringly bore the trace of a smile, had discarded the uncertainties of his BSA form a year earlier to take home the *Daily Herald* trophy, the biggest prize of his sporting life. Men have gone to heaven singing Hosannas for much less.

BAETEN vs NILSSON

One man still singing, but who tragically was to be called to heaven much earlier than he would have wished, was Baeten. With Nilsson failing to score at Hawkstone by virtue of his second heat altercation with Curtis, Baeten and the Swede were now tied on 26 points; seven ahead of Scaillet, with Draper and Lundin still on 12 and Jeff Smith sixth with ten points. Gustafsson of course had his precious eight, and Don Rickman four. With four countries yet to be visited there was still all to play for. The next two rounds would be crucial. They certainly were for Nilsson.

At St Anthonis, south of Nijmegen, at the end of the month, the Dutch tie was run in deep sand and the organizers had adopted the two-heat system introduced firstly by the Salop club in 1955. John Draper won the first, after the pack concertinaed shortly after the start eliminating many of the favoured riders, including Dave Curtis and Jeff Smith – though not the championship front-runners, who later had a pile-up of their own to allow Draper into the lead. At halfway Baeten had just passed Nilsson and promptly fell. Nilsson was unable to avoid his fallen foe and crashed himself. Although Baeten was able to restart, Nilsson had bent the front forks of the Crescent and broken the frame for good measure. Nilsson's discomfiture was exacerbated as he, Johansson and Gustafsson with nothing serviceable to ride, had little option but to spectate during the second heat, which Baeten won to give him third overall behind Albert Dirks of Holland on a BSA and Draper. The Englishman thus scored the first ever grand prix victory to be decided by a tie-break, as the sum of his elapsed times was lesser than that of Dirks. This was the sixth and last of Draper's grand prix triumphs, though there was still another Moto-Cross des Nations win in his satchel.

Seven days later Bill Nilsson must have felt that fate, rather than René Baeten, was pulling the title from his grasp. There were 25,000 or more spectators at Namur as Baeten, Nilsson and John Draper took a grip of an absorbing race. Baeten broke the lap record repeatedly as Nilsson clung tenaciously to second place. As Draper tired, Sten Lundin – who loved the Citadelle and who won there in 1957 and 1961 – came into the picture and was closing on the Crescent as the last lap signal went out. In the furious couple of kilometres that remained, Nilsson tumbled, allowing Lundin up to second as Baeten coasted to victory. Nilsson only had enough time to make third place, just ahead of Draper. Baeten was now on 38 points and to have a hope of retaining his crown Nilsson – with 30 – needed to win in Luxembourg. Draper's only chance of adding a World to his European title was to take the last two rounds and hope Baeten and Nilsson would no-score in both. This prospect, even the irrepressible Draper thought too improbable to take seriously.

Nilsson's third fall – and, as it transpired, the knock-out and submission – was delivered at Ettelbruck in front of an expectant crowd even larger than had attended Namur. The 18-lap

Top **John Draper's victory in the French Grand Prix at Cassel, lifted him to fourth in the standings. Although he went on to win the Dutch GP at St Anthonis, Draper was still nine points adrift of the FIM Bronze Medal place at the season's end.**

Above **Brian Stonebridge was runner-up in the first British 250cc Grand Prix, at Beenham Park on the factory Greeves.**

69

Right The British contingent making their way to the parade before the French Grand Prix at Cassel. (From left to right) Geoff Ward, Les Archer, Mike Jackson, Dennis Bickerton, Terry Cheshire, Dave Curtis, John Draper, Jeff Smith, and ACU official Harold Taylor.

Below Derek (left) and Don Rickman preparing a BSA in their New Milton workshop where, within a year, the Metisse story unfolded.

Luxembourg GP soon became a race between Baeten, Draper and Nilsson, with Jeff Smith and Sten Lundin ready to move up if only one of the title hopefuls were to slip. Lundin briefly snatched second as Draper weakened, but Nilsson had asserted himself by halfway and was noticeably pulling ahead of Baeten. With six laps remaining and a lead which had grown to seven seconds from Baeten and a minute on Lundin, it began to rain. There was only a lap to cover in worsening conditions when Nilsson's incautation struck again and the title was prised from him by the eager and deserving Baeten.

The final acts to conclude what had been an enthralling international season were both played to Scandinavian audiences. On Sunday 17 August near Uddevalla, a west coast shipbuilding town, Sten Lundin won the Swedish GP, with only Jeff Smith preventing a clean sweep of the points by home riders as he battled to fourth after a poor start. Lundin's victory settled the dispute for third place in the standings - and with it an FIM bronze medal - as Draper was concussed by a first lap crash. The dashing west countryman, despite his wins in Holland and France, was pushed down to fourth, five points ahead of Scaillet, who in turn was one better than Smith.

BAETEN TRIUMPHS

Three weeks later at Knutstorp under a baking sun, Lars Gustafsson, Bill Nilsson and Ove Lundell lifted the Moto-Cross des Nations, to bring Sweden her second success in the competition, on a day when even the brilliant Baeten was powerless to interrupt their supremacy. Britain were second thanks to Draper, Curtis – who was runner-up to Nilsson in the final – and Ron Langston, who rode his heart out on the big Ariel. What a year it had been for British GP

Above **Mighty Matchless; available off the shelf to private entrants, this heavyweight G2CS scrambler was only distantly related to the machine Dave Curtis rode to victory in the British Championship.**

winner Lars Gustafsson and his compatriots. When Sweden had first won the team prize in 1955, Nilsson, Gustafsson and Sten Lundin all rode British-built BSAs. Three years later all their riders were on Swedish machinery. How times were changing.

They had changed irrevocably for René Baeten, whose world championship triumph was saluted with a civic reception in his home town of Herentals near Antwerp. Baeten, stocky and fair-haired, was awarded the Trophy of Sporting Merit, Belgium's highest honour for achievement in sport, and a public holiday was declared. From the outset of his moto-cross career in 1948, Baeten intended to climb as high as his talent would allow. He learned quickly from Victor Leloup and Auguste Mingels – who was in Baeten's pit when he clinched the championship – and his dedication to fitness, diet and a miserly consumption of alcohol established a lofty bench-mark for prospective champions. Baeten's victory at Namur in the presence of Prince Albert, brother of King Baudoin, did much to establish his popularity. In Jeff Smith's opinion: 'There was no-one faster. Baeten had uncanny skill and rode the FN with effortless ease. He was the supreme stylist. Often in his early days he showed glimpses of greatness. He soon ironed out the flaws in his riding and even when he lost, René's attempts were serious and noteworthy.'

Baeten won a third national title to add to his world championship, but it was insufficient to dissuade the FN factory from closing their competition's department after a decade of glory. The honours in that compelling 1958 season were almost equally divided between Sweden and Belgium. But, despite their starring roles in the summer-long drama, Lars Gustafsson and René Baeten were never to share another podium; and neither would again stand atop one.

1959

JEFF SMITH victorious at Hawkstone. Don Rickman is individual winner of Moto-Cross des Nations as Great Britain again get the better of Sweden at Namur. Brian Stonebridge is runner-up in European 250cc title-chase, but then loses his life in a car crash. Arthur Lampkin wins British Championship.

Motorcycle sport was booming. There seemed to be no restriction to the number of events for the enthusiastic spectator to choose from each weekend and limitless numbers of those wishing to attend the principal races. In Britain, moto-cross – or scrambling as it was still quaintly called – had accumulated a huge following. Even open-to-centre meetings attracted several thousand spectators; more if there were a few big-name riders among the

Left **John Draper negotiates a left hander riding his BSA at the British Grand Prix, where he finished fifth overall.**

Opposite, below **Derek Rickman gave the prototype Metisse – with a Triumph engine in a BSA frame and Norton front forks – its debut at the Sturminster Newton Club's Spring Scramble at Bulbarrow Hill in March 1959.**

entry. A weekly newspaper, *Motor Cycle News*, had been launched in 1955. Aimed essentially at the sporting market, it soon became the biggest-selling motorcycle periodical in the world. Extensive coverage of race meetings big and small, at home and abroad, so helping to fuel the rapid popularisation of the sport. Well before the final polish had been applied to the trophies awaiting presentation to 1958 World 500cc champion, René Baeten, and Czechoslovakia's Jaromir Cizek – who had become the first winner of the *Coupe d'Europe* – the FIM were finalizing their radical plans for improving the presentation and appeal of their championships.

Buoyed-up by the success of the previous year's discussions, when all the recommendations of the national representatives were accepted by the Federation's Sporting Commission, a second meeting was held, Namur once again being the venue immediately following the Belgian GP. Twenty experts from nine countries sought approval for changes to prize fund and starting money amounts before asking the FIM to ratify a 500cc division which from 1960 would be limited to only eight rounds, with each rider's five best performances to count towards his final total. With 11 events scheduled for 1959 this meant dropping three rounds; the countries losing their championship status being decided upon at the autumn congress in London. It was agreed to abandon the practice of requiring a national prefix on number plates and the meeting endorsed a call for a rule change which would forbid outside assistance on the course while racing was in progress. Heats and finals were to be discontinued and results gained either in single races or by the collective times in two separate heats. Finally the *Coupe d'Europe* would be restyled the 250cc Championship of Europe. Remarkably, the two-race-rule, modified along the way and interrupted in the mid-1970s by an aggregate of heats provision, lasted until 1991, after which time races were shortened and grands prix were decided by

73

Above **Derek Rickman, the elder brother. A talented rider and innovative motorcycle engineer.**

Below **Supreme stylist. René Baeten, four times winner of the Belgian 500cc Championship, bounces his AJS out of Hawkstone's famous sandpit at the British 500cc Grand Prix.**

three heats, or motos as some called them. For the most part the law changes made sense, but the attempt to limit the number of qualifying rounds in either tournament never took root. If the object was somehow to emphasize the quality by reducing the quantity, it was a failure. The 500cc division, like Topsy, just grew.

At the same time the 250cc class, though in only its second season, was also experiencing growing pains. For the first year the majority of 250cc rounds were scheduled for identical dates and at the same venues as the 500cc grands prix. The 250cc races were run as an adjunct to the main event and little attention or publicity was accorded them. But as consumer demand for smaller-engined road bikes was on the increase, so interest in the quarter litre class intensified. By 1959 the *Coupe d'Europe* was comprised of no fewer than 13 ties – two more than the 500cc competition – and had almost doubled in size from the previous year, when five of the seven rounds were incorporated in the 500cc itinerary. The effect of the enlargement was to give mass appeal to the activities of the manufacturers and their contracted riders. They could compete on one front but not on both. This was especially so in 1959 when only two rounds of the 250cc competition were staged alongside the larger class – the opening and penultimate ties in each tournament – in Austria and Luxembourg respectively. For those competitors concentrating on the World championship there were two benefits. Rolf Tibblin, who was to become the scourge of British riders on the big-engined Husqvarna, chose to remain in the 250cc class and so did Brian Stonebridge. This left the remainder of the experienced Britons to deal with the other two-thirds of the redoubtable Swedish threesome: Bill Nilsson and Sten Lundin. It was a Sisyphean task from which only Jeff Smith, Les Archer, Dave Curtis, the Rickman brothers and John Draper emerged with their reputations intact. Arthur Lampkin had still to make his.

There was a fever of British championship activity over the Easter weekend, a fortnight before the 11-country 500cc series began in Austria. At Good Friday's Hants Grand National there was a real buzz in the paddock as Don and Derek Rickman confirmed their intention to discontinue riding for BSA by taking the wraps off a pair of specials which they had imaginatively named 'Metisse'. Built in their own workshops at New Milton from a mixture of BSA, Norton and Triumph components, their crossbreed machines were so named after the French word for mongrel. Derek, the elder Rickman, gave his new bike a sparkling debut, winning the main event from John Draper and Jeff Smith, before Don took the 500cc race by a length from his brother. These victories were the precursor to another vibrant episode in British moto-cross history when the big factories were all successfully challenged by the gifted Hampshire brothers whose mechanical ingenuity, matched by innate riding skills, justly earned them fame. Two days later they shared the spoils at Hawkstone, Derek winning the main event with Don second, with the positions reversed in the 500cc race. The brothers ventured no further north over the holiday weekend, leaving Arthur Lampkin – who had won the 350cc race at Hawkstone from BSA team-mate Brian Martin – to mop up at Brownrigg Fell in a bitterly cold Cumberland Grand National on Easter Monday. This triumph set Lampkin on the way to his only ACU Scramble Drivers' Star. The Yorkshireman, who loved the northern nationals, also took the Lancashire GN that season and benefited – like Dave Curtis the year before – by concentrating on home events.

The Swedes focused their attention on Sittendorf and it was Sten Lundin who drew first blood – with Broer Dirks runner-up and Hubert Scaillet third – which Sten followed up with a second behind Bill Nilsson in the Swiss GP two weeks later. Les Archer opened his account in Switzerland with third place, ahead of Dave Curtis on the Matchless who was having his first concerted effort in either the European or World tournaments. The British champion's reward, although he completed the series without a victory, was three seconds, two thirds and two fourths, which was good enough to earn him third overall in the final standings. But by the end of May Norton led the world as Archer beat Baeten's AJS and Dirks' BSA and a week later trounced Nilsson and Lundin at the French GP, where Jeff Smith was fourth. Lundin won his third Italian GP and turned west for England after winning the introductory West German Grand Prix at Bielstein with 14 points in hand at the top of the leader-board. Nilsson and Archer were tied on 20 and Dirks was next, four points up on Curtis with 15.

Like British Rail, Jeff Smith could not be counted on to time his arrival with any regularity, but when he was within sight of the British Grand Prix, his ambition glowed as if

Above **Jeff Smith riding the factory BSA to victory in the British 500cc Grand Prix.**

75

Right **Bill Nilsson astride the 7R AJS-engined Crescent in the British 500cc Grand Prix. Nilsson was out of the points that summer, but won the event and the world 500cc title the following year riding a Husqvarna.**

ignited by spontaneous combustion. Before unloading his bikes at Hawkstone he was, as he had been in the two previous years, without a grand prix victory. Elsewhere his form hardly encouraged unbridled optimism. Dave Curtis had again won the Junior and Senior at the Cotswold, and Don Rickman lapped everyone at a wet and muddy Sunbeam, after John Draper had annexed the Junior in front of Dave Bickers' Greeves and Lampkin's BSA. It was not until a fortnight after the British GP that Smith won his first English national of the year, the Experts' GN at Rollswood Farm. But Hawkstone was different, and Smith always did his utmost to show just why.

While most of England basked in sweltering sunshine there was some rain over Shropshire to damp down the dust, though it did little to dilute the enthusiasm of a gigantic crowd of 73,241 who were treated to a programme of marches and military favourites by the CWS Manchester Brass Band under their much-respected musical director Alex Mortimer. As a native Lancastrian, who always wore the red rose on his helmet, Jeff Smith must have felt he was at home. The *Daily Herald* once more lent their support as the one national newspaper with a moto-cross correspondent - the hearty Laurie Burills - thus providing further proof of the growing acclaim for an activity by now attracting attendances greater than those for many mainstream sports. In all it was an occasion to savour, with racing to match.

HAWKSTONE PARK

As Jeff Smith had discovered in 1954, there was no better shop window for a battling rider keen to display his abilities than Hawkstone Park on grand prix day. Offered a similar opportunity, John Burton, from Lutterworth in Leicestershire, took his chance imperturbably. Riding a BSA, Burton won the first invitation final from Tim Gibbes' AJS in straightforward fashion and then had a runaway victory in the second when he defeated Ivor England, who was also BSA mounted. Burton's performances were sufficiently encouraging to earn him a place in the official BSA team where he remained until 1963.

Very few of the mammoth crowd had seen the new Rickman Metisse but, within half a lap of the opening 12-lap heat, there were two of them in the first four places. It was Don who headed the field up the hill for the first time, with brother Derek fourth. Sandwiched in between the two hybrids were Jeff Smith and Dave Curtis, with Bill Nilsson, Lars Gustafsson and Rolf Tibblin spearheading the Scandinavian challenge. Already missing from the original 25 who came to the line was Les Archer who had fallen, while bringing up the rear was the champion Rene Baeten who, having been forsaken by FN, was riding a 7R-engined AJS. Within a lap, the front-running four had been reduced to three as Derek Rickman clashed in the sandpit with Nilsson. The Briton continued, albeit with a badly gashed arm to trail in 13th, a lap in arrears. Nilsson eventually recovered to work his way up to ninth.

Jeff Smith worried Don Rickman for five laps until he found the opening for which he had waited and chopped ahead of the Metisse.

Left **The programme for the eighth British 500cc Grand Prix.**

Below **Jeff Smith was runner-up to Sweden's Rolf Tibblin in the British 250cc Grand Prix at Beenham Park. Tibblin won the European 250cc Championship in 1959, riding a works Husqvarna. Smith concentrated on the 500cc class that summer, but was blisteringly competitive whenever he appeared on 250cc machinery.**

Above **Phil Nex was still competing in 1959, but by then he avoided the British nationals and concentrated on overseas events.**

Below **All part of the fun of competition. This Velocette-based scrambler is typical of the home-made specials ridden by enthusiasts unable to afford the latest BSA Gold Star or Rickman Metisse.**

Opposite **Brian Stonebridge, 12 weeks before his death, crests a brow on his Greeves at Beenham Park during the British 250cc Grand Prix, where he finished sixth overall. Stonebridge was still not fully recovered from a shoulder injury sustained in the Dutch 250cc GP a month earlier.**

Curtis was still third then came John Draper, Ron Langston's Ariel, Broer Dirks, Gustafsson, Tibblin – taking a day off from his World 250cc championship commitments – Nic Jansen, Nilsson and series leader Lundin, who was experiencing gear-selection problems which ultimately were to prove terminal.

Both Draper and Langston had suspension difficulties. The BSA's front forks would no longer damp effectively and Langston's rear shock absorbers were blown. So too were Don Rickman's hopes of holding on to second place as he slipped twice letting Curtis through to chase Smith. The engrossing dog-fight between Draper, Langston and Dirks went to the Dutch rider, but poor Langston paid for his endeavours with a badly jarred back which prevented him from starting the second heat. Smith's electric charge had placed him firmly in control, and though Curtis gave his all to try and reel in the leader, the margin at the flag was a wholesome 15.8 seconds.

Those who had seats for the first heat had been on the edge of them throughout. In the second race it was standing room only as Don Rickman carved out an early lead only to be hauled back by Broer Dirks, who had Archer, Nilsson, Curtis, Gustafsson and Smith towed close astern. At half distance Nilsson led from Dirks with Rickman and Curtis next in line, the leading quartet fighting tooth and nail in a 20-metre-long convoy, just ahead of the watchful Smith. Two laps later and Smith had joined them as Archer and Nic Jansen enlisted with the spectators. In his eagerness to demote Curtis, Nilsson tumbled, giving Curtis a clear

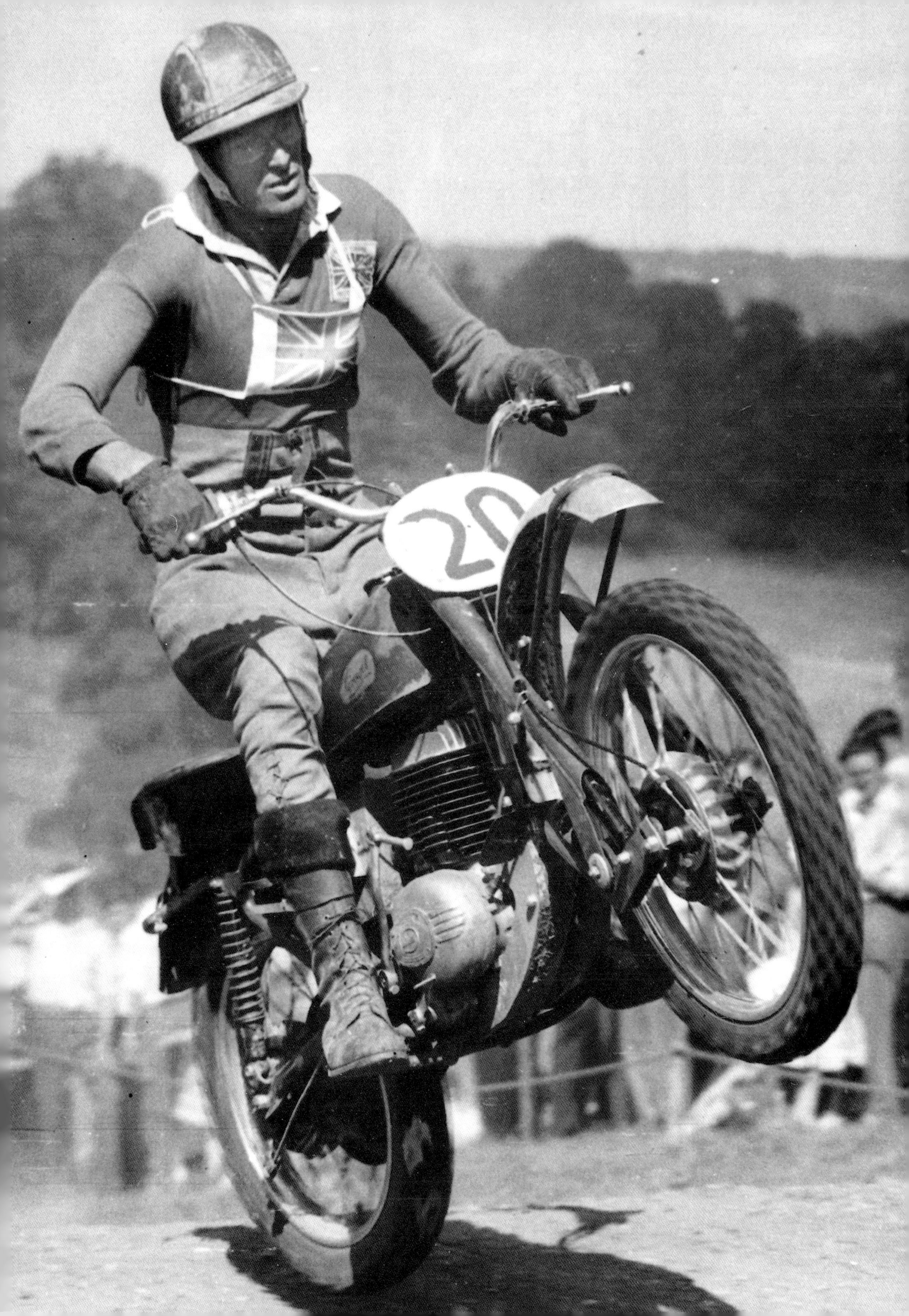
20

Right **The field strung out behind eventual winner Rolf Tibblin (Husqvarna, 26) during the British 250cc Grand Prix at Beenham Park. Over Tibblin's left shoulder is Brian Stonebridge (Greeves, 20), while next up are Jeff Smith (BSA, 40), Triss Sharp (Greeves, 18), Dave Bickers (Greeves, 8), and Mike Jackson (Greeves, 19).**

Below right **Don Rickman made the best individual performance in the Moto-Cross des Nations at Namur, where Great Britain gained revenge on Sweden. Rickman reckoned this was one of the finest rides of his career.**

field from Smith, Rickman and Dirks, who was now under pressure from Tibblin and Draper. In the climactic closing stages Smith knew he could not get beyond Curtis and the timekeepers would be called upon to separate them. He dare not lose to the Matchless rider by more than he had beaten him by in the first race. He didn't. The margin was 3.6 seconds and on the aggregate of times, Smith had shaded it, after well over an hour's racing, by just 12.2 seconds.

Afterwards, Mrs Mirabelle Topham, the owner of Aintree Racecourse, likened grand prix racing to the Grand National as she presented the *Daily Herald* trophy to Smith. In fairness to the equine brigade, Hawkstone had hosted racing every inch of which had been contested with a dramatic fervour that Liverpool's famous course would have envied. What is more, everyone present knew it, including the redoubtable Mrs Topham, who continued to visit Hawkstone to present the famous silver pot.

Lundin, tall and dark-haired, was nicknamed 'Storken' because of his long neck and considerable height. With an effortlessly unruffled riding style, Lundin had kept his lead in the table and though it was the Monark's gearbox which undid him, July 1959 was not a good month for the courteous, affable Swede. Lundin never really came to terms with Hawkstone's demanding corrugations and its intimidating hill. After another disastrous attempt to conquer the Shropshire fortress a year later, Lundin refused to ride there in 1961, despite the fact that he again led the standings.

In the seven post-Hawkstone weeks it took

to conclude the series, only Nilsson and Curtis could stop Lundin taking the title. They had four rounds in which to do so. Curtis came closest at Norg where Broer Dirks was a popular winner of the Dutch GP, just beating the British hopeful, with Lundin fourth. As the Moto-Cross des Nations was scheduled for Namur, the Belgian GP had been moved to Houlpaix where Nilsson triumphed in a thrilling, single-race event, which René Baeten seemed certain to win, until his AJS threw its chain. Nilsson then took over, winning from Lundin and Curtis.

ADVANTAGE 'STORKEN'

With nine rounds completed and only the six best scores to count, riders were now discarding points. Lundin's net total for three victories, two seconds and a third, was 40. Nilsson was on 28, Curtis 27, Dirks was next on 26 with Archer – who hadn't scored since his French triumph in May – on 23. Nilsson needed to win both remaining rounds and hope Lundin would finish no better than fourth in either. Curtis couldn't win and the best he could expect was second. However, Lundin was to disappoint both his rivals as he skated to victory at Ettelbruck to win a sodden Luxembourg GP from Jeff Smith and Don Rickman so ending the uncertainty. All that remained in the closing round at Saxtorp was to split Nilsson and Curtis, who were locked together on 28 points apiece in the conflict for the Silver Medal. Nilsson did so with a surgeon's precision, winning his fourth Swedish Grand Prix; where Curtis could only finish third behind Lars Gustafsson, and a place ahead of the newly-crowned Lundin.

Before any plans for revenge in the Moto-Cross des Nations could be consolidated, the team originally selected for Namur had to be changed when Derek Rickman broke his arm at the Ipswich club's Shrubland Park Scramble, which Dave Curtis won from the younger Rickman and John Draper. John Burton was brought into the six-man British line-up and though he didn't feature in the results, Great Britain won – for the ninth time – Sweden were second and Belgium third. Don Rickman's

Below **Jeff Smith's BSA heads an English 1,2,3 at Hawkstone Park in the British 500cc GP. Dave Curtis brought his Matchless home in second place, and Don Rickman was third riding a Metisse.**

81

Right **Bill Nilsson monowheels the Crescent out of the sandpit, where he clashed with Derek Rickman in the first heat of the British Grand Prix. In the second race, Nilsson fell while attempting to overtake Dave Curtis.**

Opposite, below **Out on his own. Rolf Tibblin won both heats of the British 250cc Grand Prix at Beenham Park, riding the Husqvarna which took him to the world title.**

second heat victory earned him the individual award at the Citadelle as he had beaten second-place man Ove Lundell of Sweden by over 50 seconds. Jeff Smith and John Draper did the rest – just as they had done there in 1956 – this time clinching a particularly sweet victory, with the Swedes just under half a minute behind the triumphant British trio.

Before the warm after-glow of the rejoicing had completely evaporated there was tragedy.

The main attention throughout the year had, as always, been the 500cc class, whether in world or national competition. But within the space of two seasons the 250cc division had become firmly established in Europe, and at home the lightweight races were attracting a significant increase in interest. The Coupe d'Europe did much to develop the relevance of competition for the growing breed of two-strokes and British riders and motorcycle makers played their full part in this evolution.

Britain's standard bearer in the 1959 *Coupe d'Europe* was Brian Stonebridge. Having worked so assiduously on the development of the Greeves Brian knew better than most how to get the best out of the bike on the track. He was also superbly equipped to do so and by now the Stonebridge-Greeves combination was at its zenith.

In the important English nationals, if Stonebridge was beaten it was usually by the second work's Greeves of his close friend and ally, Dave Bickers. Stonebridge soon showed he had the measure of the title-holder Cizek on the factory Jawa by taking an early lead in the European series with victories in Switzerland and Belgium. On circuits in Eastern Europe less familiar to Stonebridge, the locals held sway and the champion superseded him. But a brilliant win in Italy at Pinerolo followed by a second place behind Rolf Tibblin at Cassel in northern France during June, enabled Stonebridge to pull back to within a single point of the Czechoslovakian, in advance of the Dutch round at Lichtenvoorde. Weeks of hot sunny weather had reduced the course to a carpet of fine, sandy dust; well over a foot deep in places. It was to prove the undoing of many, including Stonebridge, who was felled by a German competitor – also on a Greeves – whose bike lay in the track for Dave Bickers to slam into. Stonebridge had dislocated his shoulder in the incident and was not properly fit to ride again for a month. By then Rolf Tibblin had taken a decisive hold on the title race by winning the final three rounds including the British tie at Beenham Park in Berkshire, where some 30,000 attended. By finishing runner-up to Tibblin in Luxembourg at the penultimate round, Stonebridge had beaten Cizek but was forced to make do with second place in the *Coupe d'Europe*. His crash among the trees in Holland had probably cost him the title.

But it was typical of Brian Stonebridge to put the set-back out of his mind in order to concentrate on the next event, where he would demolish the opposition. The last big meeting of the year – and of Stonebridge's life – was the trade-supported Lancashire Grand National at Cuerden Park on 29 August where he routed a quality entry in both the 250cc and 350cc races. Seven weeks later Brian was dead.

TRAGIC ENDING

On Wednesday 21 October he was returning home by car from a business trip north with his friend and managing director Bert Greeves, when they were involved in a traffic accident, near Retford in Nottinghamshire. Mr Greeves, who was driving, sustained multiple injuries but ultimately made a full recovery. Brian died two hours after the crash in Retford Hospital. He left a widow Janet and two young children.

The death of Brian Stonebridge was profoundly felt by moto-cross enthusiasts, for he had been among them long enough to engender genuine grief. His untimely death marked the first moment when the sport felt it had been deprived of someone for whom it harboured a genuine heartfelt affection. Those fortunate to have seen him ride will forever testify to his enduring skills and terrific determination. All who knew him were witness to his good nature and quiet humour; how he took his failures without distress or rancour. Brian Gerald Stonebridge was an exceptional moto-cross rider. His outstanding record will never be forgotten.

1960

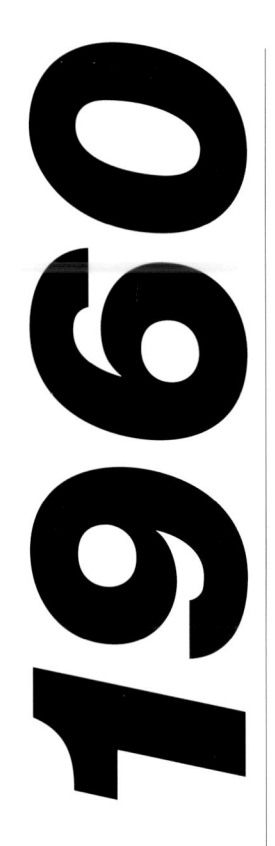

BRIAN STONEBRIDGE Memorial Scramble attracts 84,000 crowd to Hawkstone. René Baeten killed at Stekene. British Grand Prix marred by dust. Dave Bickers is European 250cc Champion and collects first British 250cc title. Great Britain triumph in soggy Moto-Cross des Nations at Cassel.

Motor sport and motorcades of black cars bearing flowers have been tragically inseparable since the idea first took root that it would be interesting and fun to pit groups of motorcycles and their riders against each other in organized races. The participants and those within their orbit are close-knit communities; and when a death occurs, especially of a competitor, the sense of loss is familial. If a rider is killed while competing it serves additionally to highlight the risk inherent in all motorised sport where speed is the prime ingredient. There are occasions when tragedy strikes beyond the competitive arena. Graham Hill's death in November 1975 was mourned no less genuinely because it was the result of an air crash, than it would had he been at the wheel of a Formula One racing car. Although Brian Stonebridge came to his untimely end in a road accident, rather than on the track, it in no way minimized the melancholy of his going.

But mere sadness was an inappropriate emotion as the 1960 season got under way, not to the echo of open exhausts, but to the strains of 'The Last Post', ululating out across the Shropshire countryside.

A PERFECT FAREWELL

Some 84,000 souls bared their heads as a minute's silence was observed before the start of the Brian Stonebridge Memorial Scramble at Hawkstone Park on Sunday 20 March. The event was run along grand prix lines with two six lap races, the result to be decided on aggregate time. The cream of Britain's moto-cross riders fought both exciting heats; the first going to Dave Curtis by 100 yards from the BSAs of Arthur Lampkin and Jeff Smith. The second went to Smith by an even narrower margin from Curtis, with Lampkin third.

It seemed fitting somehow that Curtis should win. Although he and Smith were separated by a mere two seconds, Curtis was from similar farming stock to Stonebridge and they shared the same Corinthian values. To each, moto-cross was important, but not the whole world. They rode to win, but not at all costs. Both were supreme sportsmen, generous in victory and always charitable to their opponents.

Brian Stonebridge rode in an era when it was possible to succeed and have fun at the same time. We look at a life like Stonebridge's now and see the comparative absence of humility and humour in contemporary sport. Most sportsman stand out like grey against a darker grey; and some are grotesquely inflated by retrospective verdicts. Brian Stonebridge was merely illuminated by a clearer, stronger light.

In bright sunshine Stonebridge's widow Janet presented the *Daily Herald* trophy to Cur-

Opposite, below
Sweden's Bill Nilsson. Twice world 500cc champion, who won his native Grand Prix six times.

Left **Geoff Ward, three times British 500cc champion, rockets his AJS out of the Hawkstone sandpit during the Brian Stonebridge Memorial Scramble.**

tis, as Brian's Greeves team-mate Dave Bickers looked on, disappointed he could finish no higher than 16th overall. Bickers was not the only rider affected by the poignant nature of the occasion. Nevertheless, by the end of the year, the wiry East Anglian had more than made amends, ensuring that the hours of development work Stonebridge had put into the Greeves had not been wasted time.

The enormous crowd at Hawkstone – by far the largest in British moto-cross history – had paid their final tribute to Stonebridge's memory and also seen some fine racing. The proceeds of the meeting, together with hundreds of donations from others unable to be present, were given to his dependants. It had been a remarkable start to a season which, well before it ended, had embraced almost all the emotions.

Within a few weeks the spirits of those with the well-being of British moto-cross at heart were lifted unexpectedly – though not by riders

Right **The programme for the Brian Stonebridge Memorial Scramble.**

Below right **Getting crossed up. Bill Nilsson exchanged his Crescent for a Husqvarna in 1960, and it carried him to the world 500cc title.**

in the 500cc category, where Swedish competitors won every one of the nine grands prix – but in the European 250cc Championship.

Apart from his family and friends, no-one could be expected to feel Stonebridge's loss more acutely than Greeves. They were now without their star rider. With only a handful of good results in national races Dave Bickers was thrust into the limelight as Stonebridge's chosen successor. Bickers' rise to prominence began in 1958 when he took second place behind Triss Sharp's Francis-Barnett in the 250cc race at the Sunbeam, which he followed with wins in the lightweight category at the Cotswold and Shrubland Park nationals. A year later, with Stonebridge injured, Bickers was given his first real taste of international competition, and responded with third place in the Luxembourg 250cc GP and fifth in the Swedish 250cc round, to add to his third in the British 250cc GP.

By 1960, the European 250cc competition was staging rounds in more countries than either the 500cc moto-cross or road racing tournaments. Its burgeoning popularity would soon bring the new competition world status. Bickers' new status as Greeves number one rider was soon to earn him widespread renown and respect, as he became number one in Europe.

THE GREEVES' SUCCESSION

Dave Bickers was the son of a garage proprietor from Coddenham, near Ipswich. Encouraged by his father, Bickers Jnr, then aged 16, won his first race at Burstall in his native Suffolk riding a 197cc DOT. He graduated to a works bike for the Manchester concern at the age of 18, before being offered some limited help by the Greeves' factory in 1958. The story from then on could have been written for the pages of *Boy's Own*. Bickers won the opening tie in Switzerland and by the time the end of May was reached – which he celebrated with victory in the Polish GP – Bickers was 14 points clear of Czechoslovakia's Miroslav Soucek on a works Eso. Although the Czech rider won his native grand prix, he eventually faded under pressure from Jeff Smith and Arthur Lampkin on the factory BSAs, who between them secured a victory each in Finland and Luxembourg. Smith took the British GP on Bickers' home ground at Shrubland when the Greeves went sick in the first heat, even though Bickers was the comfortable winner of the second. With the best seven scores to count, Bickers wrapped-up the championship with wins in Sweden and West Germany. Ultimately he was only eight points short of the maximum; 13 ahead of runner-up Smith, who in turn was nine up on Soucek. Lampkin was fourth.

Bickers' victory was as extraordinary as it was unprepared for. In a few months Dave Bickers had not only softened the blow of Stonebridge's death but replaced him in the affection of British fans who immediately warmed to the newcomer's dare-devil tactics, platinum nerve and crouched riding style. Apart from the significance of his title-win, Bickers had accomplished it by beating Jeff Smith. No mean feat, as Smith was the best rider in Britain at the time. Greeves were swamped with orders.

Before Bickers was able to relax in triumph, there was the not inconsiderable matter of the

Above **Sten Lundin, the reigning world champion, keeps his Monark ahead of Josef Aufrerter's AJS. The Austrian rider was involved in the accident on the hill where Derek Rickman suffered a broken leg. Lundin failed to score at Hawkstone, having been lapped in both races.**

Above **Arthur Lampkin hurries his BSA Gold Star past the Hawkstone timekeepers' tower in the British 500cc Grand Prix. Lampkin led the second heat until his engine developed a misfire.**

Opposite **Jeff Smith keeps his nose in front of John Clayton (BSA, 3), and the Matchless of eventual winner Dave Curtis during the Brian Stonebridge Memorial Scramble.**

World 500cc Championship, plus the domestic competition which, for the first time, had a 250cc category added to it.

At home, defending 500cc champion Lampkin, hardly got a look-in as his BSA team-leader Smith strode to his third crown, so embarking on an unbroken six-year title-winning sequence which has never been equalled, even in the Graham Noyce, Dave Thorpe and Kurt Nicoll eras. The Sunbeam was cancelled and did not re-appear on the calendar until 1966. Smith won almost everything else worth winning, except the Cumberland Grand National, which went to Lampkin, with Bickers second in both Junior and Senior. Smith for once got the better of Curtis in the Cotswold – so denying the Matchless rider a sixth consecutive victory – though Curtis would have exacted revenge in the Experts' GN but for a loose plug lead. Smith went on to win for the third time at Rollswood Farm.

The World 500cc Championship was an exclusively Scandinavian contest in 1960. The best five performances were to count from nine ties. There was no round for Switzerland or Denmark this year. Had there been, it is unlikely to have altered the outcome. The British GP was the sixth, with the Dutch, Belgian and Luxembourg rounds to follow. By the time Hawkstone Park was reached, the defending champion Sten Lundin looked well on his way to a second title, after wins in West Germany and Italy, and a second in France. Lundin had 26 points.

The inaugural champion Bill Nilsson's opening flash of brilliance came in the Swedish round, to coincide with Rolf Tibblin's first piece of bad luck. Earlier it looked as if it might be Tibblin's year when he won the French GP at Vesoul. In the first heat Don Rickman was beating Tibblin fair and square when the Englishman knocked a plug lead off on a straw bale on the last lap. Despite carburettor problems, Tibblin won the second race in pouring rain. He had already won in Austria,

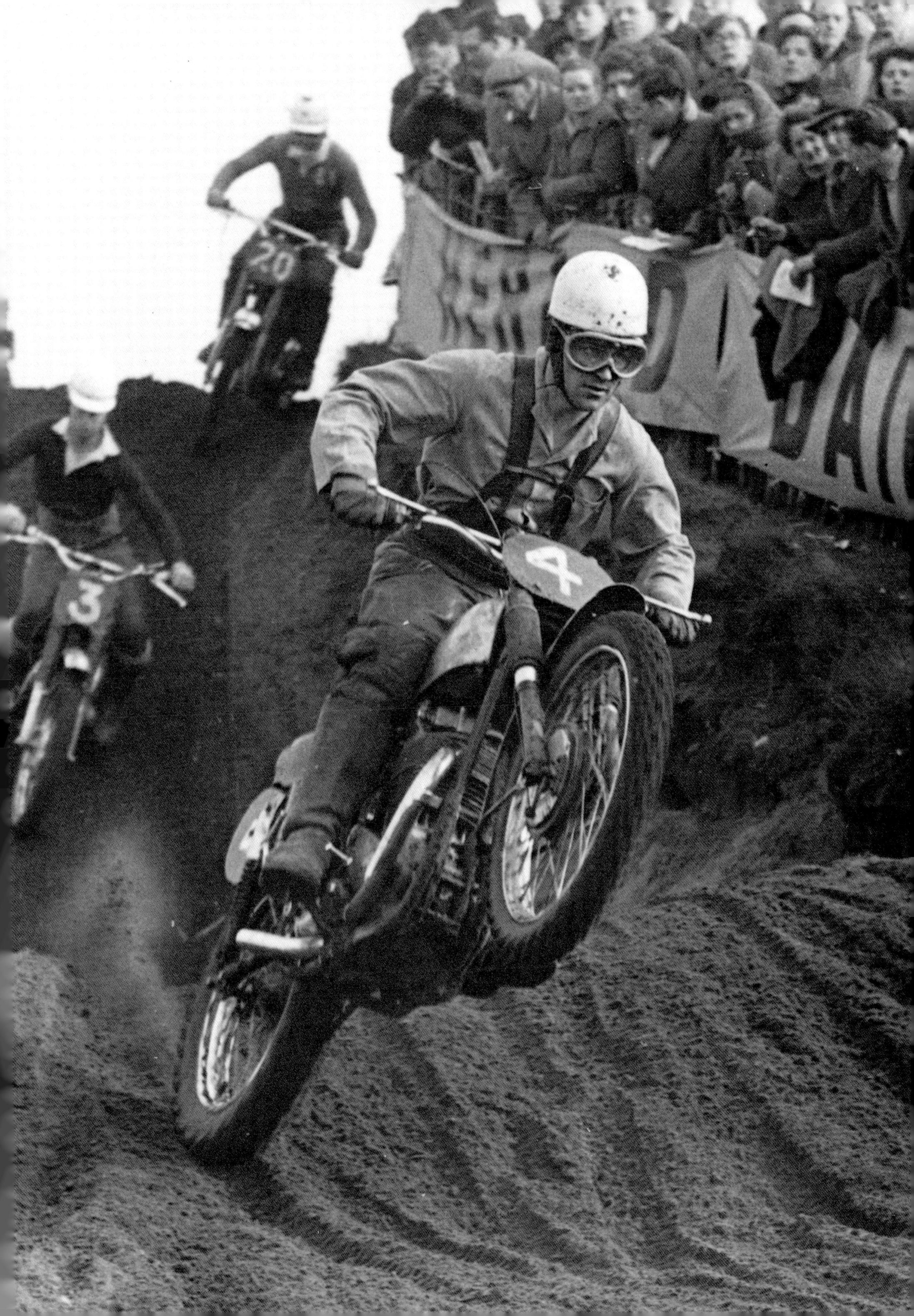
20
4
3

Above **Dave Curtis takes the chequered flag on his Matchless at the end of the first race of the Brian Stonebridge Memorial Scramble.**

but at home, an argument with a tree and concussion ruined his chances. Nilsson seized his with an inspired ride in the second heat, to add to a third in the first behind Lundin and Gunnar Johansson's Lito. It was the turning point for Tibblin, and for Nilsson, who by July was the principal contender. Coming to Hawkstone Nilsson had 18 points, Tibblin 16, Johansson 13 and Rickman 12.

HAWKSTONE BATTLE

In the six years since they first assumed responsibility for running the British GP, the Salop Motor Club had played an enviable and worthy role in helping to establish the World 500cc championship as a relevant competition. Their slick organisation, attention to detail and useful innovation were bywords for excellence, as the youthful tournament searched for recognition. In 1960 at Hawkstone it all went wrong.

A system of awarding one point to the winner of each heat, two for second place and so on, was first introduced at Hawkstone in 1955; thus the lowest aggregate score would determine the winner. This simple arrangement is still in widespread use today in many events; though not in the World Championship. But it wasn't the adoption of this novel marking method which caused the trouble – it was dust. Great, swirling, all-enveloping, blinding clouds of it. The Salop club were forced to confront two new problems: controversy and discontent.

There had been rumblings among the riders after Saturday's practice, and the worst fears of the organizers were realized in the two supporting heats and final which opened the meeting in chaos and confusion. The problem was worst on the hill where mid-field men stalled, fell and came to a halt, in a suffocating turmoil of choking uncertainty.

The organizers couldn't be persuaded that it

would be prudent to cut out the hill, so the first of the two 12-lap heats started as planned. Les Archer was the early leader, but his Norton was soon displaced by Bill Nilsson's red and silver Husqvarna, as the Swede sought to squeeze every advantage out of the conditions. Nilsson quickly opened up a gap on the Metisse of Don Rickman, as visibility dropped and the chasers were forced to grope their way round the circuit in semi-darkness.

Derek Rickman had been robotically tailing his brother when, near the top of the hill, he was halted by a tail-ender, Josef Aufrerter of Austria, who had dropped his AJS. As Derek struggled to keep himself upright he stretched out his right leg only for Jeff Smith – who was virtually blind to the pair – to ride over it and effect a nasty break. Smith was blameless, but the damage was done. It was remarkable that there weren't more accidents of this sort. Brother Don - who had finished second over a minute behind Nilsson, and was one of only three riders on the same lap as the winner – canvassed the support of his fellow competitors in the interval as Derek was ambulanced off to Shrewsbury. Edward Damadian and Harold Taylor - the two senior ACU officials on

Below left **European 250cc Champion Dave Bickers, guns his factory Greeves to second overall in the lightweight class of the Hants Grand National at Matchams Park.**

91

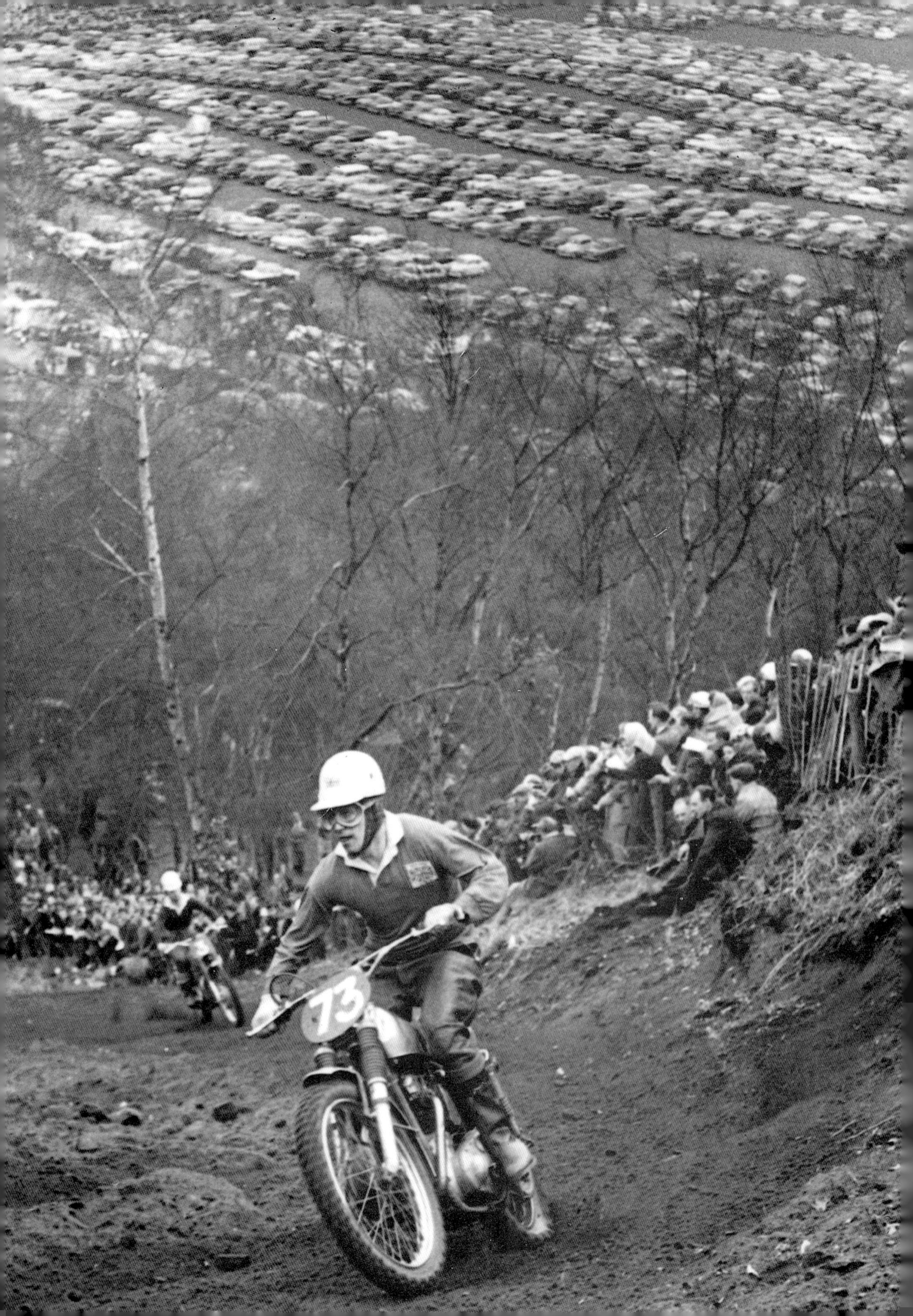

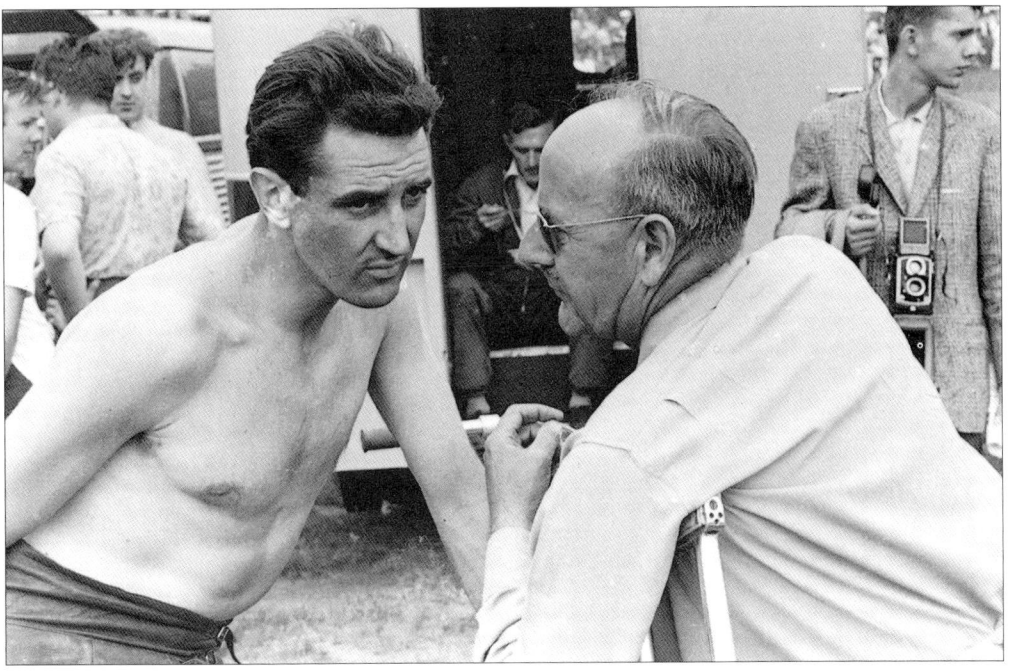

Opposite **Derek Rickman nears the summit of Hawkstone's hill in the Brian Stonebridge Memorial Scramble. Giving chase to Rickman's Metisse is John Clayton (BSA, 3).**

Left **A bare-chested Sten Lundin in earnest conversation with the Auto-Cycle Union official Harold Taylor.**

Below **Les Archer had an unhappy Grand Prix. The engine of his Norton succumbing to the clouds of dust billowing across Hawkstone Park. Within a year Archer had pulled out of world championship moto-cross, and concentrated on continental events. He retired from the sport in 1967.**

duty – were left in no doubt that unless the hill was eliminated, they could abandon the meeting. The riders' protestations were upheld and the second race was scheduled for 14 laps over a shortened course, looping right after the finish line and before the foot of the hill, to meet the original circuit, just west of the end to the start straight.

Nilsson took to the new lay-out as he had the old. John Burton's first race was brought to a premature end when his carburettor clogged with sand; but he led the second – being soon overhauled by the stoic Lampkin, and flying Nilsson – before his BSA's gearbox broke. Lampkin and Gunnar Johansson who, along with Don Rickman, were the only riders to go the distance with Nilsson in the first heat, remained well to the fore in the second, until

93

Right **The British team, led by their manager Ron Baines, parade before the start of the Moto-Cross des Nations at Cassel.**

Centre **Three crashes and bent forks in the first heat of the British 500cc Grand Prix, proved too much of an obstacle for Jeff Smith. He finished fifth overall on the works BSA, one place behind Arthur Lampkin.**

Lampkin's engine went off-song. Even so, the Yorkshireman finished seventh, to give him fourth overall, one place behind the green and chrome Lito of Johansson. Smith and Rickman annexed second and third respectively as Nilsson lapped all but they and four others.

LUNDIN'S BOGEY COURSE

Poor Sten Lundin once again fell victim to his Hawkstone jinx. Lapped in the first race, he was fifth. In the second he was 12th, almost two minutes behind Nilsson, which relegated him to eighth overall and without a point. Lundin had thereby lost the outright leadership of the championship which he now shared with Nilsson. In a ten year international career during which he twice won the 500cc title, four times finishing third and being runner-up twice, Lundin scored only three points at Hawkstone; for fourth place in 1957. He hated the place.

'The course is murderous,' reflected an angry Lundin afterwards. 'I cruised round at walking pace; I would not take the risk. People say I don't like Hawkstone. I don't think Hawkstone likes me.'

The ACU's Harold Taylor, a member of the international jury, told the press: 'I have advised the Salop Club that a new course would be desirable.'

'Frankly, what it needs is every scrap of fencing to be removed, the whole place completely cleared and then we can get down to laying out a really great moto-cross circuit. I've told them that they must, if necessary, forget all about the hill. Famous though it is, the hill is unimportant. We want good racing and we want safety.'

Echoing Taylor's thoughts, Les Archer, by now the longest-serving international rider in the world, said: 'Unless something is done about this course, moto-cross here will be finished.'

Whatever the extent of lasting damage to British moto-cross, contemplating the survival of Hawkstone without the hill would be like predicting a future for the Winter Olympics in Saudi Arabia.

Left **Torsten Hallman relaxes between heats at the British 250cc Grand Prix.**

It had been a pretty bleak afternoon for almost everyone and a painful one for Derek Rickman. His younger brother Don was one of few who could have counted his day a success. He was runner-up for the third successive grand prix of the year and had moved up to third in the standings, eight points behind the joint leaders.

Don Rickman barely got the credit he deserved – especially from the press – for his Hawkstone performance or his season. He had put together two brilliant rides full of skill, phlegm and tenacity. With valuable support from Smith and Lampkin, Rickman had prevented a complete rout by the dominant Swedish competitors.

Don Rickman was now a fully-fledged challenger for world honours. A fourth grand prix second was to earn him the FIM Bronze Medal for a share of third place in the championship – he tied with Rolf Tibblin on 26 points – before his year ended in triumph as a member of Britain's victorious Moto-Cross des Nations team and, for the third time in a row, he was runner-up in the British Championship.

Before then, there was more controversy, in the Dutch GP at Berharen, Sten Lundin's Monark had been tampered with and water was discovered in the fuel tank. The culprit

Above **Fourth place in each heat of the British 500cc Grand Prix, was sufficient to earn Gunnar Johansson third overall with his Lito.**

was never found. Although the start was delayed to allow Lundin time to rectify the problem, he was soon sidelined with engine failure. Nilsson took his third grand prix win of the year, after a race-long battle in the second heat with Rolf Tibblin, to go to the top of the leader-board with eight points in hand.

Lundin now needed to win the penultimate rubber at Namur to have any hope of retaining his crown. The event consisted of a single 39-mile race around the Citadelle circuit where dust was again a problem. Mustering every ounce of the determination which had taken him to the top of the ladder, Nilsson made a perfect start. Although Lundin worked his way from sixth to second and had Nilsson in sight by the final lap, it was Nilsson's race and title, for he now had an unassailable lead.

The British contingent, including John Draper, John Burton and Les Archer, were looking like an embattled and tattered band of defenders in a doomed fort. Only Don Rickman in fifth place and Belgium's Nic Jansen on a Matchless in sixth, prevented a complete Swedish whitewash.

In the final round, in Luxembourg, Lundin gained a consolation victory from Don Rickman – with Ove Lundell third on a Monark and John Draper's BSA fourth – as Sweden prepared to conclude their year of overwhelming supremacy by regaining the Moto-Cross des Nations trophy surrendered to Britain at Namur the previous September. The 14th in the series of popular and keenly contested team competitions was staged at Cassel in Normandy in atrocious conditions. Two days of continuous rain had effectively rendered the grassy hillside track virtually impassable to all but Don Rickman, Dave Curtis and Jeff Smith; the only team to qualify for the final. Against all the odds Britain had vanquished the Swedes to lift the trophy for the ninth time. It was almost the stuff of legend. For Cassel the result was lasting infamy among Swedish supporters.

There was one last act to conclude an unforgettable season. The year would end – as it had begun – in tears. Belgium's René Baeten, who had been World Champion in 1958, was killed while competing in a national championship event at Stekene, five days short of his 33rd birthday. A memorial moto-cross was held at his home town, Herentals, where Baeten ran a motorcycle dealership. The Belgian Royal Family, who had honoured Baeten when he won his world title, donated six solid gold fruit cups as first prize. These were carried back to Stockholm to join the rest of the silverware on Nilsson's groaning sideboard.

Lundin, as he had in the championship, finished second, Dutchman Broer Dirks was third on a BSA ahead of Jeff Smith and Dave Curtis. The René Baeten memorial meeting that October had provided an emotional end to a tumultuous year. Nilsson had brought a master's touch to his virtuoso season. As Bill Nilsson's name was now woven permanently into the fabric of Hawkstone folklore, so his monogram, for the second time, was deservedly emblazoned on the World Championship tapestry.

1961

DAVE BICKERS beats Arthur Lampkin to the European 250cc title, but Lampkin edges out the Greeves maestro at home. Jeff Smith denies Dave Curtis in British 500cc series, though Curtis wins the British Grand Prix.

Les Archer had been competing continuously since 1946. There were few who knew more about the sport than the 1956 European Champion. From the mid-1950s, Les contributed regularly to the now bygone magazine *Motor Cycling*, with his views on the international moto-cross scene. Archer's intelligent, reflective articles made absorbing reading. In his review of the 1960 season, which appeared in *Motor Cycling*'s popular annual – *Sports Yearbook* – Archer sought to given an insight to the reasons for the recent domination of the World championship by Swedish riders.

'In previous championships we have often had individual riders who, during that particular year have been supreme,' averred Archer:

'But I cannot recall any other nation suddenly producing a complete team of world beaters to match Sweden's efforts during 1960. What conclusions can we draw from studying the results? Why have they been so superior?'

'Bill Nilsson, Sten Lundin and Rolf Tibblin have been familiar names in moto-cross for some time and have been improving their riding skills year-by-year; but they had never before won their races so effortlessly.'

'So often the major races developed into a struggle between these men and when they really started to scrap among themselves they quickly out-distanced all other competitors; and often lapped the majority. In fact, the lap times differed so much that while obviously

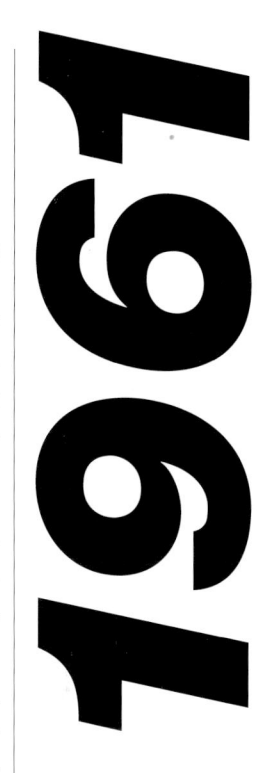

Left **Matchless Man. Dave Curtis heads the pack out of the trees at Hawkstone. Leading the chasers is Don Rickman (Metisse, 23), followed by Derek Rickman (Metisse 24), Gunnar Johansson (Lito, 3), Bill Nilsson (Husqvarna, 1), Albert Dirks (BSA, 16), Gordon Blakeway (Triumph, 27), Lars Gustafsson (Monark, 4), and Broer Dirks (BSA, 15).**

Above **Lars Gustafsson, the popular Swedish rider.**

Right **Big man, bigger bike, biggest victory. Dave Curtis slides the Matchless across the finishing line to win the British 500cc Grand Prix at Hawkstone Park.**

paying tribute to their exceptional ability, we must seek other explanations. Naturally this means their machines.'

'Until recently the Swedes rode English-made bikes. Then, after Nilsson's modified road-racing lay-out, the Swedish factories – Monark and Husqvarna – decided to build some specials. At first the Monarks weren't very successful, but later, the ease with which they tackled the various hazards of a moto-cross circuit pointed to a great reduction in weight.'

'Here I feel sure we have unearthed a major contributing factor. I may be wrong of course, but it seems to me it is along these lines that development has run. Bill Nilsson's Husqvarna weighs about 290lb [131.5kg]; the Matchless Dave Curtis rides weighs some 370lb [167.8kg]. You cannot in my opinion give an opponent of Bill's capabilities this sort of start.'

Archer's words had a messianic ring about them, even though the Associated Motor Cycles' literature of the period claimed that the G80CS such as Dave Curtis campaigned weighed only 329lb [149.2kg]. But AMC were not terribly reliable or accurate about this sort of thing and it was not until the G80CS

– introduced in 1965 – which felt smaller and handled better than previous AMC machines. Even so the new model still couldn't prevent the needle from rising until it touched 318lb [144.2kg].

Though Archer didn't say so in his article, there was also a significant matter of the singular input from an exceptionally talented young engine builder from Sweden : Nils Hedlund.

In the seven years from 1957 – Sweden's golden era in World Championship moto-cross – six titles were won by three riders : Bill Nilsson, Rolf Tibblin and Sten Lundin. They each appeared to be riding different bikes – Husqvarna, Monark and Lito – except in the first year, when Nilsson rode his AJS. In fact they all used similar engines assembled by Hedlund, which were based on a 1935 Husqvarna unit designed by Folke Mannerstedt.

In the Husqvarna pre-war range was a British Sturmey-Archer engine which Mannerstedt modified into a modern ohv 500cc unit.

Husqvarna were then too busy with the manufacture of armaments and allied products. But they agreed to allow their tools and plans to be used for production by a company with widespread marine interests called Albin, who supplied the engines to bicycle manufacturers Monark on Sweden's west coast at Varberg. The Monark-Albin was a robust piece of tackle, and hundreds of army despatch riders would use them in military service over a number of years.

HEDLUND'S ENGINES

Hedlund used an Albin engine in a Velocette frame to make his racing debut in 1952. Though the result of his own toil, the enthusiasm for the project came from Mannerstedt's ambition to produce a Swedish racing engine. By 1955 Hedlund had produced two engines for Monark's managing director Lennart Warborn who loved moto-cross.

Two years later Hedlund, still only 24, purchased the small tuning business where he worked, from the owner Gunnar Hagström. Within 12 months, Sten Lundin's Monark was fitted with a Hedlund-modified motor which powered him to the 1959 title. That year, Rolf Tibblin won the European 250cc crown, but when he switched to the 500cc class Husqvarna became interested and, in their tiny competitions department, built moto-cross racers for Nilsson and Tibblin. Once Warborn died, the Monark factory lost their relish for racing and the machine campaigned by Lundin in 1961, though in reality a Monark, sported a Lito badge.

Nils Hedlund stopped building the old Albin engine when a unit bearing his own name was ready to go into production. However, by then, Hedlund-prepared engines had earned three World titles for Husqvarna, and one each for Monark and Lito. Though this gave the impression that these successes were a direct result of the Swedish factories' interest in the sport, in truth it was Hedlund's fascination with engines and his skill as a tuner, which gave his compatriots a vital edge.

Well before Hedlund's extraordinary contri-

Above **Yorkshire's finest. Arthur Lampkin, despite a demanding moto-cross schedule, still found time to win the Scott Trial in 1961.**

Below left **Arthur Lampkin was runner-up to Dave Bickers at the British 250cc Grand Prix, held at Shrubland Park. The BSA rider also had to settle for second place in the European 250cc Championship, won that year by the brilliant Bickers.**

99

Right **Dave Bickers listens out for the opposition. There was plenty from Arthur Lampkin and Jeff Smith on the factory BSAs in the European 250cc Championship. But Bickers led them home in triumph.**

bution, the power-to-weight pennies had begun to rain down. At Thundersley the penny had dropped even earlier, and the square-barrelled Greaves 24SCS which was introduced after Dave Bickers had won the 1960 European championship on a prototype, weighed 225lb [102kg]. Compared to Arthur Lampkin's 250C15 BSA – 40lb [18kg] heavier at somewhere near 265lb [120.2kg] – Bickers was another rider with a handy power-to-weight advantage at his disposal.

The benefit had not been wasted by Bickers who, in addition to his European triumph, supplemented his acquisition by taking the maiden British 250cc championship. By the end of the 1965 season Bickers had won another four domestic 250cc titles; a record unequalled in the competition. Although 1961 was another celebratory year for Bickers, who retained his European crown, the East Anglian wizard was almost thwarted in his quest for major honours by Arthur Lampkin. The Yorkshireman won a low-scoring contest in the national 250cc class to add to the 500cc title he had won two years previously.

In the 14-nation European 250cc division, despite a blistering opening which netted Bickers five wins from six starts, Lampkin chased Bickers the length and breadth of the Continent, winning three grands prix in the second half of the competition to close to within three points of the champion on aggregate. But with only a rider's best seven performances to count, Bickers eventually edged out Lampkin in a thrilling series with a net score of 56, to the BSA man's 48. Lampkin's team-mate Jeff Smith – who headed the standings in early July – had played a full part in an absorbing summer-long duel, to finish third with 40 points.

BRITISH INTEREST

From a purely English perspective, the high point of the competition had been the British round at Shrubland Park where some 20,000 spectators were engrossed by the Bickers-Lampkin-Smith battle. Bickers won both 15-lap heats, but Lampkin was now at the head of the leader-board by a point, on 44; with Smith a further two adrift on 41. Sweden's Torsten Hallman, who was to break the domination of the English trinity and lift the title the following year, was on 33 points with the Husqvarna.

The new tournament had very quickly captured the imagination of the sport's followers, as between them Smith, Bickers and Lampkin had won 11 of the 13 rounds. Hallman was the only rider to interrupt the British trio's supremacy with a solitary mid-season victory. Jaromir Cizek, riding a Jawa, took the final round in East Germany, but by then, Bickers had wrapped up the championship and he and the other Englishmen were absent. The consolation for Smith was another British 500cc title which he won by four points from Curtis, with BSA's Lampkin – whose sole important domestic win of the year was the Gloucester Grand National – third, ten points behind the Matchless rider.

SWEDISH SOVEREIGNTY

Inevitably, the loss of the three Britons, together with John Draper – who had at 32 decided to see out the remainder of his career riding for Cotton – diminished the likelihood of a British rider breaking the Swedish hegemony in the 500cc division. There was, therefore, ample justification for expecting another clean-sweep by Bill Nilsson, Sten Lundin and Rolf Tibblin in the new season's 11-part championship – which, for the first time included a round in Czechoslovakia – with only a rider's six best scores counting.

Eventually, like Bickers in the lightweight category, Sten Lundin – notwithstanding his abhorrence of Hawkstone – lifted the 500cc title with a maximum. John Burton was flying the BSA flag in the big capacity class and, despite the inspiration of being runner-up to Lundin in the second round in Austria, a third in Luxembourg and fourth at Hawkstone was all the big midlander could muster as he finished sixth in the final classification.

Lundin, this time riding a Lito, collected his second 500cc title, comfortably ahead of Nilsson, who added another three grands prix victories to his tally – winning in Czechoslovakia, Italy and his native Sweden – with Gunnar Johansson improving on fifth place of the previous year, to claim his first FIM Bronze Medal for third.

To complete another season of Swedish sovereignty, Nilsson, Tibblin and Ove Lundell gained ample revenge for the drubbing they received at Cassel, by taking the Moto-Cross des Nations back to Scandinavia after a convincing victory in deep Dutch sand at Schijndel. Britain, in the shape of Jeff Smith, Dave Curtis and Les Archer were worthy – but well beaten – runners-up, four minutes adrift of the Swedes.

This left the rest fighting for leftovers. Only two 500cc podiums were topped by non-Swedish riders: the Dutch GP at Bergharen, where Broer Dirks provided BSA with their only victory of the campaign, and at Hawkstone when Dave Curtis proved the exception. It was a singular season for Curtis, born into an Oxfordshire farming family almost 30 years earlier – forever associated with the heavyweight Matchless – but now on the brink of retirement.

Tom Curtis was a farm manager with charge of a thousand acres near Bicester. He encouraged his two sons Roger and David in their motorcycling, and both started their competition careers on BSAs. Dave was indisputably the more talented of the two Curtis brothers and, at the close of a brief attachment to Ariel, Hugh Viney offered Dave a factory Matchless shortly after Harold Taylor had provided Curtis with a 350cc AJS for the 1954 Experts' GN at Rollswood Farm. Thereafter, Dave Curtis remained steadfastly loyal to Matchless until he retired in October 1961, having been narrowly prevented from denying Jeff Smith his fourth British title in a confusing climax to the domestic season at Boltby, north Yorkshire.

Dave Curtis drew much of his inspiration from Geoff Ward and for a time it seemed as if it seemed as if it was the pair of them fighting a lone battle for Associated Motor Cycles – Matchless and AJS respectively – against the accumulated might of BSA. In 1954 Ward had won the ACU Star contest in front of eight BSAs. The previous season he had headed home four Small Heath runners. When Curtis won his title in 1958 there were five BSAs trailing in his Matchless's wake. These battles between the big two British makers was a feature of the domestic championship, and the

Big John Burton. The BSA man missed out on the top honours, but was equal second on points with Don Rickman in the 1960 British 500cc Championship, runner-up to Jeff Smith in 1962, and third a year later. The biggest moment of Burton's career came when he appeared in the winning British team at the Moto-Cross des Nations in 1963.

101

crowds adored every moment of it. When the celebrated Hungarian composer Franz Liszt wrote his first piano concerto, he did so having it in mind that only the most accomplished would be able to play it. The man who devised the Matchless must have a had a similar proviso for those expected to win on an uncompetitive, outweighed motorcycle, which had little chance of success as bikes were getting lighter and faster. Curtis, and before him Ward on the AJS, proved the exception.

Comparisons between Ward and Curtis are inevitable. Both made their names on AMC machinery. Each was blessed with an uncomplicated disposition, a good sense of humour, and were decent, fair-minded competitors who loved their racing. On their day Curtis and Ward were good enough to beat the best; and they had plenty of good days.

Their career records have a striking similarity. Ward won the domestic 500cc title three times; Curtis only once. In mitigation however, Curtis had to cope with Jeff Smith in his pomp and the Matchless maestro was twice runner-up to Smith. Moreover, from 1955 until he retired, Curtis was never out of the top five.

Ward was in four Moto-Cross des Nations winning teams; Curtis in three. Curtis twice – 1956 and 1958 – won a gold medal for Britain in the International Six Days Trial. They each won a similar number of big races at the major UK nationals, but whereas Ward never won the British GP (his best efforts were a third place in 1953 and sixth in 1955) or ever dominated a trade-supported event in the way his AMC rival did the Senior race at the Cotswold, Curtis was able to crown his career with victory at Hawkstone.

THE RISE OF DAVE CURTIS

Having no budget or time for an assault on the World 500cc championship, Curtis had not been abroad for any of the five rounds which preceded the British Grand Prix. He had risen from his bed after a bout of influenza to wrest the Baughan Trophy from Jeff Smith's grasp by winning his sixth Cotswold Senior race. Invigorated by this unlikely triumph he was, a week later at Hawkstone, a little more certain of a good performance against the Swedish contingent but was not touted as the winner, even

Right **The winning habit. Dave Bickers won seven rounds of the 13-nation European 250cc Championship in 1961, to annexe the title with a maximum score of 56 points. Here the Greeves ace entertains his home supporters by winning the British Grand Prix at Shrubland Park, a few miles from Bickers' Suffolk base.**

Brothers in arms. Arthur Lampkin (left), and Jeff Smith, who between them appeared in the winning British team at the Moto-Cross des Nations on no fewer than ten occasions.

though the standings' leader Sten Lundin had decided to give the event a miss. There was still Gustafsson, Johansson, Nilsson and Tibblin to contend with, as well as the BSAs of the improving Dutchman, Broer Dirks and the great trier Burton.

Farmwork and the outdoor life had contributed fully to Dave Curtis's natural fitness. Although only 5'8" [1.72m] tall and weighing about 168 pounds [76.2kg], Curtis was immediately recognizable, with a round, open face, receding hairline and shoulders and forearms broad enough to shore up a sea wall, with hands like hams. By 1990s standards he might not be considered aerobically fit. You would not, for instance, think him a candidate likely to win a Three Peaks race. However, if you wanted someone alongside you to *defend* a peak, then Curtis would be your man.

Immensely strong, Dave Curtis was tenacious and always wanted to win. The rougher it was, the more Curtis liked it. The conditions at Hawkstone Park that Sunday in July were ideal for him. A heatwave gave rise to speculation that another sandstorm event was in the offing after Saturday's dusty practice. However, overnight rain and cool, grey skies extinguished the threat of a re-run of the 1960 friable pantomime. There were 33,500 present as the Ransome & Marles bandsmen picked their way through the various national anthems during the riders' presentation, before Don Rickman headed the pack into the tunnel of trees on his Triumph-engined Metisse.

Rickman was soon supplanted by Curtis and, much later, by Sweden's Lars Gustafsson; now in his third season as a Monark rider. This rapid threesome were never headed once the halfway point of the heat was reached, though Broer Dirks and John Burton on their works BSAs, Derek Rickman on the second Metisse, Gordon Blakeway's Triumph and the two Swedes, Rolf Tibblin and Gunnar Johansson – on Husqvarna and Lito respectively – were all in the shake-up at one time or another.

Far too shaken-up for his own good was Bill Nilsson, who was forced to pull out suffering from food poisoning, his dreams of a second successive Hawkstone triumph clouded by nausea.

103

Above **Holland's Broer Dirks rode his BSA to fifth place in the first heat of the British 500cc Grand Prix. But was forced out of the second race on the first lap with an engine malady. Over the Dutchman's left shoulder is Bill Nilsson, who had an unhappy day on his Husqvarna.**

The sun was shining on Curtis by the time the second race began, literally. Nilsson – a retiree within two laps – was no longer a threat. Nor, two laps later, was Don Rickman, who collided with Gustafsson and broke the Metisse's gear lever. This left Gustafsson to dispute second place with compatriot Johansson, leaving Burton, Tibblin and Les Archer on his Norton to haggle over the rest of the points.

With the sour flavour of the ill-managed Nilsson episode still in the memory, no victory tasted sweeter for AMC and their ex-road racer director Jock West. Curtis never had a contract with Matchless. The provision of bikes, spares and expenses depended on no more than a handshake with West, whose most memorable piece of advice to Dave Curtis was: 'Remember my boy – you do it for the love of the sport.'

Fortunately for AMC, the cherubic Curtis was not one to be seduced by money – what little of it there was for trade-supported riders in his time. What mattered to Curtis was that he would be treated by others as he would treat them. Honour, fairness and personal integrity were central to Curtis's code of conduct. He rode, as he conducted the other parts of his life, to the highest standards available to him.

History records that in the ensuing 35 years after Curtis's triumph, only five other Britons were to win the British GP. Jeff Smith had already made out a case for building a hall of fame. The others later entitled to enter it were: Don Rickman, Vic Eastwood, Graham Noyce and, much later, Smith's illustrious successor, Dave Thorpe.

When considering those most conspicuously qualified as all-time British greats, the name of Dave Curtis would not perhaps spring readily to mind. But no one moved to consider the record of English riders in the distinguished history of the British Moto-Cross Grand Prix ought to overlook his achievements.

1962

Sweden take all the major prizes. ROLF TIBBLIN wins the British 500cc Grand Prix, again clouded by controversy, and the World title. Torsten Hallman wins 250cc crown, which is now World ranked, but brilliant Dave Bickers denies the Swedes at Tor, which hosts its first British 250cc Grand Prix. Bickers and Jeff Smith reign supreme in the domestic competitions.

There was no reason to suppose that British riders would not be in a position to challenge for major honours in world moto-cross, though before the new season began Dave Curtis announced his retirement and there were doubts about Dave Bickers' commitment to a chase for the 250cc title which had been elevated to world grade after five years as a European competition.

Writing in *The Motor Cycle*, Jeff Smith, looking ahead to the two major competitions, expressed the view that if Bickers were to be absent, Joe Johnson and Brian Leask would spearhead the Greeves challenge. Rolf Tibblin was expected to partner Torsten Hallman in a strong, all-Swedish assault by Husqvarna. BSA would field himself and Arthur Lampkin, as they had done the previous year.

In the 500cc class, Smith predicted in his magazine article that the running would be made by Bill Nilsson or Sten Lundin, with Holland's Broer Dirks as the most likely outsider. In the big-bike category, according to Smith, only Lutterworth's John Burton of the British contingent had any sort of chance of upsetting the Swedes.

Smith was partly right. There was no one capable of rocking the seemingly unsinkable Swedish boat, and the twice European champion Bickers stayed at home in order, as the

Left **Rolf Tibblin won five grands prix in 1962 to win the world 500cc title with 52 points; four shy of the maximum. All his victories were achieved riding a Husqvarna; including the British GP at Hawkstone Park.**

105

Greeves factory decreed, to concentrate on the British 250cc championship. Having conceded the national title to Lampkin's BSA the previous year, one could understand Greeves' thinking; though not sympathise with it. Instead of exploiting Bickers' European successes by mounting a full-scale sales effort on the Continent, Greeves could see no further than the Channel ports as they sought only to improve their share of the UK market.

For Bickers, it was hardly the brightest move of his career. Still only 24, but already with 11 grand prix victories and three major titles to his name, he was denied the opportunity of maintaining the momentum and adding to his triumphs, just as he was reaching his prime. It was a transparently narrow, parochial tack by

Above **Women competitors have been very few and far between in any era of British moto-cross. But this Greeves-riding representative seems fairly pleased with herself.**

Right **John Harris keeps his BSA ahead of the Metisse ridden by Ivor England in the Hants Grand National at Matchams Park. Harris finished second overall behind Jeff Smith, and went on to finish third in the British 500cc Championship in 1962.**

Far right **Versatile Bickers. Just for a change, Dave Bickers swapped his Greeves for an ex-Dave Curtis Matchless in the Hants Grand National. He finished third overall. Riding his usual Greeves, Bickers won the second of his five British 250cc titles in 1962.**

106

Greeves, typical of the short-sightedness that afflicted so many of Britain's motorcycle manufacturers and which contributed towards the industry's sad decline. Within little more than a decade, the weight of this sort of thinking was too much to bear. The construction of motorcycles in England became an uncompetitive trade and the business imploded.

For the moment, BSA were unaffected by the short-termism which blighted Greeves, and the Small Heath concern lent their full weight in support of an offensive to capture the World 250cc crown. Where Arthur Lampkin had so narrowly failed the previous year, BSA were determined that either Lampkin or Smith would triumph in 1962. They were nearly right. There were 13 rounds in the inaugural World 250cc Championship, with a rider's seven best scores to count. Thus, there was every indication that one would need a maximum to be certain of the title.

AN IMPRESSIVE START

The British BSA duo began brilliantly. Lampkin won the opening round in Spain – to put down an important historical marker – Smith the second, in Switzerland, then Lampkin the third in Belgium. By the time the half way mark had been reached, Smith – with three victories, two seconds and a third – headed the standings with 40 points. Lampkin was next on 31 with Sweden's Hallman – a single victory to his credit – trailing in the Britons' slipstream with 18 points.

Within a month the Swede had wrested the initiative from the English pair with four victories, including one at the first grand prix ever staged in the Soviet Union. Held at Yukki, near St Petersburg, an estimated 100,000 spectators were enthralled by Hallman who won both heats, as Smith and Lampkin were respectively second and third in each.

Smith badly needed a win but, as in Russia, he could only finish second as Hallman won in Luxembourg, Sweden and West Germany. When it came to the British round, Smith was again upstaged, though not this time by Hallman, but by Bickers, who was well on his confident way towards a second British 250cc title.

Having been comforted by the organizational successes with two British 250cc grands prix at Beenham Park and two at Shrubland, the ACU awarded the 1962 event to the Tor club. Their Higher Farm circuit at Wick, near Glastonbury, was popular with spectators, and 30,000 of them found space on the grassy slopes of the Somerset countryside as Bickers won both 15-lap heats by decisive margins. Considering he was so short of international competition, it was a quite stunning comeback for the raw-boned East Anglian.

TIME FOR CHANGE

Poor Jeff Smith could only manage eighth in the first race, though third in the second was sufficient to earn him a point for sixth overall. In both races, Smith's was the leading four-stroke. Lampkin's mount was beset by a misfire and he no-scored.

Hallman, though unable to catch the irrepressible Bickers, was second overall and clinched the title for Husqvarna in his native GP at Enköpping, where Smith was 2nd and Lampkin third. It was a familiar story, which for the BSA riders will be almost as painful in the re-telling as was the reality. The truth is, that by the end of the 1962 campaign, the well-prepared two-strokes in the hands of Hallman, Valek, Aarno Erola and others possessed power-to-weight advantages which BSA were unable to match.

A fundamental re-think was needed by BSA. At Glastonbury, they had been embarrassed by some of the lightweight bikes, including Don Rickman's Bultaco-engined Metisse which, despite making only its second appearance, beat Smith's BSA into fifth overall. However, there was a benefit gained for the competitions department at Armoury Road, who learned the lessons of 1962 to develop what eventually became the 420cc Victor, which was to convey Jeff Smith to more glory within another season.

The 250cc class had in five short years not only established itself, but had taken centre stage. From a purely British point of view, the 500cc category had only limited appeal, with

Above, far left **Torsten Hallman closes on second place during the British 250cc Grand Prix at higher Wick Farm, Glastonbury, which was won by Dave Bickers on the factory Greeves. But Hallman lifted the world title for Husqvarna.**

Left **John Giles takes the flag at a club event on his Triumph. Giles, a brilliant all-rounder, was no stranger to gold in the International Six Days Trial, but in international moto-cross was no match for the works riders. Though he was good enough to win the Experts Grand National in 1961, the year he finished fifth in the British 500cc Championship.**

Below left **The British team before the Moto-Cross des Nations at Knutstorp (actually taken in the following year). From left to right: Team Manager Peter Wigg, Arthur Lampkin, Don Rickman, John Burton. Jeff Smith, Derek Rickman.**

Right **The British 250cc Grand Prix moved to Somerset for its fifth running, and the grassy slopes of Higher Wick Farm, Glastonbury accommodated some 30,000 spectators who witnessed some fine racing and a home victory. Dave Bickers won both races by decisive margins on the factory Greeves.**

Below right **Malcolm Davis was unplaced on his privately-entered Greeves.**

John Burton the sole English representative with a realistic chance of scoring some points. There were ten countries participating in the bigger capacity division, with the best six scores to count. Once again there was a tie scheduled for Czechoslovakia. Somehow, squeezed in among the plethora of dates for rounds which constituted the two main competitions, were the British championships – still in the main made up of the trade-supported events.

Whatever his disappointment in the European and World 250cc Championships, Jeff Smith was in no mood to relinquish his hold on the British 500cc crown. With a hat-trick of titles as his subsidiary target, Smith took maximum points at Glastonbury and Hawkstone, before winning his third successive Hants GN, on Good Friday. At this early stage of the season Smith was already 14 points clear of his team-mate Lampkin. Victories at Shrubland, and in the Experts' Grand National – for the sixth time of his career – plus the Jackpot at Beenham, were to guarantee Smith his fifth ACU star, 24 points ahead of John Burton, with BSA privateer John Harris third on 11.

Set alongside the intoxicating World 250cc series, the 500cc competition in 1962 must have seemed an anodyne affair. Unless you were Swedish, it was. Not until August – when

Left **John Burton** was a stalwart competitor on the British scene. the Lutterworth rider finished in the top three of the national 500cc championship in 1960, 1962 and 1963.

Below **Rolf Tibblin (Husqvarna, 4)** chases Don Rickman at the British 500cc Grand Prix. Tibblin won both heats and went on to lift the world title. Rickman was third overall at Hawkstone, riding the Triumph-engined Metisse.

Above **Oscar Bertrum "Bert" Greeves at the gates of Buckingham Palace after his investiture. He received the MBE from HM The Queen Mother in February 1972.**

Below right **Vivid action from the start of the British 250cc Grand Prix. Sweden's Olle Pettersson (Husqvarna, 21) has the inside line from his compatriot, Torsten Hallman (Husqvarna, 20), Don Rickman (Metisse, 27), Vlastimil Valek (CZ, 5), Brian Leask (Greeves, 29), Billy Jackson (Cotton, 39), and Alan Clough (DOT, 36).**

John Burton became the first Briton to win a World Championship grand prix at Namur – were the Swedes beaten. Instead of returning to the 250cc class as Smith had predicted, Rolf Tibblin stayed aboard a 500cc Husqvarna and took control of the tournament from day one. Having triumphed in Austria and France, the 26 year-old from Sollentuna, near Stockholm, was only seriously challenged by Gunnar Johansson on the Lito.

Fifth in the final roll-call in 1960 and third the year later, Johansson won in Switzerland and Czechoslovakia, where Tibblin's frame broke. By the time the circus had reached Shropshire, Tibblin was on 30 points, Johansson 24. When they pulled out of Hawkstone, en route for the Dutch tie at Lichtenvoorde, it was 38-30, and Johansson had scored in all six events.

There was another huge crowd at Hawkstone – though no larger than the attendance at Glastonbury – the *Daily Herald* again lent its support and, for most of the first 12-lap race, it looked as if there would be another home win. The mirage soon evaporated.

Don Rickman on the Triumph-engined Metisse and his brother Derek, riding the Matchless-powered version of the Mk3 New Milton specials, were the early leaders of the event, which once again was polluted by clouds of dust. The organising Salop club had not adequately come to terms with the problem, which eventually led to the ACU's decision to have it staged elsewhere, despite the great affection for Hawkstone among British fans. Dust was not only intolerable, it was dangerous.

Johansson was the Rickmans' first pursuer, but as Derek fell back, Tibblin relegated his

112

compatriot and gave chase to Don. It took the Swede until the sandpit on the last lap to get by the sweet-sounding Metisse, but Rickman could do nothing about it, and Tibblin took the chequered flag with 4.4 seconds in hand. The elder Rickman was fifth, behind Johansson and Bill Nilsson, riding a home-made device he called a Bilsson. Per-Olaf Persson's Monark was sixth.

With Tibblin in such form, the second race was an anti-climax once the Swede had forced his way past Don Rickman and Johansson, by third distance. From then on it was a matter of whether Rickman could hold the second Swede and claim the runner-up spot on aggregate time. But Johansson was further ahead of the Briton than Rickman had been of him in the first heat, so it was a Swedish one-two. Don Rickman, second two years earlier, had to settle for third, as he did in 1958 and 1959.

Rickman senior, Burton and John Harris all expired, but Triumph's Gordon Blakeway and Dave Bickers riding Dave Curtis's old Matchless could be well pleased with their performances. So too could Tibblin and his countrymen, who finished the season in the top five places in the championship and then won the Moto-Cross des Nations at Wohlen. The only point of contention was why John Burton – who was the highest placed Briton in the championship – should be left out of the British team. Ultimately it didn't really matter – except to Burton – for there was very little satisfaction for those wearing Union Jack bibs, as Tibblin, Nilsson, Johansson and Ove Lundell took the flag in line-abreast, six minutes ahead of the British team.

In the summer of 1962 the Swedish juggernaut had been unstoppable.

Above **The pain of victory. Rolf Tibblin looks completely drained after his double-race triumph at Hawkstone Park.**

113

1963

DON RICKMAN takes a heat at Hawkstone but Jeff Smith collects the winner's garland. Rickman's consolation is to wrest the Moto-Cross des Nations trophy from Sweden's grasp with the support of his brother Derek and the redoubtable Smith. Vic Eastwood falls two points short in his bid to take Smith's British 500cc title.

Recovery from the disappointments of the previous summer – after the pounding they had received at the hands of Swedish riders in both major championships and the team contest – was a painfully slow experience for the leading Britons. Nonetheless, 1962 had not been entirely without hope and, before Jeff Smith, Arthur Lampkin, Dave Bickers, the two Rickmans, John Burton and the others spent the winter absorbing the lessons of the season and preparing for new challenges, Smith had struck a blow for Britain by winning the Swedish 500cc GP at Hälsingborg. True it was the final round in the 1962 championship, and Tibblin had already been chapleted as the first rider to win both the European 250cc and World 500cc titles. But winning in Sweden had been an exclusively Swedish privilege, except in the days of the European 500cc series when Smith's brother-in-law John Draper, John Avery and Belgium's Nic Jansen all won on Swedish soil. In strictly world terms, Smith's was a singular triumph. There were also signs that a new crop of young English riders was beginning to flower. Vic Eastwood, Dave Nicoll, Chris Horsfield, John Banks, Alan Clough and John Griffiths were soon to make their mark.

After two years of trying to capture the European 250cc crown and another chasing the World 250cc title with their C15S, the BSA factory decided on an attempt at the World 500cc Championship with a B40, enlarged to 420cc. Smith and Arthur Lampkin would spearhead the attack, with John Burton on hand with a Gold Star in case either of the factory's leading riders succumbed to injury.

Smith gave the new machine a winning debut at the Hants Grand National having a fortnight earlier won at Hawkstone in front of the television cameras on a 343 cc version, to claim maximum points from the first two

Right **It really was wet for the Moto-Cross des Nations at Knutstorp. Derek Rickman (Metisse, 14) leads from Arthur Lampkin (BSA, 11), and Don Rickman (Metisse, 35). Jeff Smith (BSA, 12) is the next British rider in sight.**

Left The shape and size of things to come. Torsten Hallman tests the prototype 360cc Husqvarna in practice for the Moto-Cross des Nations at Knutstorp. Husqvarna had previously made two-stroke engined bikes with a capacity no larger than 250cc.

Below Vic Eastwood tries a spot of snow-cross at Hankom Bottom, riding the factory-supported Matchless. The hard winter of 1962-63 saw the first BBC screening of scrambles for the Grandstand Trophy.

Above **Broer Dirks (Lito, 6) and Rolf Tibblin (Husqvarna, 1) at the British 500cc Grand Prix. Arthur Lampkin – who finished second overall riding a 420cc BSA – is partly hidden behind Dirks.**

rounds in the British 500cc Championship. Unfortunately the scheduling for national championship rounds resulted in clashes with the international competitions, which meant that Smith, Lampkin and Bickers were often overseas, thereby allowing some of the newcomers to shine at home.

Vic Eastwood won the principal race at the Wessex, over Tor's Glastonbury course watched by a crowd of 20,000, and Bryan Goss took the first maximum of the season in the five-venue domestic 250cc title-hunt. Goss and Eastwood were to run the main protagonists fairly close, though in the end Bickers – despite his eventual fall out with Greeves – sealed his second successive 250cc bid by winning the Wingfield Trophy at Ashbourne.

In Smith's absence, Eastwood needed victory at Elsworth to end the BSA star's three-year run of title successes. But Metisse-mounted Andy Lee – who had spent most of the summer competing in continental races – pushed Eastwood into second, so the main prize once again went to Smith; though this time by a narrow two points.

In 1963 the world 250cc series comprised 14 rounds set as far apart as Spain and Poland. Having decided on some sort of strategy for Europe, Greeves once more entered the fray with Dave Bickers and newly-recruited Alan Clough from Cheadle Hulme as their riders. John Griffiths and John Banks rode for DOT, while Chris Horsfield and – far less frequently – Dave Nicoll campaigned

Opposite, top **Early in the first race of the British 250cc Grand Prix at Shrubland Park, overall winner Torsten Hallman, leads on the works Husqvarna from Alan Clough (Greeves, 14) and Ernie Greer (DOT, 33).**

Left **The British team before the Trophée des Nations at Lac de Loppem, near Bruges. From right to left: Don Rickman, Arthur Lampkin, Dave Bickers, Jeff Smith, Alan Clough and Team Manager Harold Taylor. Great Britain were runners-up to Sweden.**

James Starmakers from the AMC stable. By contrast to the 500cc class – where Lampkin Burton, Smith and Rickman were able to restore British prestige – the second World 250cc championship proved to be an unrewarding arena for the English factory runners. Dave Bickers won the initial round, in Spain, though thereafter it was a disheartening season – especially for Greeves – despite flashes of promise from Clough.

TROUBLE AT GREEVES

The British 250cc GP returned to Shrubland where Don Rickman on the Bultaco-Metisse was the only British rider to complete both 15-lap heats. With his campaign in tatters after a sequence of mechanical failures, the deeply frustrated Bickers bought a Husqvarna. He offered to paint it Moorland blue, and pass it off as a Greeves, but quite properly the founder and managing director of the company, French-born Bert Greeves would have none of it. 'We regret that our association with Dave Bickers has come to an end,' said Bert Greeves. 'But ours has always been a 100 per cent British concern, and if Dave is determined to ride a foreign machine we have no alternative but to release him.'

In point of fact Bickers was not contractually-bound to the Thundersley factory, as he explained: 'I'm really sorry to have to break with them and I hope there won't be any hard feelings. But I'm not under contract and I think it will be in my best interests if I continue as a privateer.'

Torsten Hallman had no such contractual problems. By the end of the season, when he had won eight of the 14 grands prix, hammering home his invincibility in the most uncompromising fashion, it is almost certain that he had a contract with Husqvarna which, for 1964 and beyond, was nothing less than watertight.

In July of 1963 as the youth of Britain were rocking to the sound of the Beatles and the Tory government was rocked by the Profumo scandal, moto-cross fans were still reeling from the effects of Bickers' dispute with Greeves. As Hallman had underlined so tellingly, without Bickers, Smith and Lampkin, the British challenge in the 250cc class was limp and ineffective. During the next three decades and more, there would be far too many seasons when similar accusations were to bear a familiar validity.

A week after Smith gave the lightweight unit-construction B40 its winning debut at the Hants GN, he and Lampkin were both soundly beaten by John Burton's 500cc Gold Star, which in turn was seen off by four Swedes and a Russian, in the Austrian GP at Sittendorf. It was not an auspicious start for the new model, or a very heartening way to begin a challenge for the championship, which was enlarged to 12 events, with rounds in the USSR and East Germany. The best seven scores would count.

Outpaced in Austria – where Smith was seventh overall and Lampkin ninth – the B40 was among the points in Switzerland and very much on the pace in Denmark, where Smith was victorious. It took Lampkin a little longer to come to terms with the characteristics of his new mount, but third place at Imola in the Italian round, added to his fourth in Denmark, were welcome tokens of improvement.

SCANDINAVIAN DOMINATION

The Swedes meanwhile were rolling inexorably towards another title. Sten Lundin won the first two rounds, but after Smith's Danish intervention, Rolf Tibblin strung four successive victories together in Holland, France, Italy and Czechoslovakia – a feat not previously achieved by any rider in one season – to take a grip on the championship which was never loosened. Lundin, who had come close to setting this record – by winning the final round in 1960 and the first three in 1961 – managed only a second and two thirds as his compatriot assembled this impressive sequence, but was still holding second in the standings when he decided to forego another tilt at his least favoured circuit, Hawkstone Park.

Given that fewer than 10,000 had turned up at Shrubland Park for the British 250cc GP a month earlier, officials of the Salop club were a shade apprehensive about the prospect of a larger crowd for the 500cc grand prix on 7 July. In fact it was another monster, as 43,000 enthusiasts were there to witness the first British one-two-three since 1959.

The Scandinavian threat never materialized. Lundin's unwillingness to travel, coupled with the non-appearance of 1958 winner Lars Gustafsson was further diminished by injuries to Bill Nilsson and Gunnar Johansson. Nilsson had begun the year well with two second places, but a broken leg in Italy put him out for the season. Johansson also suffered a broken leg before the championship began and nothing was seen of him until the following year. The new boy in the Swedish line-up was Jan Liljedahl, riding a similar Husqvarna to those in the hands of Tibblin and Per-Olaf Persson. The Swedish trio left Hawkstone empty-handed as Don Rickman – now riding a Matchless-engined Metisse – and Jeff Smith led an all-British offensive with a race-win apiece.

If it hadn't been clear before the grand prix that the system of marking was incompatible with fairness, it most certainly was afterwards. Both Tibblin and Don Rickman had cause to regret the arrangement which required a rider to complete both 12-lap heats in order to be classified as a finisher. In other circumstances, if Rickman were contesting all championship rounds, or had Tibblin needed the points from his second place in the first 35-minute race, the procedure would have given rise to even greater controversy.

Not that Smith complained, for his afternoon's work had proved to be entirely satisfactory and the eight points he obtained for victory lifted him above Lundin, to take over second place in the standings, 11 points behind Tibblin. With three rounds remaining, Smith would be World champion if he won them all, even if Tibblin was thrice runner-up. Ultimately this unlikely hypothesis was to fail its first test when Tibblin won at Namur, and Lundin in Luxembourg. Smith brought the series to a close by winning in East Germany to conclude a gratifying first season for the development B40, with third place for him and fifth for Lampkin.

Notwithstanding Smith's understandable delight at recording his fourth overall victory in Britain's premier event, it was the least satisfying of the five in his remarkable career. Heavy overnight rain had left the course in near perfect condition as John Burton set the early pace in the first heat, with Don Rickman, Vic

Above **Fast and furious in the Hants Grand National at Matchams Park. From left to right: Robin Cox (Cochise, 81), John Giles (Triumph, 4), Don Rickman (Metisse, 74), Ivor England (Metisse, 75), and John Burton (BSA, 43). Derek Rickman's rear wheel can be seen to the far left of the picture, a familiar sight to many riders through the years.**

119

Right **The programme for the British 500cc Grand Prix at Hawkstone Park. Some 43,000 enthusiasts paid to witness the first British 1-2-3 since 1959.**

Eastwood, Smith and Lampkin in close pursuit. Tibblin was disputing ninth place with John Giles' Triumph and Derek Rickman's Metisse. Burton's BSA soon developed a misfire, and Smith took up the leadership as Don Rickman wilted under a fierce attack from the British champion. Tibblin hauled himself up to third, as Don Rickman's Metisse surrendered with a timing malady. This left Smith to win without any pressure from Tibblin. Lampkin, who had ridden a competent, sensible race was third, well ahead of Derek Rickman and the Matchless of Eastwood and – riding in his first British GP – Chris Horsfield. Only eight riders completed the full distance.

Dave Curtis, who had come out of retirement to ride in the invitation races, sportingly loaned Don Rickman the magneto sprocket from his Matchless so that Rickman could repair his stricken Metisse. With a fit motor, Don Rickman showed what might have been, when he turned the second heat into something of a procession. One of Smith's beliefs was that a good rider need only go as fast as was necessary to win a race. He had no necessity to chase the Metisse, for second place was good enough to earn Smith outright victory. So the BSA team-leader rode with intelligent restraint; especially once his pit informed him that Tibblin had retired with a sticking throttle.

THE BRITISH FIGHT BACK

The British Grand Prix in 1963 proved two things. Firstly it confirmed that with newcomers like Eastwood and Horsfield, England was producing young riders capable of making a big impression in world moto-cross. Less attractively it re-affirmed the view that there was an inherent unfairness in the scoring system at all grands prix where there were two heats. Although scoring values were changed before the start of the 1969 season, it wasn't until 1977 that scores from all races completed by a rider counted towards his aggregate. Things move slowly in the administration of world moto-cross.

Not so slow was Britain's team in the Moto-Cross des Nations, held at Knutstorp in Sweden, on a track made treacherous by incessant rain. The cornerstones of Britain's 11th victory in the immensely popular international team competition were laid by the Rickman brothers. Dispensing with the usual two heats plus a final format, the 1963 contest was decided over two gruelling heats - each took almost an hour for the winner to complete - with a team's best three placings in each race added together to decide the winner.

Although Sweden were without Johansson, Nilsson and Tibblin – the world champion was injured at the Luxembourg GP – as host nation they put up a tremendous fight and only failed to retain the trophy by two points. Apart from the Rickmans, Smith, John Burton – who had replaced Bickers from the 1962 team – and Lampkin all played important parts at an event which revived soggy memories of Cassel in 1960.

Although both major championships had been won by Swedish riders, Britain were indisputably number two. For the first time in the world 500cc class there wasn't a Belgian in the top 15. How times change.

120

JEFF SMITH is World 500cc Champion. He and Dave Bickers pocket the national spoils, but the Greeves rider is outpaced by Joel Robert in the British 250cc GP at Cadwell Park. Great Britain win the Moto-Cross des Nations at Hawkstone.

1964

Anyone who has competed in sport, at any level, will readily acknowledge that some successes are more easily earned than others. Whatever it takes to win a grand prix, Jeff Smith was in need of rather less of this precious commodity at Hawkstone Park in July 1963 than was required by him on the other four visits when he collected maximum points, or on the countless occasions he did so elsewhere in the world. By temperament rather than upbringing, Smith – like almost all champions – was markedly different from his peers and he required more than grudging commendation from them, or the approbation of his native people.

Jeff Smith was now in his 30th year and to a considerable extent his ambitions until then had only seriously been affronted by the succession of exceptionally talented Swedish riders. Inwardly Smith believed he had the wherewithal to beat the best of them though, like the vast majority of sportsmen and women who aspire to breathe the rarefied air on top of the world, he realized it would require a monumental effort to do so.

He also understood that he couldn't get there on his own. The competitions department at Small Heath would have to play their part in the continuing development of the B40, with the considerable support of BSA's dynamic, new managing director Harry Sturgeon, who recognised the sales value of racing successes, but who still had to source a budget for their programme

The responsibility for seeing moto-cross projects through fell to Brian Martin, who

Belgian bombshell. Joel Robert was simply irresistible in the British 250cc Grand Prix, held for the first time at Cadwell Park. The 20-year-old Robert, from Chatelet, near Charleroi, went on to become the youngest winner of a world title when he clinched the title at the Finnish GP; and completed the season with a maximum score of 56 points.

121

Above **Dave Bickers** was the only rider to mount a serious challenge to Joel Robert. Bickers won the first heat of the British 250cc Grand Prix, but was well beaten by the Belgian in the second race.

Below right **Sten Lundin**, who won the World 500cc Championship in 1959 and 1961, scored only three points at Hawkstone Park, a circuit he hated.

enthusiastically managed the competitions department. Martin had ridden in national trials as a 15-year-old. To fund the purchase of his first machine, a 350cc B25, he took a job as a pusher at Birmingham Speedway. After serving an apprenticeship with a small engineering company Martin joined the BSA comp shop as a fitter. 'It was the sort of job you dreamed of in those days,' reflected Martin. 'These were the glory years of Gold Stars; when BSA were winning trials and moto-cross events throughout Europe.'

Martin's contribution to those results included three gold medals and a silver in the International Six Days Trial, and membership of the winning British team in the 1957 Moto-Cross des Nations at Brands Hatch. With a wealth of competition experience to draw on, Martin was convinced that for BSA to lift a world title, greater power-to-weight improvements would have to be made to their moto-cross bikes. Over the following seven seasons, until the competitions department was closed abruptly in 1971, Martin's theories were vigorously tested in the major international tournaments. Harry Sturgeon was also alive to the potentially lucrative promotion possibilities for his company's products, should the BBC continue to televise close season moto-cross events from England and Wales.

MOTO-CROSS ON TELEVISION

Television and moto-cross had first made contact in December 1954 when, at the instigation of Harold Taylor, the BBC broadcast a special meeting from Beenham organized by the South Reading Club, and won by Les Archer. Before then, the BBC had screened speedway and road racing, but moto-cross was an untried subject. Almost a decade later, after Independent TV had broadcast some events from the north of England, the BBC had the bright idea of showing moto-cross when frost and snow ruled out any soccer on a Saturday afternoon.

The winter of 1962/63 was particularly severe and played havoc with traditional outdoor sports, especially ball games. Thus was born the BBC's *Grandstand* TV scrambles series, which was to make household names of Jeff Smith, Arthur Lampkin, Dave Bickers, Chris Horsfield and Vic Eastwood. Here was a marvellous opportunity to broaden the appeal of the sport and widen its audience. There was also a welcome spin-off for the motorcycle makers and the careers of up-and-coming

Left **Malcolm Davis looked the obvious successor to Dave Bickers when he finished third overall at the British 250cc Grand Prix, but never quite took the mantle. By the time Davis won the first of his three national 250cc titles, in 1968, Bickers was semi-retired.**

young riders such as Dave Nicoll, who were guaranteed regular appearances on the nation's most watched sporting programme.

Building a bike capable of winning the world 500cc title was Martin's principal objective and it was handy to have the winter TV series to continue the development work on Jeff Smith's bike, and iron out any niggling fallibilities without the long-haul travel between grands prix. It was also very handy to have Smith as his leading rider. Quite apart from his other qualities, Smith was, in Brian Martin's words: 'A brilliant development rider, and a very dedicated, professional and fit competitor.'

Jeff Smith had served a five-year apprenticeship at BSA. In the years 1951 to 1955 he worked in the service department, toolroom, mechanical test shop, heat treatment, Gold Star engine and machine build, then a spell in the competitions department, in advance of departure for Hampshire and two years National Service. On completion of his stint in the army, Jeff worked in his father's engineering consultancy business and then returned to the BSA competition shop to assist in the development of the C15S in preparation for an attack on the European 250cc series. There was not much Jeff Smith didn't know about off-road BSA bikes.

At a time when most of his rivals rode to get fit, Jeff Smith got fit to ride. Maurice Herriott was a production line worker at Armoury Road, who won an athletics silver medal in the 1964 Tokyo Olympics. Herriott devised a fitness programme to aid Smith's stamina and enable him to withstand fatigue in arduous grand prix races. Herriott's share of the input that underpinned Smith's commitment and dedication was to earn an impressive dividend.

Before the opening championship round, Smith's confidence was high. He had appropriated the winter *Grandstand* TV series and won his fifth Hants Grand National on the trot, while thinking his BSA – which now scaled 228lb [102.6kg] – was as much as 80lb [36kg] lighter than Rolf Tibblin's Hedlund special. Smith reckoned he would start with a big advantage over his Swedish rival, though what evidence there was to support this was put through the shredder by Tibblin in the opening tie at Payerne in the rolling hills above Lake Neuchâtel, near Bern.

If Smith was concerned by his infelicitous start on 12 April, he and BSA could be

Alan Clough (Greeves, 15) tries to take Pat Lamper (DOT, 20) on the outside during the British 250cc Grand Prix. Clough was fourth in the second race.

excused for feeling downcast in mid-May, by when Tibblin had repeated his earlier feat and peeled off four successive victories to demoralise the British champion.

Memories of the vain chase of Hallman for the 1962 World 250cc title must have crowded Smith's mind. It was almost two years since the BSA rider held a 22-point advantage over Hallman, only to lose out when the Swede mounted an unassailable charge in the second half of the competition. Was Smith again to be thwarted or could he repeat Hallman's stratagem?

The answer now, as then, lay in events following the Dutch tie. Smith won in Holland in 1964, as he had done 24 months earlier. But whereas he was never victorious after the Dutch 250cc round in 1962, the Netherlands proved to be the crossroads for the Briton in the 1964 500cc tournament. Having collected his first eight-point score of the year, Smith felt he was somewhere near the right track.

The odds, however, still favoured Tibblin. With 14 countries to be visited, there were more rounds in 1964 (and again in 1966) than any other years in the history of the 500cc championship. With only the seven best to count (it was eight in 1966), Tibblin required just three more victories from the remaining nine grands prix.

He got the first a week later in France, where Smith punctured and could only finish third. Smith won the next two – in Italy and at Lvov in the Soviet Union – as Tibblin's good fortune deserted him, and he failed to score in either. Smith was now two points ahead of Tibblin; though not for long. Seven days later, Tibblin won at Prerov in Czechoslovakia, so with six wins and a second he led Smith 54 points to 48. There were still five rounds to go as the riders took a break from criss-crossing Europe, before the series resumed in Belgium in early August.

It gave Brian Martin and the team a welcome breather and an opportunity to make one or two changes to the B40 to make it more reliable. Crankcase failure, with a resultant power loss, had been a constant worry. When Smith appeared at Namur for the first of the five tumultuous rounds which climaxed the tournament, a more powerful engine had been fitted with a beefed-up casing which eliminated the problem.

Smith's solitary grand prix victory at the most gladiatorial circuit in world moto-cross brought him enormous satisfaction. Tibblin twice crashed in the first heat and Sten Lundin won the second, with Smith runner-up. This triumph, as Tibblin again failed to score, was the turning point for Smith.

Either side of Lundin's West German win, Smith took maximum points in Luxembourg and at Schwerin, East Germany, where he pipped Tibblin by a mere fifth of a second. The leading pair were now tied on 54 points, with double champion Lundin, 20 points behind them. It would all be decided at the 14th, and final, heat round at San Sebastian in northern Spain.

There were two weeks in which to prepare for the Spanish showdown on Sunday 13 September. Smith approached the last few days with a thoroughness and attention to detail which typified his application and tactical planning for grand prix moto-cross. It had been a long, wearing summer with tens of thousands of road miles accumulated in the cramped van Smith shared with Arthur Lampkin or John Harris, who between them had acted as Smith's mechanic and pit-signaller. Jeff Smith had come too far to be

Below **Derek Rickman guns his Bultaco-engined Metisse up the hill away from the road racing circuit at Cadwell Park. Rickman finished fifth overall in the first moto-cross grand prix to be held at the Lincolnshire venue. It was the first time in two months that the elder Rickman had gained a place on a grand prix leaderboard.**

Right **Chris Horsfield (James,17) tries to get the better of Derek Rickman (Metisse, 22) in the British 250cc Grand Prix. Horsfield failed.**

Centre **Joel Robert (CZ, 3) and Dave Bickers (Greeves, 12), during their epic dice in the first heat at Cadwell Park.**

denied the big prize a second time, even though the reward for Rolf Tibblin would be a unique hat-trick of world 500cc titles.

While Tibblin returned to the cool of Sweden, Smith arrived in Spain, four days before the grand prix, to acclimatize and get accustomed to local conditions. With temperatures in the high 30s Celsius, Smith and John Harris trained in the hot sun, tested the Spanish fuel to jet the carburettor correctly, walked every inch of the course and generally left nothing to chance.

Tibblin by contrast, arrived tired late on the Saturday evening, after journeying the length of Europe. On race day he was not satisfied with the Spanish petrol supplied by the organisers so, taking the tank off his bike in lieu of a can, he sent his mechanic across the border to buy some premium grade French fuel. This little shopping trip took longer than expected, and when the first race was due to start, Tibblin's Hedlund was still without its petrol tank

The whole exercise sounds like a chapter from one of Michael Palin's *Ripping Yarns*. The anguish and suspense this must have caused in Tibblin's mind, was no way to prepare for the year's most important grand prix. Tibblin fretted nervously while the start was delayed. It was the only time he was close enough to Smith to see if the tension had got to his archrival. If it had, then it certainly wasn't apparent as Smith disappeared into the distance from a perfect start. Tibblin got up to second within a couple of laps, but overdid things in trying to wind Smith in, and damaged the Hedlund's front wheel forcing his retirement. Although the Swede sportingly appeared for the second heat – being the first to congratulate the BSA man as they crossed the line together – the Spanish GP had been something of an anti-climax. Belgium's Hubert Scaillet was second, riding a Metisse, with Lundin third. Jeffrey Vincent Smith was world champion.

Smith's triumph entirely vindicated BSA's decision to discard John Burton and Arthur Lampkin from the team, so the factory could put its full weight behind Smith's title endeavours. At the end of an exhausting season Smith was quick to pay tribute to Lampkin – who had accompanied him to the early rounds, dutifully accepting the mechanic's chores – and John Harris who was with Smith throughout the closing stages. Despite Jeff Smith's pre-occupation with the World championship, he still found time to win his seventh ACU 500cc Star, once again beating Vic Eastwood into second place, with Chris Horsfield third.

Dave Bickers completed a hat trick of domestic 250cc title wins, though it was not a particularly productive year for the Greeves teamster, apart from his national success and the 250cc class win he enjoyed in the *Grandstand* TV series. In the 14-round World 250cc championship, Bickers and the title holder Torsten Hallman had their hopes buried under an avalanche of victories scored by 20-year-old Belgian new boy Joel Robert, who rode a very rapid works-prepared 246cc CZ. Included in his haul of championship firsts, was a hard-fought win in the British 250cc GP, staged for the first time at Cadwell Park, Lincolnshire.

BELGIAN COMEBACK

Bickers had the 15,000-strong crowd on their feet, by winning the first 18-lap race as he and Robert continually swapped places. But the Belgian had the last word, winning the second heat by more than half a minute. The day had not been without encouragement for some British riders. Malcolm Davis and Bryan Goss were respectively second and third overall – each riding the latest Greeves Challenger – but the threat of CZ machines to both Greeves and Husqvarna was ominously clear. After Cadwell, there were five CZs in the top 10 of the standings, which Robert headed by a comfortable 16-point margin. Bickers, with only one win in the competition was in fourth place, and effectively out of the title reckoning.

The FIM had ruled that when a country was awarded the Moto-Cross des Nations, they would lose the right to stage a round of the World 500cc championship. Generally the team contest came after the individual classes

Right **Hawkstone Park staged the Moto-Cross des Nations in 1964. In the second race, Sylvain Geboers (Metisse, 4), of runners-up Belgium, leads Denmark's Mogens Rasmussen (Metisse, 11) and the burly Dutchman, Broer Dirks (Lito, 28).**

Opposite **Rolf Tibblin was challenging Jeff Smith and Don Rickman for the lead in the first heat of the Moto-Cross des Nations, until he broke the rear brake rod on his Hedlund.**

had been completed. But in 1964 the final round of the extended 500cc itinerary was not scheduled until mid-September, so the Moto-Cross des Nations was slotted into a gap in late August. For the fourth time Britain were hosts, though after three visits to Brands Hatch, this time Hawkstone was chosen as the venue.

Anxious not to jeopardize his championship chances, Jeff Smith opted to use his old B40 rather than the newer version which was fitted with a quicker motor and strengthened crankcase, which had been unveiled at Namur. After three grand prix wins in as many weeks, Smith was virtually walking on water at Hawkstone Park, as he and his British teammates overwhelmed the opposition.

Smith was invincible. The only survivor from the winning team when the event was previously held in England, he won both 16-lap heats at his own pace. Don and Derek Rickman on Matchless Metisses were second and third in the first race. In the second, Sylvain Geboers and Herman de Soete ensured that Belgium would finish as runners-up, bringing their Matchless Metisses into second and fourth places respectively. The Swedish challenge dissolved when Bill Nilsson crashed his Metisse and Tibblin retired with brake trouble.

From a British point of view it had been another staggeringly successful day. From the Salop club's perspective, the afternoon could have gone much better. Many among the crowd of 42,000 were reduced to jeering and slow handclapping after four false starts disfigured the first race. In the last false start, Nilsson and Vic Eastwood crashed together at the head of the pack. Eastwood's footrest knocked out two of Nilsson's teeth and Eastwood broke a bone in the back of his hand. Once again dust was a major problem and Hawkstone was clearly on borrowed time.

Still having the time of his life was Jeff Smith. A fourth individual award for him, as Britain won for the 12th time in 18 years, was followed by the 500cc title to be added to the TV and domestic championship trophies he had already pocketed that season. It had been some year for Jeff Smith.

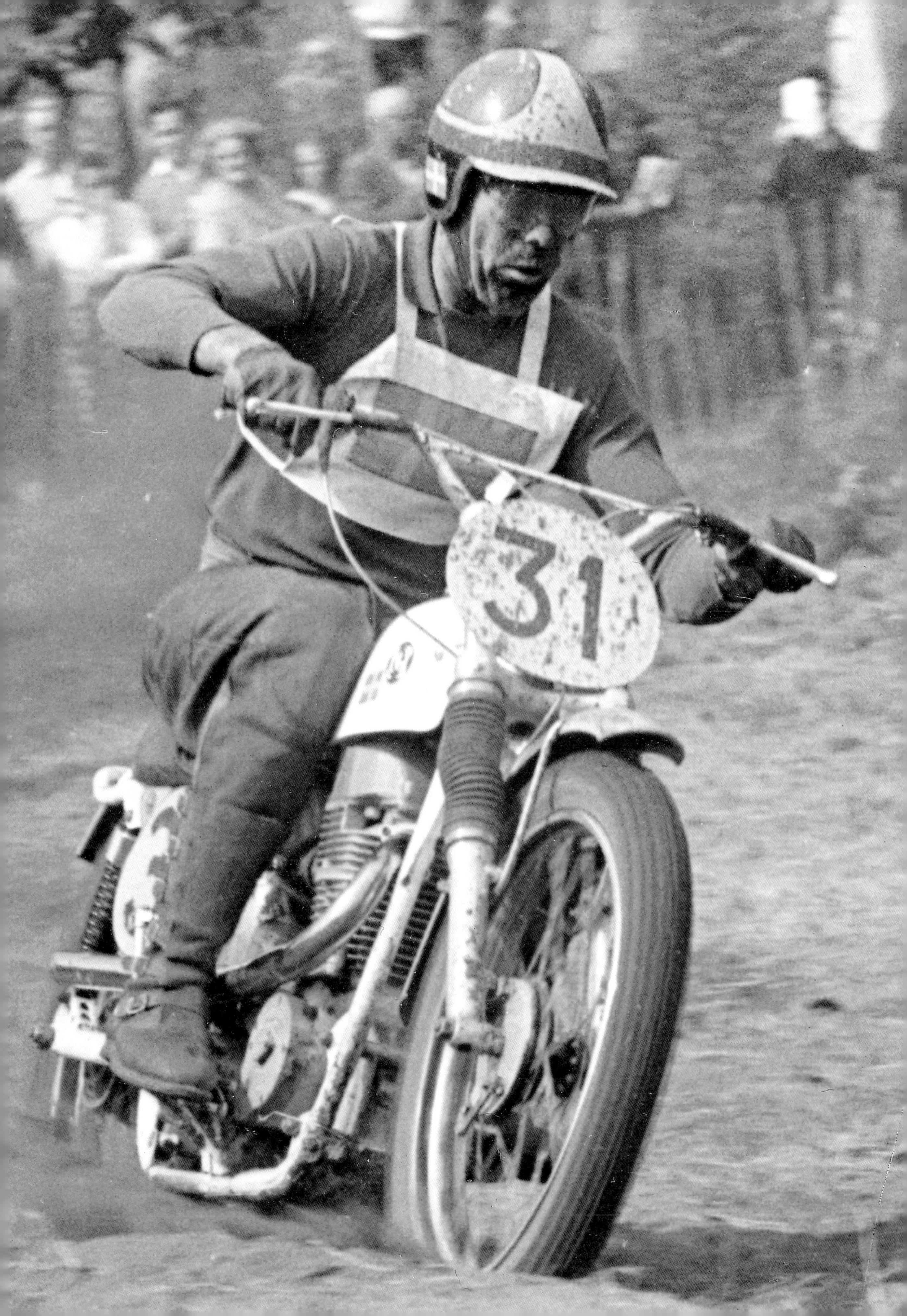
31

1965

A British GP win apiece for JEFF SMITH and DAVE BICKERS. Smith retains his world and national titles. Great Britain complete their second hat trick of Moto-Cross des Nations victories.

At the end of his world title-winning season, Jeff Smith was drained, both physically and mentally. He contemplated retirement. After all, he had achieved everything within his compass in 1964, and there seemed nothing else to do. Perhaps the key to a change of heart lay in the answer to a question put to him by Norman Sharpe, a journalist with the weekly, *Motor Cycling*. 'What did you learn?' asked Sharpe.

'Well, I used to think that international competition was a grim, dedicated sort of business, in which the only purpose was to win,' replied Smith. 'Now, I really believe that there's true sportsmanship in it. You might say it's mellowed me a lot.'

The suggestion that if Smith continued, he would somehow be more carefree in his approach was not one to be taken seriously. The truth is that Smith was dedicated to winning; he saw no purpose in competing otherwise. It was this obsessional quality that made him what he was: the finest moto-cross rider of his era, if not the best Britain has ever produced. Across the span of all generations, Jeff Smith was unquestionably the greatest of a distinguished line of British all-rounders.

It's a peculiarly perverse trait of the English media to be less than generous to those of their fellow men who have made it to the top of the sporting pile. One only has to look at the hatchet job done by some commentators on Nick Faldo who almost single-handedly

Right **Rolf Tibblin** forsook his Husqvarna for a two-stroke CZ in 1965. But there was to be no repeat of his 1962 Hawkstone victory, and the talented Swede had to settle for second place behind Jeff Smith's BSA.

Opposite **Vic Eastwood**, for whom the journalistic plaudits were reserved, after the British 500cc Grand Prix.

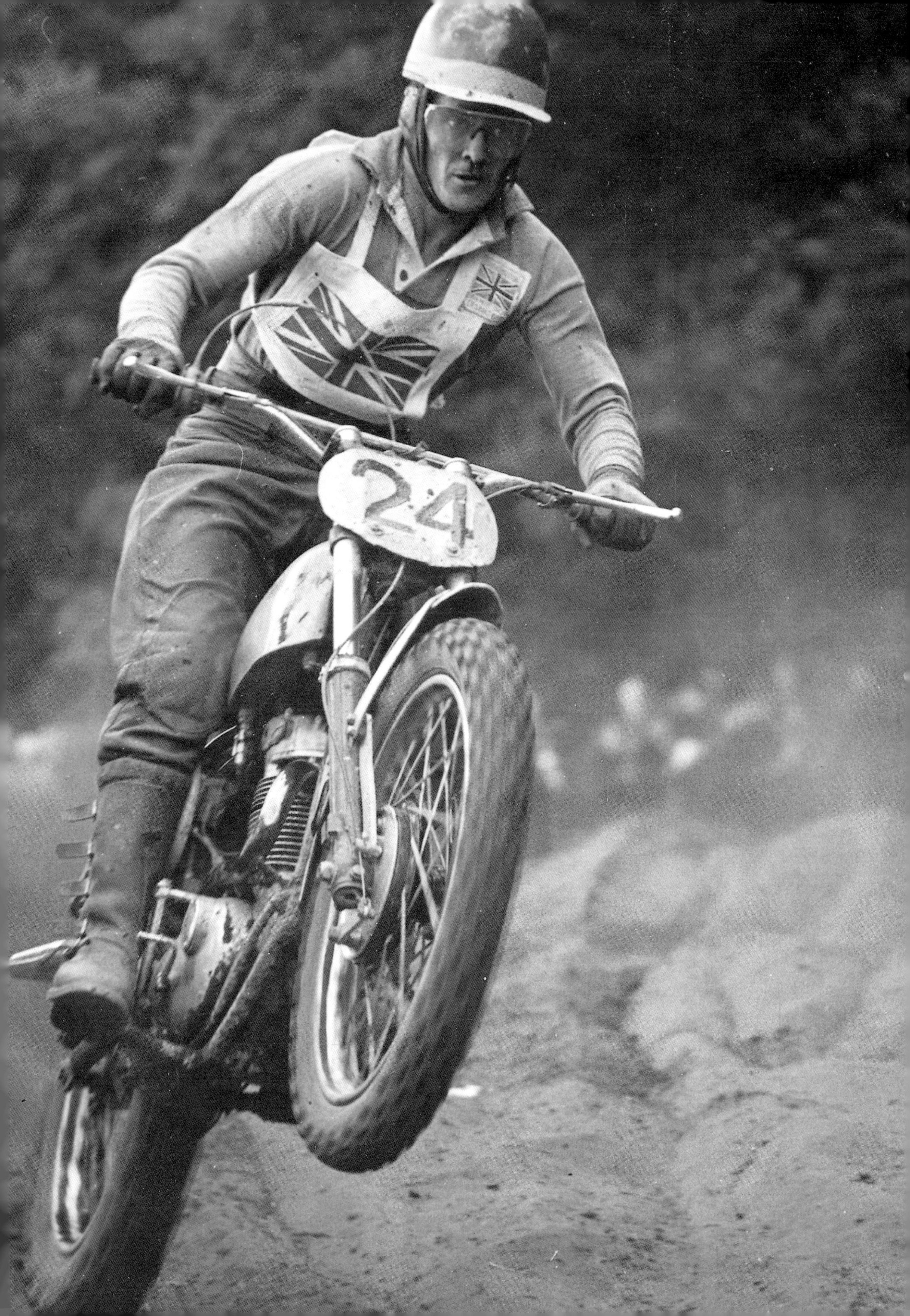
24

Right **Dave Bickers bustles his Greeves to victory in the British 250cc Grand Prix. The Tor track at Higher Wick Farm, was one of his two favourite circuits.**

Below **Jeff Smith gave a masterful display of racecraft in winning the British 500cc Grand Prix for a fifth time.**

restored British golfing pride, which had been becalmed for a long period in the doldrums. At the same time they laud the transparent mediocrity in others like boxer Frank Bruno – who was so obviously out of his depth against world-class opponents – yet turned him into a national hero.

To a considerable extent the public fall for it; mirroring the prejudices of those sporting journalists who should know better. In a high-profile game like golf, with a media circus scrummaging for exclusive stories, the kind of exposure the player gets depends almost entirely on his continual availability for interviews and how affably or otherwise the subject comes across. The animus that exists between Faldo and some sections of the media is a direct result of his lack of embrace for them. Despite Faldo's stature in world golf he has, in the eyes of some, failed to turn the admiration he earned into affection.

In the 1960s the searching interview of leading riders was not a trend in moto-cross culture, any more than it is now. Had it been in 1965, Jeff Smith would no doubt have told it as it was. Although there was no question of any animosity between Smith and the motor cycling press, they never greeted his world championship victory with unrestrained delight. Why, isn't clear. Maybe they sensed that Smith appeared not to care a great deal about anybody who wasn't on his chosen path. Friendships did not then play a part of his life, except those at BSA where Brian Martin, Arthur Lampkin – who was to become a lifelong friend – and John Harris, were cocooned with Smith in mutual ambition.

Jeff Smith had immersed himself in moto-cross and neither sought nor offered much else. He couldn't remember a time when it was different, for his had been a life dedicated to a pursuit, the sort of life that seems shamefully shallow to those with no sporting passion. While others who aspire to sporting eminence have either the vanity or discretion to apply cosmetics to their character, Jeff Smith was going through life playing himself straight, without compromise or disguise. If you peeled off a layer of Jeff Smith, you would only have found Jeff Smith beneath it. What you saw was what you got.

Left Another angle on Jeff Smith, a record nine times British 500cc champion.

THE GREAT JEFF SMITH

The British riders, more out of envy than malice, thought he was lucky. Smith had the best bikes, the might of BSA behind him, better engines, Brian Martin's know-how, and so on. They had conveniently overlooked the fact that much of the development of the B40 was attributable to Smith's own engineering aptitude.

Others resented his style. It is true Smith could never be described as flamboyant, but some suggested he was a cold-hearted assassin who picked off his rivals as if they were victims. There are petty jealousies in all sports. Some, like it or not, are transmitted and amplified by the press. Not with the open hostility that football managers are sometimes

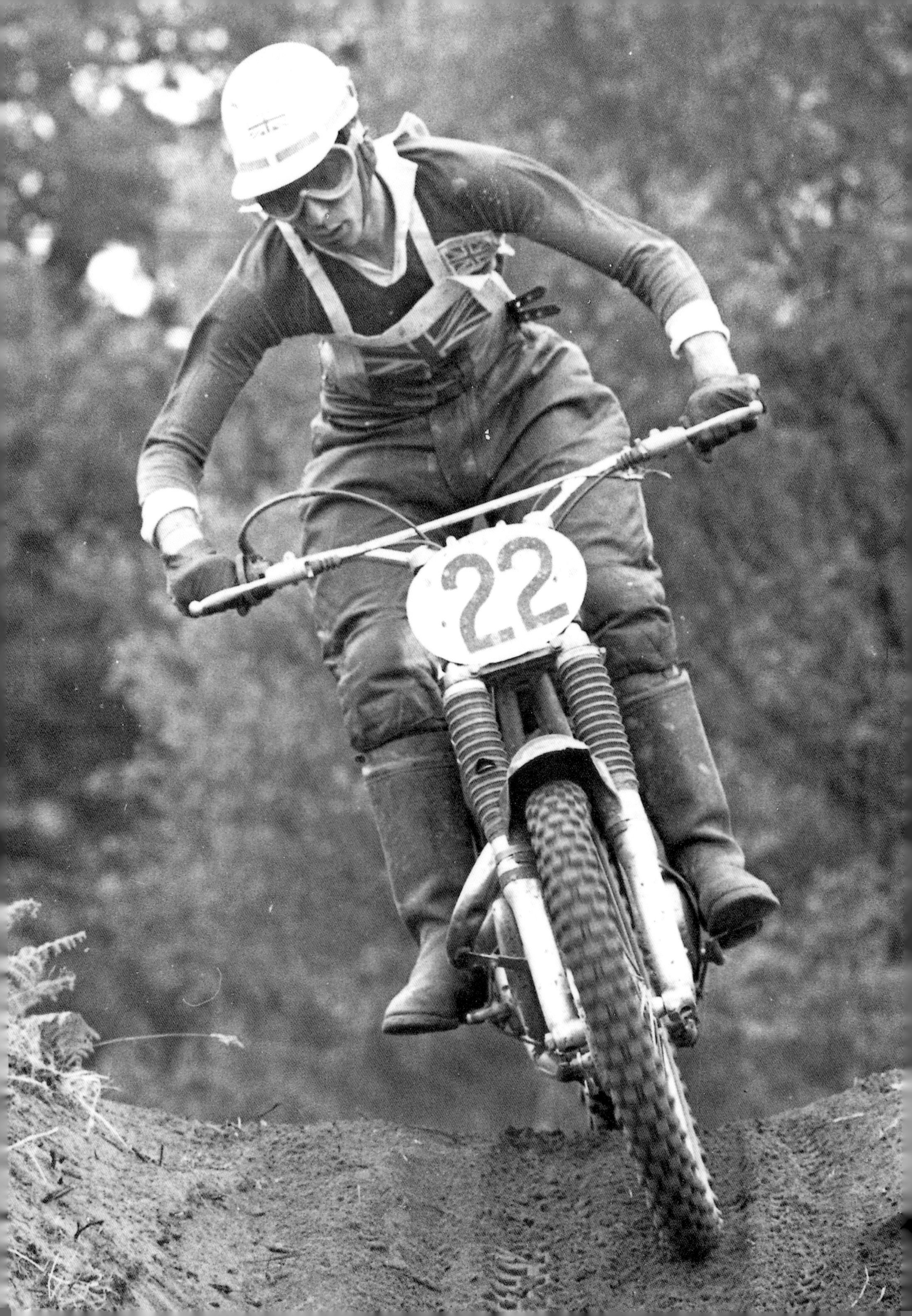
22

targeted, but in a way which fosters a coolness edging toward enmity.

There is no better evidence of this than the reports of Smith's fifth British GP victory at Hawkstone, in 1965. Instead of acknowledging Smith's acute tactical awareness, his triumph was described as lucky. The journalistic plaudits were reserved for Vic Eastwood and Rolf Tibblin, for whom Smith was apparently no match.

EASTWOOD'S TOUGH LESSON

You don't have to possess a fortress mind to be a champion, even a world champion, but the ability to endure periods of mental solitary confinement is a great help. Some riders win their races from the heart. Dave Bickers is an example of one who did so frequently. The emotional verve which supplemented his aggressive technique, allied to a cheeky, laid-back manner, made Bickers a great favourite with British crowds.

Smith's approach was altogether more cerebral. Like Lester Piggott, he thought through his race wins. Being in the correct position, at the right time, was what mattered. Towards the end of a race, when Smith looked out of it, and the riders at the front were counting their prize money, Smith would pounce to steal victory. He could also lead from the front. As the chasers edged closer, sure they would catch him in the closing laps, Smith would pull away, certain his superior stamina and fitness would see him through. It invariably did. At Hawkstone Park on 4 July, Smith gave a perfect demonstration of his racecraft. Though for many of the 30,000 present, including the press, it was all down to his good fortune.

While Smith was undecided about his future, BSA made the decision to recruit some fresh talent. With Arthur Lampkin and John Burton put out to pasture, Brian Martin lured Vic Eastwood from Matchless, while still providing some support for Lampkin at specific events. In the search for new blood, Eastwood fitted Martin's requirements to the letter. Seven years Smith's junior, Eastwood had twice been runner-up to the champion in the ACU 500cc Star competition and was handling the factory Matchless with all the aplomb Dave Curtis had shown in earlier seasons. Of the great Swedish quartet who had once dominated the heavyweight division, only Gunnar Johansson remained loyal to Hedlund-engined machinery. Tibblin had acquired one of the new 360cc CZs.

In the first 12-lap race Eastwood had pulled out a ten-second lead on Smith, with Tibblin struggling to get on terms after a poor start. With two laps to go, and Smith biding his time, Eastwood went down in a moment's carelessness as he was about to lap Dave Nicoll. Smith seized his chance and, though Eastwood recovered, it was the world champion who took the flag, three seconds ahead of his new team-mate. Tibblin was third, 11 seconds adrift of the woebegone Eastwood.

Don Rickman led the second heat (he had been tangled up in the starting elastic in the first, but eventually finished 13th) and maintained his advantage till lap five, when he fell. Tibblin then took up the leadership with Smith second and Eastwood third. Smith knew all along that whatever distance Tibblin won by, what mattered was keeping the youthful Eastwood at bay. If Eastwood could get past Smith and within 11 seconds of Tibblin, then the tie would be broken in Eastwood's favour, on the basis of time taken for both races. But the canny Smith was never sharper than when there was a big prize at stake, and he staved off Eastwood's late surge to claim a shrewd victory. Smith had given Eastwood plenty to think about, at the same time reminding those who may have forgotten, who was the master of Hawkstone Park, and the British 500cc Grand Prix. Tibblin and Eastwood had all the time in the world to reflect on Smith's luck.

Meanwhile, Smith had the moto-cross world at his mercy. With the B40 enlarged to 441cc, Smith missed out in the first of the 13 events which made up the championship, and it was Sten Lundin who won in Austria, riding a Matchless-Metisse. Thereafter Smith assumed command, winning in Switzerland, France, Finland and Sweden – becoming the first overseas rider to win the Swedish GP more than once – to pull out a 24-point lead over

Opposite **Don Rickman threads his way through the ferns at Hawkstone Park, en route to fourth place in the second heat of the British 500cc Grand Prix.**

Right Jerry Scott was fourth in the British 500cc Championship in 1965. Scott gets his BSA airborne at the British 500cc Grand Prix, where he finished sixth overall. This was Scott's most productive season, in a life which was tragically foreshortened by a racing accident.

Eastwood. Tibblin revived his chances in the second half of the campaign with maximum points in Italy and West Germany, and newcomer Paul Friedrichs won in Luxembourg to augment his CZ victories in East Germany and Czechoslovakia.

With the seven best scores to count, Smith retained his title by winning the Dutch GP at Druten, near Nijmegen. Although he hadn't achieved a second maximum (he was two points short) the BSA rider had no need to, as Friedrichs and Tibblin were a long way adrift and realistically had only the FIM Silver Medal as their target. Eastwood was a creditable fourth, with three grand prix runner-up finishes to his name. Not at all bad in his first full season among the big boys.

Smith's achievement seemed an age removed from the uncertainty over his future in the sport. When the *Grandstand* TV series commenced, Smith was still undecided so the 12-part tournament started without him. With results from all venues to count, many saw the TV competition – with a regular Saturday audience of 12 million – as more important than the five-round ACU Star contest; especially the publicity-hungry motorcycle industry.

Having decided to defer retirement, Smith took a long holiday and was off-form on his return, failing to make up for a poor start. Although he won only one of the 12 rounds, Chris Horsfield on the prototype 1965-production Matchless carried off the BBC trophy. Dave Bickers lifted the 250cc TV class once again.

BICKERS WINS FOR GREEVES

Greeves had made up their minds to develop a 360cc engine in order to compete with CZ and take a tilt at the World 500cc Championship. With the new motor as yet untried, they were keen that Bickers would focus his attention on retaining his ACU 250cc crown and win the World 250cc championship. The former task proved much easier than the second, as one would expect, though there were one or two alarms for Bickers before the silver polish was eventually called for. Reliability was still a problem for Bickers, which enlivened the rivalry between Greeves and Bryan Goss, on the factory Husqvarna. Fortunately for Bickers, when Goss outpaced him at the Experts' GN, second place on the Greeves was sufficient to earn Bickers his fifth successive title.

Despite his fame at home, the consistency required to win a world title continued to elude Bickers and, at 27, time would soon run out for the Coddenham flyer and for Greeves. With only a single grand prix victory in each of the previous three years, Bickers had been having a fairly thin time since he won seven in 1961 to retain his European 250cc title.

He began with a bang in Barcelona, winning the first of the 15 rounds in the category and led the standings at the end of April when he won the Belgian GP at Hechtel. But after this morale-boosting start, there were only four third places, a second and one more first, as Bickers finished third behind Joel Robert and Podolsk's Victor

Arbekov, who at 23 became the Soviet Union's first world moto-cross champion. Arbekov, with five victories, and Robert with three, topped the final table in a CZ one-two, though it was Bickers' third win which brought most pleasure to British fans.

The 12th round in the competition was the British GP which returned to Glastonbury where it had only once previously been held, in 1962. Bickers had no-scored in each of the earlier three rounds, and with Arbekov a non-starter due to a dislocated thumb, the Greeves frontrunner was up for his third British 250cc GP.

Glastonbury and Shrubland Park – where Bickers won his first British – were his two favourite circuits. From the outset things didn't look too bright for the Briton as Robert's CZ appeared to be much quicker than the Greeves. But the Belgian developed chain trouble and trailed in eighth as Bickers headed Don Rickman's Bultaco-Metisse over the line.

Robert was tremendously quick in the second heat, lapping all but the first seven competitors. After Robert came Bickers, who again beat Rickman to the tape, so the Greeves' rider took the overall from Rickman and Jawa's Vlastimel Valek. A crowd of 36,000 greeted Bickers' effort with prolonged applause. It was as well they made the most of it, for home victories in the British 250cc GP were to become depressingly rare occurrences.

Within another three years the same would be said of British triumphs in the Moto-Cross des Nations. But not in 1965. Belgium hadn't won the competition since 1951 when it was first held at Namur, though they were strongly fancied to repeat that success; which if they were to, would only be their second in the 19-year history of the event.

The home team were given masses of encouragement by Joel Robert, who won both 12-lap races over the Citadelle course, to take the individual award. However, Don Rickman led a marvellous second-heat fightback with

Below **Chris Horsfield (CZ, 6), holds off Dave Bickers (Greeves, 1), during a round of the televised Grandstand series. Horsfield had won the previous winter's competition riding a Matchless. Bickers won the lightweight class four years on the trot.**

Above **The going gets heavy for Chris Horsfield as he ploughs his CZ through the Kentish mud, at a Grandstand round held over the Canada Heights circuit.**

valiant support from Jeff Smith – appearing in the competition for the 11th time – plus Vic Eastwood, to register Britain's 13th victory.

A week later Smith, Arthur Lampkin, Don Rickman and the two factory Greeves' riders, Dave Bickers and Alan Clough were in Switzerland for the Trophée des Nations. This was the team contest for 250cc machines. Much less important, or anything like as well attended, as the Moto-Cross des Nations in the early years, there was some interest in the competition which Great Britain won in 1961 and 1962, though never again in its original form. After prolonged torrential rain, the course became impassable and the event was abandoned after the first heat. Amid chaos and confusion it appeared that Britain had won, but the FIM jury decided to invoke a ruling of force majeure and no result was declared. It had been a long wasted journey.

The next trip Jeff Smith made from his Birmingham home was shorter and more meaningful. Only a fortnight before the *Grandstand* TV winter series was scheduled to start, there was the unfinished business of the ACU 500cc Star competition, and the final tie, at the national Jackpot Scramble. Organized by the Mortimer Club at their Padworth,

Berkshire circuit Smith, Vic Eastwood and Dave Bickers still had everything to play for.

Were it not for a late change of date, the Experts' Grand National – which Bickers won, giving the 360cc Greeves its long-awaited debut – would have been the final round. However, the change meant a loss of status for the Experts', so the outcome went to the wire at the aptly-named Jackpot. After four events, Smith topped the charts with 22 points, Eastwood was on 20 and Bickers 16. For Bickers to beat Smith to the title he would need to win, and hope his BSA rival would finish no higher than fifth. But the real danger was posed by Eastwood. If he were to defeat his team-mate and could count on someone else doing so as well, the championship would be Eastwood's.

A DEFINITION OF EXCELLENCE

The atmosphere at the start of the 20-lap race was electric. Jerry Scott was leader for 14 laps, doggedly resisting Keith Hickman's BSA, and Smith. After clinging to Scott for eight laps, Hickman was forced out with chain trouble. Bickers, 11th on the first lap, had carved his way through the field on the 360cc Greeves until, on the 13th lap, he had caught the three BSAs. First, he displaced Eastwood, before setting about Scott, who by then had been relegated by Smith.

For five laps, Bickers climbed all over Smith, twice pulling level, but in a pulsating finish, the champion held on to win the most exciting race of the domestic season, to pouch his sixth successive Star, the eighth of his career. Eastwood was third and so, for the third year on the trot, was runner-up to the unyielding Smith.

Another summit-stakes' occasion had once again drawn a superlative performance from Smith, before the curtain was lowered on arguably the finest season of his long reign at the head of British moto-cross. Kenneth Tynan, the famous drama critic when asked for his criterion of a high-definition performance, described it as: 'The ability – shared by great athletes, sportsmen, bullfighters and conversationalists as well as stage performers – to communicate the essence of one's talent to an audience with economy, grace, no apparent effort and absolute, hard-edged clarity of outline.'

Apart from economy, it is the final six words of Tynan's portrayal which most appositely describe Smith's talent. Jeff Smith was the yardstick not only by which all other riders were judged, but by which they judged themselves. For the other stars, matching or beating Smith was the highest possible triumph; an endorsement of their own celebrity. Few were capable of achieving it, let alone aspired to it. To lesser lights, finishing second to Smith was as good as victory.

1966

DON RICKMAN wins the first British 500cc Grand Prix to be staged at Farleigh Castle. Dave Bickers triumphs in the British 500cc Championship, Fred Mayes is 250cc winner. Paul Friedrichs takes World 500cc title. Rickman, Bickers and Vic Eastwood bring home the Moto-Cross des Nations trophy from Normandy. Jerry Scott killed at Boltby.

Three new words were admitted to the lexicon of world moto-cross in 1966: Farleigh Castle and titanium. Throughout the year one of them dominated the headlines, though by early July the two words which had actually left the greatest impression on the memory were: 'Don Rickman'.

After the lessons of Jeff Smith's double world title triumph had been assimilated, Brian Martin and his team in the competition shop at BSA were convinced that more work had to be done to improve the power-to-weight ratio of Smith and Vic Eastwood's bikes, if they were to retain their competitiveness. This was the genesis of the great titanium project.

Brian Martin well remembers its birth. 'We had to do something dramatic for 1966 if we wanted to keep winning. We needed a bike that was lighter still, but had more power. The management thought we could buy the world championship and the job was taken from us in the competition department. The titanium bike was designed by committee, though it was my responsibility to get it built, tested and launched.'

However, Martin refused to lay the blame for the venture's ultimate failure at the door of BSA's senior management. 'It seemed a fantastic project at the time, and while we were involved we were all tremendously enthusiastic. Titanium seemed to be a magic metal – just what we wanted. But I didn't know enough about it, and we should not have gone grand prix racing with such an untested bike.'

Titanium's appeal was that, strength-for-strength, it was 65 per cent lighter than steel.

Right **Vic Eastwood leans his works BSA into a right hand bend during the first British 500cc Grand Prix to be held at Farleigh Castle. The first five riders in the finishing order were British. Eastwood was fifth.**

Opposite **Eastwood was a shining talent in a cast of English stars. He was in the great Britain team on four occasions when they won the Moto-Cross des Nations, and was six times runner-up in the British 500cc Championship; in five of those years Jeff Smith won the title.**

140

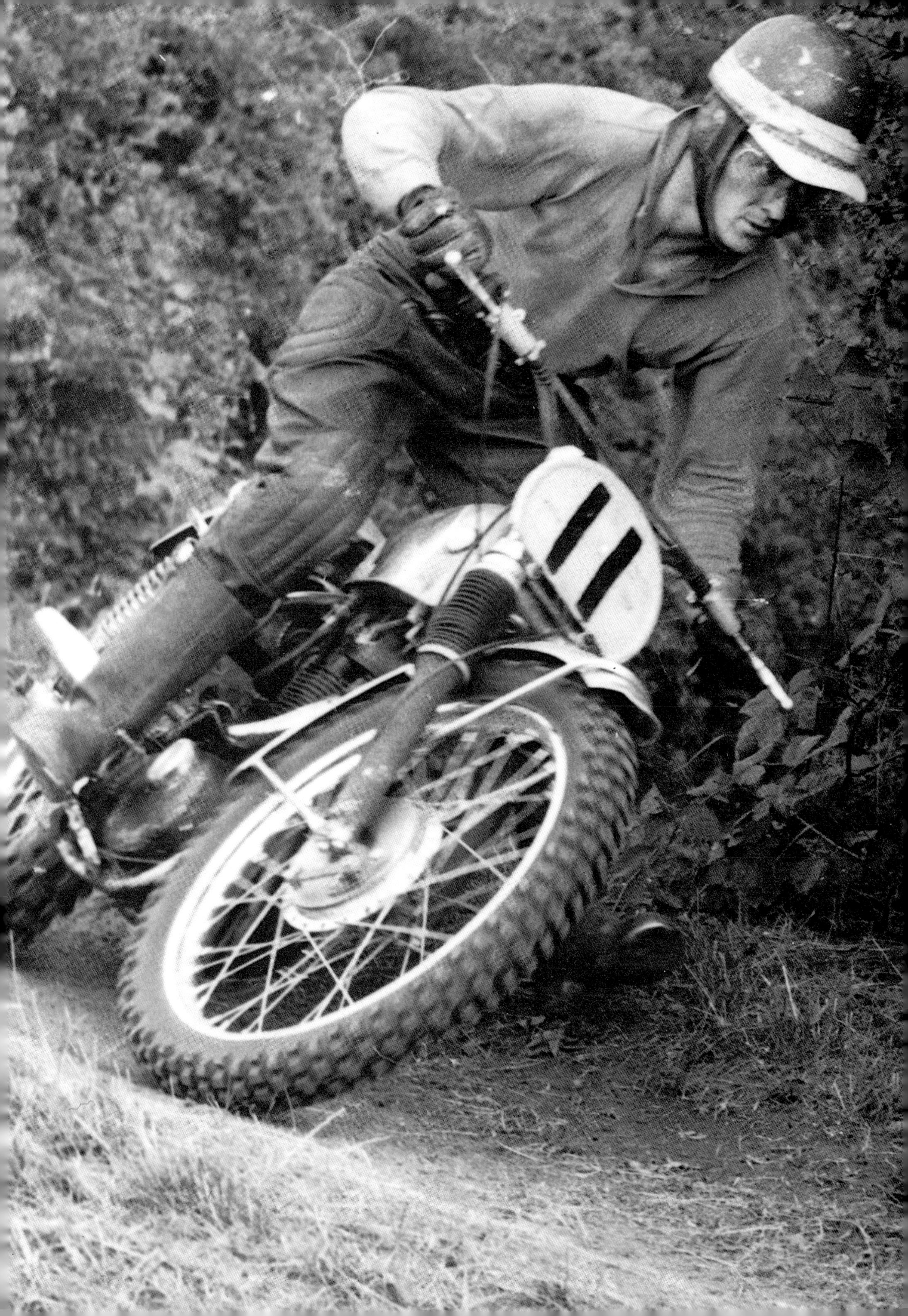

Above **Don Rickman.** His victory in the 1966 British 500cc Grand Prix assured him a place in the Hall of Fame.

Right **The programme for the 1966 British 500cc Grand Prix; the first to be held at Farleigh Castle.**

Centre **Bryan Wade** leaps over a crest on his Greeves. Wade had yet to make his mark as a championship contender. But his ebullient riding style made him a favourite with the crowds, well before he won the first of his five British titles, in 1969.

142

This allowed BSA to build a machine with a 494cc engine which produced an extra two bhp more than the 440cc unit in the 1965 bike, and at the same time bringing the dry weight down from 267lb (121.1kg) to 212lb (96.1kg). Unfortunately, there were many more disadvantages with titanium than the obvious weight-saving benefits, as BSA were to discover.

When heated, titanium absorbed oxygen and hydrogen from the atmosphere and became brittle and useless. This meant that conventional welding practices couldn't be used, and the solution was to place components in a sealed chamber in which air had been replaced by argon, an inert gas. The welder had to work with his arms in special gloves while peering into the chamber through a glass window. The titanium had to be spotlessly clean – even fingerprints were removed before welding began – and the whole process was complex, lengthy and vastly cost-consuming. If a frame cracked during practice or racing, no such fastidious working conditions were available at trackside. The titanium had to be held together with improvised plates owing to the impossibility of effecting a welded repair, until the bikes were returned to the factory.

The titanium frames also flexed to a greater extent than their steel equivalents which impaired handling. Although there were numerous other parts on the 1966 grand prix BSA – conrods, engine sprocket, footrests, rockers, brake pedal and bottom fork yoke – it was the frames, with their proneness to cracking, which caused the biggest headaches. Soon the team had to write off the year as a development exercise, and both Smith and

Eastwood finished the season riding steel-framed machinery.

There were 14 rounds to be contested in the 500cc category and, in the original schedule, 17 in the 250cc class. Eventually the counters in Denmark and Norway were axed from the smaller capacity-class programme which, for the first time since it attained world championship status in 1962, did not contain a British round. Points-scoring in both classifications was as before, and the best eight finishes in each would determine the winners.

Home interest lay almost exclusively in the 500cc section, especially as Dave Bickers had resolved his quandary over whether he should stay with Greeves or return to Husqvarna by defecting to the CZ factory. He was in good company, for joining him from Matchless was Chris Horsfield who, together with Smith and Eastwood, gave Britain a strong hand in the premier class, occasionally augmented by Don Rickman and Arthur Lampkin.

EASTERN PROMISE

The Husqvarna flag was kept fluttering aloft by double 250cc champion Torsten Hallman, who beat off the challenge from a trio of CZs to become the first rider to win three world titles. The threat from Victor Arbekov never fully materialised, although the Russian – like Czech newcomer Petr Dobry – won two rounds, so it was left to Belgium's Joel Robert to pose the greatest danger from CZ. But no sooner was the Belgian into his stride, than shoulder and foot injuries restricted his effectiveness, allowing Hallman to coast home with five victories and three second places – six points short of a maximum.

Keenly though these disappointments by the trinity of CZ riders were felt by the Strakonice factory, the Czechoslovakian manufacturer was to gain ample recompense in the 500cc class. British followers had heard of the 26

Above left **Don Rickman hastens his Metisse to victory in the British 500cc Grand Prix at Farleigh Castle.**

Above **Jerry Scott, from Parkstone, Dorset, who was killed while competing in the North v South Scramble at Boltby, north Yorkshire.**

Below **Don Rickman keeps Jeff Smith at bay during one of the most compelling races ever witnessed at a British 500cc Grand Prix. Rickman took his Metisse to victory in the first heat by 16.8 seconds. In the next race Smith won by five seconds, so Rickman was the overall winner, which effectively ended Smith's chances of retaining his world title.**

year-old Paul Friedrichs from Erfurt, who had finished runner-up to Jeff Smith the previous summer, but had been distinctly unimpressed by the East German CZ rookie who struggled to stay the pace at Hawkstone, where he had finished seventh overall. But the little-known Friedrichs, on the new, single exhaust 360cc CZ, was altogether a different proposition a season later and lost no time in signalling his intention of going one better in 1966, by winning the first three rounds of the 10th World 500cc championship.

Smith was still trying to sort out the legion of problems with the titanium-framed BSA as Friedrichs consolidated his leadership with three more victories – in Czechoslovakia, the Soviet Union and his native East Germany – before July, and the British Grand Prix were reached. While Friedrichs had scored eight times in nine events – amassing 58 points; six below the ceiling – Smith had a solitary win in Finland plus three second places to his name and trailed the shy East German by 27 points. With five rounds remaining, Smith needed to win them all and hope Friedrichs didn't finish as runner-up in any of them.

There had been comebacks on this scale, but in two notable instances, British riders had been defeated. Disputing the European 250cc championship of 1959, Jaromir Cizek and Brian Stonebridge had locked horns at the top of the table, before Sweden's Rolf Tibblin reeled off six wins in seven outings to snatch the title. Hallman himself did much the same thing to Smith in the World 250cc championship in 1962. Four years after Hallman's unforeseen triumph, Smith's dreams of reversing the deficit and becoming the first rider to win three world 500cc titles became little more than wishful thinking, as Friedrichs took the first steps towards setting this record, and on the way be the first to lift the heavyweight crown on a bike powered by a two-stroke engine.

Ever since Hawkstone Park had first hosted the British Grand Prix in 1954 the circuit had become a shrine. Enthusiasts made the trek to the Shropshire track each July as an act of faith. But the great virescent temple, which had accommodated all those colossal crowds was showing signals of wear and tear; and it wasn't just the brickwork which needed re-pointing. The danger signs were permanently on display as the structure was perennially enveloped in dust. It was time for a change.

Harold Taylor, an Oxfordshire farmer and still a prominent ACU committee member as well as manager of the British Moto-Cross des Nations team, had been among the most forceful of those articulating the case for another venue after the grimy farce in 1960. But since then, Hawkstone had continued to take prisoners with all the alacrity of an Alcatraz governor, and Taylor successfully argued the case for re-siting Britain's top moto-cross event.

Left **Meanwhile, brother Derek wins in the 750cc category at Brands Hatch on September 11 that year, on the Matchless Metisse.**

PASTURES NEW

The location Taylor had in mind was on some land which overlooked the river Frome, four miles west of Trowbridge in Wiltshire, farmed by the befittingly-named Greenhill family. In the early 1930s there were three motorcycle clubs in the area: Devizes, Trowbridge and Melksham. Devizes, the oldest, was formed in 1922 and 11 years later the three amalgamated to form the West Wilts Motor Club. Originally they staged grass track racing there on the flatter ground alongside the river. At these meetings Jack Surtees (father of road racer and 1964 Formula One champion John), Eric Oliver, Roy Zeal, Colin Mead, Ivan Kessell, Jack Difazio, Bonny Good, Vic Warlock and

145

Above **Dave Bickers who, in 1966, came within a whisker of being the first rider to win the British 250cc and 500cc titles in the same season.**

Right **The unfortunate Jerry Scott is ahead of Alan Clough in the final round of the Grandstand series, at Brill. Clough rode his Greeves to second on the day and was runner-up to Jeff Smith in the 500cc class of the eight-round winter competition.**

the legendary Lew Coffin attracted enthusiastic crowds as Farleigh Castle began to make a name for itself.

Moto-cross was first organized at Farleigh in the biting winter of 1947. Jack Stocker won the Wessex National Scramble on an Ariel and, for some years after the Second World War, the West Wilts club promoted grass track and moto-cross at the venue. Both activities were organised on the Greenhill brothers' pastures as the West Wilts club experienced fluctuating fortunes through the 1950s; and the Enfield and Frome United clubs also staged grass track meetings there.

As the popularity of moto-cross grew, so it revived the providence of the West Wilts club and helped establish Farleigh Castle as one of the premier circuits in England. In May 1963 the club ran their Maybug Scramble there, followed by the Wessex Centre team event, before the second round of the BBC's *Grandstand* TV series was earmarked for Farleigh. Beyond all doubt this secured Farleigh's position in the minds of those responsible for the custody of the British GP, at a time when the Salop club failed to come sufficiently to terms with the dust problem at Hawkstone Park.

Ken Lywood, who later rose through the administrative ranks to become chairman of the ACU, was the driving force behind the West Wilts Club's ambition to procure the grand prix for their Farleigh track. It helped of course that Harold Taylor and Lywood were good friends. But the resolution to move the event to the west country in 1966 was taken on grounds involving rather more than just friendship. The decision was to be consummated by excellent organisation and enriched with stunning British success.

ENGLAND EXPECTS ...

Before a wheel was turned in anger, Jeff Smith's chances of retaining his title were given an unexpected boost when it was revealed that the championship leader Paul Friedrichs would be a non-starter. This news was heaven-sent for Smith who, it seemed, could have the afternoon to himself with a free hand to trim eight points off the East German's advantage. Friedrichs had apparently been delayed by lengthy visa formalities in Berlin, and was left with insufficient time to travel with his bikes by road to Britain. However, Ken Lywood received a telegram from Friedrichs, less than 48 hours before the grand prix, announcing he would have to sidestep the British round because of sickness. This was but another twist to a tale which had a happy ending for almost everyone except Jeff Smith.

It was some days before the implications of Don Rickman's Farleigh victory had fully sunk in. I well remember reading the double-page spread in the following Wednesday's *Motor Cycle News*. Chris Carter's report was headlined: 'Don Rickman's Shock Victory'. Shock, I thought. For whom? Jeff Smith may have been surprised and was unquestionably disappointed, for his title had been transferred to the absent Friedrichs. Perhaps, unwittingly almost, Smith had been a mite over-confident. Whatever the wider explanation, the champion had certainly been outridden.

The Rickman brothers' story is central to the chronicle of British achievement in World moto-cross during the 1950s and 1960s. Don and Derek Rickman were the sons of a Southampton speedway rider and garage owner Ernie Rickman; who was a team-mate of 'Squib' Burton, father of BSA teamster John. In 1948, aged only 45, Ernie Rickman died, leaving his teenage sons at King's School, Bruton. Derek, the senior by two and a half years, left to serve an engineering apprenticeship and began riding his father's BSA B32 in trials. Very soon he was spotted by Harold Wakefield from Ferndown, who provided Derek with some limited sponsorship and Don with a 350cc BSA trials bike. Eventually the brothers established a small engineering business, building competition motorcycles which bore the Metisse name and were, in the right hands, capable of competing on equal terms with machinery made by the established manufacturers.

The scale of their commercial activities at New Milton, near Christchurch, on the edge of the New Forest, prevented the Rickmans from racing on a professional basis. So no time could be found for a full-blooded assault on the World 500cc title, except in 1960 when Don tied with Rolf Tibblin in third place. The infrequency of Don and Derek's international appearances was less of a handicap to the younger Rickman; though neither was quite as fit as the full-time riders and by 1966 both were nearing retirement. With their beautifully engineered and immaculately turned out Metisse bikes, Don and Derek Rickman had a special place in the hearts of British devotees, especially those from the south of England.

Their fraternal conjunction in British successes in the Moto-Cross des Nations was vital in the 1963 and 1964 victories. Don was also a member of Britain's winning teams in four other years. Only Jeff Smith had a better record in the first 20 years of the team event's existence. In the British GP, Don had three times been third, and runner-up in 1960. Derek's best finish was in 1963, when he tailed

Right **By beating Dave Bickers and Fred Mayes in the final round of the British 250cc Championship, at Builth Wells, Bryan Goss denied Bickers a sixth national lightweight title. Instead, Mayes took the title on his Greeves without having won a single round of the five counting towards the championship. Goss, twice a runner-up in the smaller class, won his only British Championship when he lifted the 500cc title in 1970.**

Arthur Lampkin and Smith to claim a highly-creditable third.

Though Don Rickman could be competitive on all types of going, he was at his best on grass. His skills were shown to their maximum advantage on the shiny surfaces of East Meon, Hankom Bottom, Bulbarrow Hill, and whenever it was wet. Don, it seemed, had inherited more of his father's speedway technique than Derek. He had an intuitive ability to control a power slide, even on the most disadvantageously cambered corners, to pull out precious distance on his opponents. Observing him at his fastest you knew you were in the presence of someone special. Dark-haired and sallow cheeked, he was leaner than Derek, though of similar height.

At times Don Rickman was like running mercury. Few, if any, ever traversed a moto-cross circuit with such languidly fluid precision. None did so with greater poise or style. He was blessed with the elusive secret of timing, which made his talent appear utterly natural to a degree which enabled him to unhinge much of the opposition in less than a lap. Witnessing Don Rickman at work on a Metisse was like watching Tom Graveney at the wicket. (Readers of a younger generation will know what I mean if I say David Gower, for the genuinely young it gets a little difficult, Steve Waugh maybe?). To strain the comparison well beyond breaking point, if Don Rickman had been a cricketer, the bars all round the ground would have emptied when he came into bat, just as they did for Ian Botham.

Don Rickman's riding had a serene, balletic quality; an almost translucent sensibility. By disposition unruffled, he was a supremely gifted natural, like Jim Clark, of the same era. As with Clark, Don Rickman's abilities were the more impressive for being veiled. He possessed a beguiling certainty – when and how to brake to earn most advantage – an almost aesthetic sense of elegance, innate balance and unhurried speed. Jeff Smith on the other hand was more like Graham Hill, self-taught, a grafter, who honed his powers to perfection by practice and application. Had Rickman not been so distracted by manufacturing bikes for others to ride – an activity which brought him and his brother Derek much pride and pleasure – and, like Smith, had been able to ride bikes made specially for him, who knows what Don Rickman would have achieved? Or his brother for that matter.

RICKMAN'S BIG PRIZE, TRAGEDY FOR SCOTT

It had taken Don Rickman a long time to come within sight of the big prize – he was three weeks short of his 31st birthday – but when it appeared on Farleigh's first grand prix podium, he seized it with typical composure. In the first 16-lap heat, Rickman led from start to finish. Initially pursued by Vlastimil Valek's 400cc Jawa, he took the flag 16.8 seconds ahead of Smith; Valek had been relegated to third, with Chris Horsfield and Dave Bickers next in line on their 360cc CZs. In the second race Jerry Scott's BSA was the early leader. But Rickman soon took it up, to be pursued by Smith and his BSA team-mate Eastwood. Although Smith dispossessed Rickman in mid-race, he never shook off the Metisse and Don was declared overall winner by 11.8 seconds. Smith was no longer world champion.

The modest Rickman, quiet and un-demonstrative, courteously received the commendations of a 21,000-strong crowd. With them he was handed a passport to the hall of fame, which Jeff Smith had been decorating in BSA's colours for more than a decade.

From that clear, sunny day onwards, the second half of the season brought only dark skies for Smith, including the black cloud of tragedy. During the North vs South meeting at Boltby in Yorkshire, Smith crashed into Jerry Scott, who had fallen ahead of him over a blind leap. It was on a very fast section of the track, and Smith was powerless to avoid the collision. Scott, 27, from Parkstone, Dorset, who had only recently signed to ride for the BSA factory, was fatally injured. Smith suffered breaks to a toe, his left wrist and collarbone in the accident and was devastated.

It was the first racing fatality involving a world-ranked rider since 1958 champion René Baeten was killed at Stekene, six years earlier. Smith had been competing at the Belgian event when Baeten was killed. 'That was upsetting because there was one of my pals who I raced with every weekend, suddenly dead and not going to be around anymore.'

'But that didn't hit me as hard as Jerry Scott's death, because I was totally involved in it, and I knew him as a good friend.'

A week before the Scott tragedy, Smith had won the penultimate round of the British 500cc Championship (the ACU Scrambles' Star label had, not before time, been dropped in favour of a more appropriate name) at Carlton Bank in north Yorkshire. But Smith still had a hard row to hoe if he was to prevent Dave Bickers from taking the title in the final episode, at Cadwell Park. Fully recovered from his collarbone injury, Smith tangled with Chris Horsfield's CZ, 200 yards from the start, fell and broke his right collarbone. Another title had gone.

Bickers had added a 500cc crown to his five sets of 250cc laurels, which would have been six had he been able to make up the four-point leeway on Fred Mayes in the lightweight series' last round, at Builth Wells a week later. Bickers beat Mayes, but Bryan Goss beat them both, so Mayes, on a Greeves, took his only British title, by a solitary point. It was an uncommon and quite unexpected coup for Mayes, whose best efforts had been as runner-up at Matchams and Nympsfield. Chris Horsfield had won the opening tie, at Nantwich, and Goss and Bickers had each won two rounds. The unconsidered Mayes had claimed the championship without a single victory to his name.

THE END OF A GREAT SEASON

Before the sacrament could be conducted to mark the end of an extraordinary, and quite unforgettable year of moto-cross, Dave Bickers led the national team to Remelard in Normandy. With Jeff Smith injured, Bickers, Don Rickman, Arthur Lampkin and Vic Eastwood destroyed the challenge of Belgium and Sweden to notch a fourth successive win for Britain in the Moto-cross des Nations. At Brands Hatch, Sweden won the 250cc Trophée des Nations contest, though Bryan Goss was the individual winner on a Swedish-made Husqvarna, as Britain took second place.

At the close of the season Jeff Smith vowed to be back. While Smith was injured, his friend Arthur Lampkin won the Belgian GP at Namur, riding the 1965 steel-framed BSA. It was Lampkin's only overseas' grand prix ride of the year and brought the Yorkshireman his first, and only, World 500cc championship win of his long career.

The folly of BSA's expensive titanium experiment had very probably cost Jeff Smith his world title. The Jerry Scott mishap almost certainly marked the start of Smith's decline.

'I have always said that I never did any good after that,' was Smith's judgement, some years afterwards. 'I did win, but it was much, much harder.'

As hard as titanium.

1967

A fifth successive victory for GREAT BRITAIN in the Moto-Cross des Nations. Jeff Smith wins his ninth British 500cc Championship. Alan Clough at last collects the national 250cc trophy, having three times been third, and twice runner-up. Paul Friedrichs and Torsten Hallman lift the world titles.

Nineteen sixty seven was a watershed year for British moto-cross. It was a season flawed by controversy and telling for its lack of success; except at Markelo in Holland, where Vic Eastwood, Dave Bickers and Jeff Smith won the Moto-Cross des Nations. It will also undyingly be remembered for presaging a 27-summer arid spell, during which Great Britain failed to win the famous team competition; as well as for Jeff Smith's ninth, and final, national 500cc title triumph. In its way, 1967 signalled the end of not one era, but two.

During the first 10 years of the World 500cc Championship the four riders who had won the title twice – Bill Nilsson, Sten Lundin, Rolf Tibblin and Jeff Smith – all improved their winning margin the second time. The first rider to prove the exception was Paul Friedrichs. But his margin of 22 points ahead of Tibblin in 1966 was the widest in the first decade of the

Right **They're off. Typical Saturday action from a BBC Grandstand Trophy round in deep midwinter; Dave Nicoll (17), Dave Bickers (23), Vic Eastwood (7) and Jeff Smith (4) head for the first corner.**

Left **Vic Eastwood tied on points with Alan Clough in the British 500cc Championship. Both were on 20, while Smith – who had dominated the competition since he first won it in 1955 – was on 21. Here Eastwood takes to the air in the third round of the five-tie series, at Dodington, where he and Dave Bickers finished the day as joint leaders.**

competition. Friedrichs didn't quite repeat it the following year, but a 21-point gap on Jeff Smith would, at today's scoring values, be well into three figures. Wide enough in other words for there to be no doubt as to who deserved to be champion.

Until 1977, when the scoring system in world championship events was changed irrevocably and all races were accumulated in a rider's total, it was still possible – when only his best six or seven finishes counted – to complete a season with maximum points. In later years the title was often won with an aggregate of high finishes, even though the winner had conceded more victories to a rival. (As recently as 1992, champion Georges Jobé was first in only two grands prix, yet runner-up Kurt Nicoll won five.) Both systems have their advocates, but in the first 25 years of the championship, if a rider was to have any hope of lifting the title, he had to race with only victory in mind.

Paul Friedrichs was a winner. In 1967 he won seven grands prix, retained his title and became only the third champion to score a full-house. Not until the great Roger de Coster appeared was the fourth – and only other – maximum recorded, or, was the winning margin greater than in 1972. Trailing in Friedrichs' wash were four other CZs and Jeff

151

Right **Although the market in ready-made scramblers had never been stronger, some riders still liked to make their own. This rider-mechanic has squeezed a Maico engine into a Greeves frame.**

Opposite **Alan Clough had twice been runner-up, and on three occasions third, in the British 250cc Championship, riding a DOT or Greeves. In 1967, Clough at last won the title, though this year he was transported by a Husqvarna.**

Smith's BSA. Bickers won in Sweden and Luxembourg, while Smith completed his tally of grand prix triumphs with victory in the Soviet GP at Kishinev, close to the Black Sea.

At the British GP, Smith, Bickers and the rest of the home faction did their best to rein in the flying Friedrichs, but to no avail. Thanks to their CZ consanguinity, Bickers came closest when Friedrichs pulled over to allow the Briton to win the second heat. Had it not been for this misplaced gesture, Smith would have been runner-up. The storm of criticism which blew up afterwards was not the only squall in a cyclonic season.

Smith showed his displeasure by refusing to attend the rostrum presentation, though both rider and BSA team declined the opportunity to make a formal protest. With a commanding lead in the 11-nation contest, Friedrichs clinched his second championship by winning at Farleigh Castle. Although there was no British winner to cheer, the 22,000 spectators had at last seen Friedrichs at his best on an English track. The Erfurt policeman turned in a quite brilliant display for them.

Don Rickman, riding only his second grand prix of the year, led the first 45-minute heat until two-thirds distance, but tired allowing Friedrichs and Vic Eastwood to overhaul the Metisse. But in the second 20-lap race, Rickman again led until near halfway, when Friedrichs forged past. Even so, Rickman was still second and with every chance of being overall runner-up until his gearbox blew. Eastwood's hopes went the same way as he toured in with a broken rear-brake pedal, so it was down to Smith and Bickers to dispute second, when the CZ pit took a hand and ordered Friedrichs to allow Bickers through to make it a CZ one-two.

Smith was able to prove there was still some gas in his tank by finishing second in the championship – nine points in front of Bickers – but it was perfectly clear at BSA that they quickly needed to find a successor for him. At first they looked to Belgium and tried to sign the hugely-promising Roger de Coster. But this attempt failed and they were left with the reliable Eastwood and another uncut East Anglian diamond: John Banks.

While Brian Martin wrestled with the succession problem, Smith's inheritance was a conundrum which masked the wider contentions gnawing away at the roots of the sport in Britain. As boom often leads to bust in corporations, and global economies, so

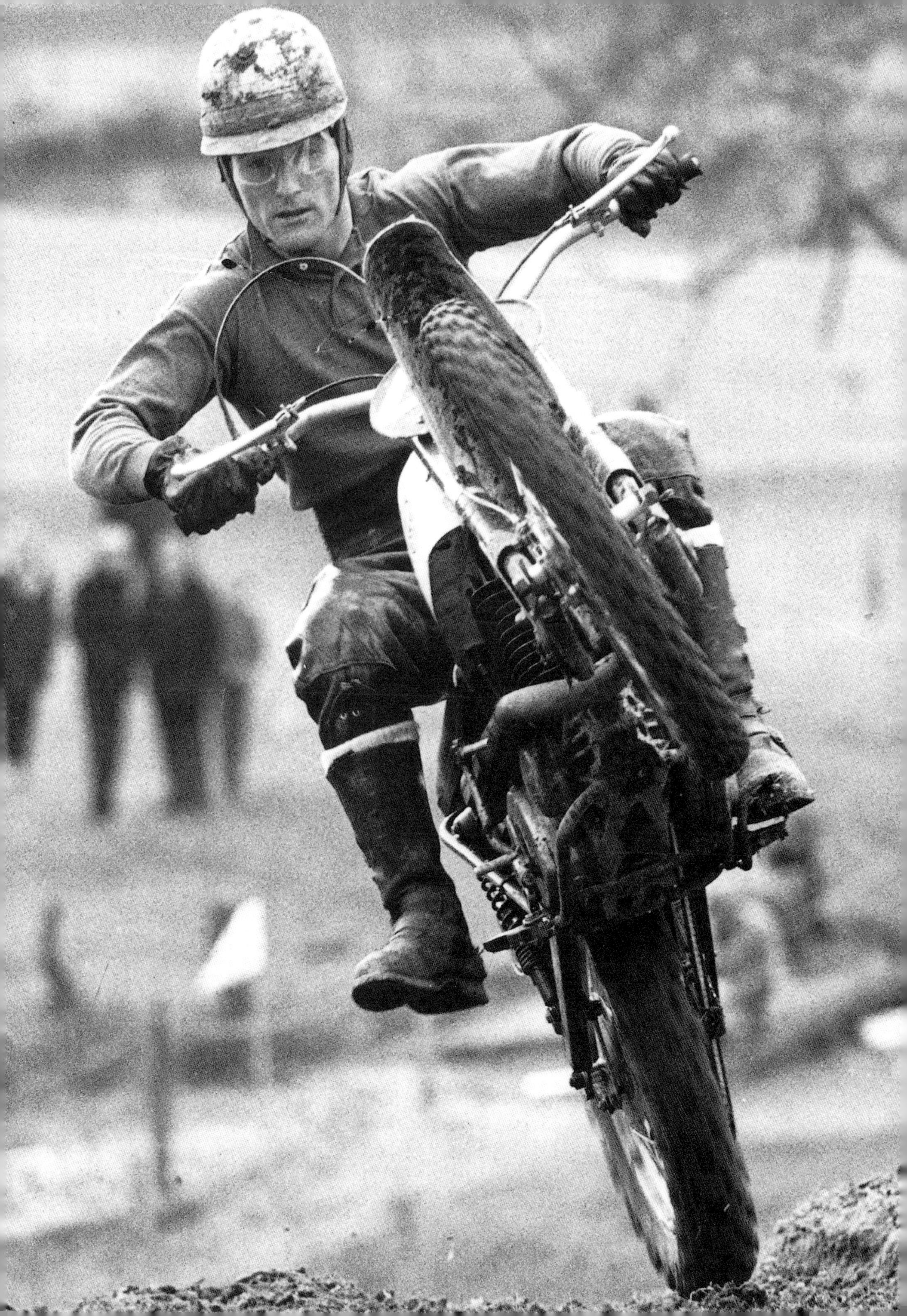

moto-cross in Britain was experiencing similar difficulties. The kernel of the dilemma was over-exposure. Moto-cross had apparently become too popular for its own good.

The BBC's Grandstand series had set the ball rolling. Soon, everyone wanted a slice of the action. Foolishly, the ACU said yes to them all. There was a warm and wide welcome to share in the mushrooming reputation of moto-cross as a brilliant television spectacle. It was armchair sport at its most exciting.

Several national newspapers had taken a benevolent interest in moto-cross. In 1955 the *Daily Herald* began its long association as sponsors of the British GP. After 1961, when the *Herald* was acquired by the Mirror group, the new owners continued their support until in 1964 the *Herald* was closed, re-emerging as the *Sun* under the slogan: 'A newspaper born of the age we live in.' (The *Sun* in 1964 is not to be confused with the tabloid version reborn after being sold to Rupert Murdoch in 1969.) When the grand prix was moved to Farleigh Castle in 1966, the *Sun* carried on with their valuable sponsorship.

This gave moto-cross a much-needed shop

window. In 1966 the *Daily Sketch* lent their name to the Trophée des Nations at Brands Hatch. A year later the *Daily Express* got in on the act and sponsored a non-championship international at Wakes Colne in Essex. By and large the endorsements from national newspapers were wholly beneficial. Not so the television companies. While the papers had the simple matter of dealing with individual organising clubs, the TV producers – who wanted to screen complete championships – were forced to negotiate with the ACU. Inevitably this led to uproar.

At first there were eight winter Saturdays earmarked for the BBC series. This was then increased to 10, after two internationals were added to the list. A further five were to be screened by ITV, when the ACU proudly announced a 13-event series of 'Winternationals' sponsored by tobacco giants John Player. It was overkill on a fairly destructive scale.

MEDIA INFLUENCE

Quite apart from the effect it had on the leading riders, who had been driving tens of thousands of miles across Europe throughout the summer, winters would be without a break. Club organizers soon found that unless they could shell out for the big names, the fans stayed at home and watched the stars on television. Consequently, dozens of well known events lost money and never again appeared on the calendar. The damage done to the ACU's own championships was at first minimal, but it was only a matter of time before the incalculable harm done to the sport as a whole began to corrode its core competition.

The commercial innocence of the ACU and their lack of judgement took the breath away. It's easy to say, but if the ACU had been rather more circumspect and not so wilfully embraced those wanting to muscle - in on the

Below left **Joel Robert was in unstoppable form in the British 250cc Grand Prix at Wakes Colne, near Halstead, where just 9,000 spectators turned up and only one British competitor – Andy Roberton, riding the experimental, Villiers-engined Cotton – scored a point.**

Left **Alan Clough, one of Britain's most experienced two-stroke experts, and a worthy British Champion, photographed at the Belgium 250cc Grand Prix in April that year.**

155

Right **Don Rickman (Metisse, 37) and Paul Friedrichs (CZ, 14)** were rarely much further apart than this in either heat of a riveting British 500cc Grand Prix. But Rickman, the hero of the 1966 GP at Farleigh Castle, was pipped by Vic Eastwood for second place in the first race. In the second, while disputing the lead with the East German, Rickman went out with a broken gear box.

opportunities created by the Grandstand series, moto-cross might still be a televised sport in Britain.

TV HEROES

In 1967 the Grandstand and British championships still had a monopoly of the best circuits in the country. The TV series had been monopolized by Dave Bickers – who won both classes with ease – but it was a different story in the two five-round national contests. Alan Clough had mopped-up the 250cc class for Husqvarna before the final round was reached at Cadwell Park. In the heavyweight category, Bickers and Eastwood held the key to the trophy cabinet, with Jeff Smith hoping to pick up the scraps after his two rivals had gone to the head of the table with the scores tied at the end of the third round, held at Dodington Park in south Gloucestershire. There was a four-month gap before the fourth round, at nearby Tirley, where Eastwood's front wheel punctured and Bickers' CZ was forced out with a condenser malady. The single 20-lap race went to Smith after a ding-dong battle with John Banks. Smith was now on 18 points with Eastwood and Bickers at 14 and Alan Clough and Chris Horsfield each with 12. Any of the five could be champion.

The final round was the Kidston at Builth Wells on 15 October, the day after Jeff Smith's 33rd birthday. A 35-minute plus one lap race would decide the outcome. Clough had the chance to make history and become the first rider to win the 250cc and 500cc titles in the same season. The Cheshire-born Clough couldn't be faulted for effort, edging his 360cc Husqvarna home ahead of Eastwood in front of 8,000 spectators on a soaking afternoon. Bickers was never in the hunt, and finished well back. Smith was hunting as usual. In his inimitable way, the wily Lancastrian had paced himself correctly, he knew exactly what he had to do once he realized Eastwood wasn't going to beat Clough, and so settled for fourth behind Arthur Browning.

The three points Smith had earned enabled him to win the 500cc championship for the ninth time; a record no other rider has come close to breaking. Poor Eastwood, runner-up for a fifth successive year, was mortified. Alan Clough wasn't best pleased either.

The World 250cc competition had one more

tie than the 500cc class, though the same number of finishes would comprise a rider's net score. The contest for the title became a two-horse race between Joel Robert and three-time winner Torsten Hallman. Apart from Victor Arbekov and Wakes Colne winner Olle Pettersson, no one other than Robert and Hallman won a round. Although the Belgian and the Swede each won five grands prix, it was Hallman's three second places and greater consistency which decided the issue. Robert was runner-up only once and, towards the end of the season, either won or was out of the points.

BELGIUM TRIUMPHS AGAIN

The duel between the two riders, who dominated the 250cc class for a decade, was still unresolved when the Halstead club staged the eighth round at their recently-christened international venue near Colchester. It was a perfect opportunity for the best of the British lightweight competitors to match their skills against the continental stars. But English riders were eclipsed as Robert took the overall lead after Hallman had punctured in the first 20-lap race of the *Sun*-sponsored, ninth British 250cc GP. Sensing that it might not be a day when British competitors would have much to celebrate, there were fewer than 9,000 at Wakes Colne to witness the Belgian's superiority.

Bryan Wade had been third in the first heat but a crash put paid to his hopes just as terminally as a fall had eliminated Bryan Goss in the second. The best Briton was Cotton's Andy Roberton, who at 19 years-of-age, completed his very first international in sixth place. Although Robert's win had moved him back to the top of the standings, he didn't score another point until after Hallman had clinched the title at Belgorod in the Soviet Union.

To underline his supremacy in the quarter-litre class, Hallman led Sweden to a fourth triumph in the Trophée des Nations. Britain's representatives at Holice, Czechoslovakia – Malcolm Davis, Bryan Goss and Arthur Browning – were fourth.

In an attempt to revive their flagging fortunes, Associated Motor Cycles had experimented with a Villiers-engined two-stroke bearing their Norton badge. Fred Mayes had forsaken Greeves to become their test rider. In October Mayes was sacked and AMC announced the signing of Bryan Goss who was to campaign the new machine – as a 250cc or 360cc AJS – in the forthcoming TV series. But after three weeks Goss – who eventually became no stranger to controversy – quit and returned to Husqvarna.

There were other signs that all was not well with the big manufacturers. With only Jeff Smith's domestic championship to gladden them, BSA had agreed to supply the Rickman brothers with engines. But in a last-minute *volte-face* by the Small Heath board, the New Milton duo were forced to abandon plans for large-scale production of a 441cc Victor-engined Metisse.

Compared with the dismemberments which lay ahead, these were only blips in the heart-rate of Britain's once-great motorcycle industry. With Greeves no longer achieving any worthwhile results, the intensive care ward was put on stand-by.

Left **Joel Robert had the World 250cc Championship sewn up, until he suffered a shoulder injury in the Swedish GP, allowing Torsten Hallman to become the first rider to win three world titles.**

1968

VIC EASTWOOD wins a wet British 500cc Grand Prix at Farleigh. John Banks is runner-up to Paul Friedrichs in world title chase, losing out by a single point. Banks is British 500cc champion – Eastwood is second for the sixth time – Malcolm Davis is 250cc winner. Dave Bickers opts out of British series. Britain pull out of Moto-cross des Nations in protest at Soviet invasion of Czechoslovakia.

Sometimes the weight of expectation can be too great. For John Banks and Vic Eastwood eventually perhaps it was. At different times, each gave the impression he was capable of picking up Jeff Smith's baton of greatness, to transfer it onward for another generation. Ultimately, both narrowly failed at what was an almost impossibly difficult task. Nevertheless, the careers of John Banks and his erstwhile BSA team-mate, Vic Eastwood, reached their apotheosis in 1968. It was over two decades since Bill Nicholson, Fred Rist and Bob Ray had secured the first of Great Britain's 16 Moto-Cross des Nations victories, when they won the 1947 event at Duinrell, Holland. In more than 20 years, British fans had neither known – nor anticipated – anything other than a steady accumulation of success.

The year began prescient with promise for Banks, Eastwood, Smith, Dave Nicoll and BSA. Not content with his ninth British 500cc title, Smith appeared in the BBC TV Grandstand series on a titanium-framed 250cc BSA and won the smaller-engine class at a canter, from the works AJS of Malcolm Davis. The early leader in the category had been Bryan Goss, but the Husqvarna rider was stripped of his points after being convicted of theft, for which he received a nine-month prison sentence.

Opposite **Bryan Wade did not finish in the top six of either the BBC's Grandstand 250cc series or the 250cc class in the British Championship in 1967. But he did take his works Greeves to fifth overall in the British 250cc Grand Prix at Dodington Park that summer.**

Goss's story was a shabby little tale, though within a year he was competing again, and his rivals did their best to ensure for him an undistracted reintegration.

Although Smith was still winning important tournaments, the old guard was about to be changed. Smith had contemplated retirement in 1964 but, now in his 34th year with 17 seasons of unrelenting competition under his belt, it would soon be time to hang up his boots. Derek Rickman had already faded from the scene, while younger brother Don, a mere 33, restricted his appearances to a handful of events, most of them on the two-stroke Bultaco. This doughty trio of riders had collected a total of 16 winners' medals in the Moto-Cross des Nations. Some score.

Eastwood was not only the most experienced of the younger brigade, but the most successful. As he approached the most important afternoon of his career, some four months short of his 27th birthday, he had appeared in four winning British teams at the Moto-Cross des Nations and had been runner-up in the British 500cc championship six times. Twice Eastwood had fallen short of the biggest domestic prize by two points and, in the 1967 season, by just one.

Over the winter Eastwood, Keith Hickman, John Banks and Arthur Lampkin, all on BSAs, had slugged it out in the five-round Grandstand competition which was concluded at Caerleon in South Wales. Banks and Eastwood were tied on 19 points each. Hickman, who won the final round, Lampkin and Eastwood, had a victory apiece. But the decision went to Banks via the tie-break, as he had won twice.

Above **Dick Clayton (22) and Malcolm Davis (17) bang their AJSs together at Naish Hill in a round of the Grandstand series. Davis was runner-up to Jeff Smith in the 250cc category of the BBC's tournament, and also won the British 250cc Championship that year.**

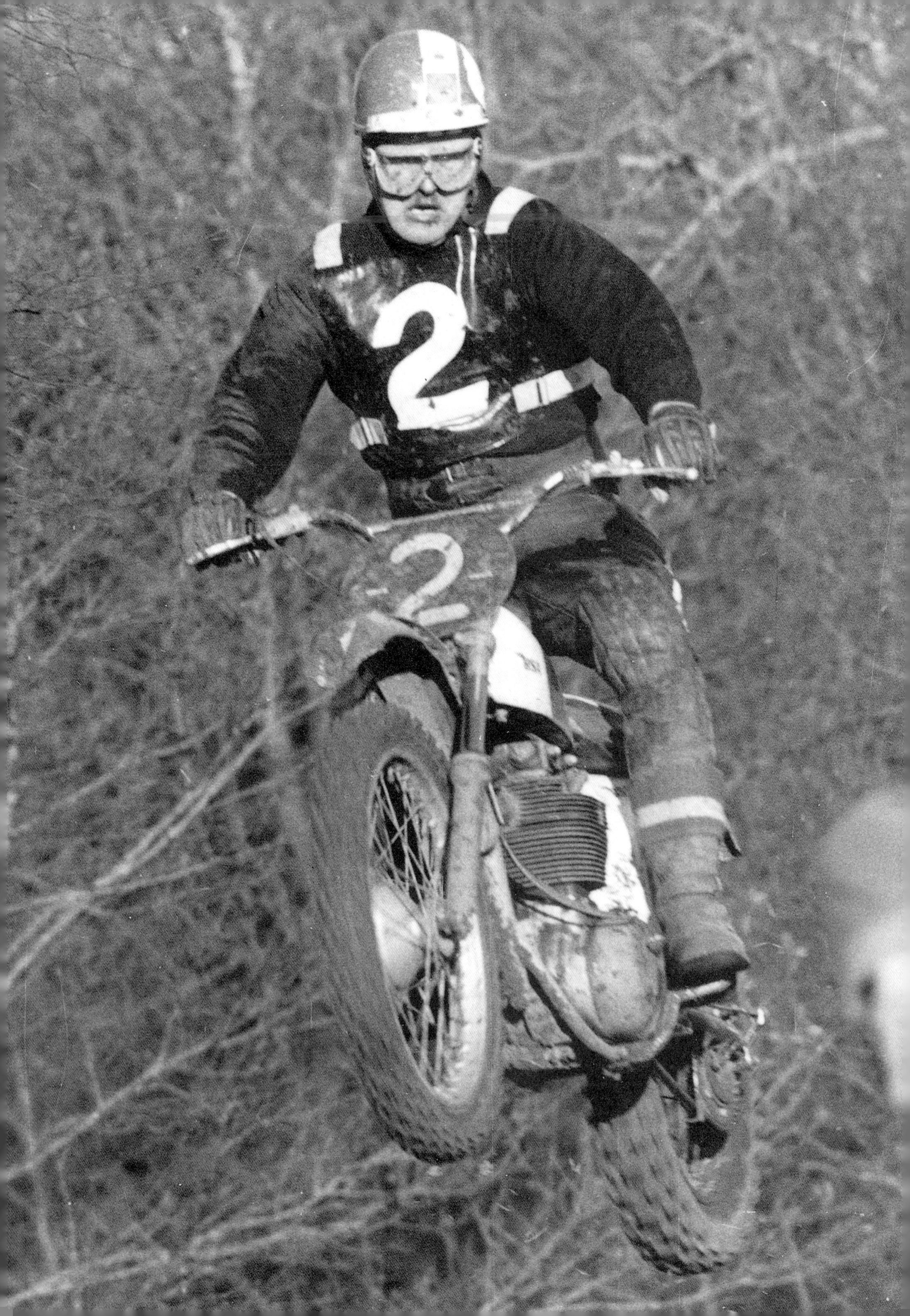
2
2

Once again Vic Eastwood was painfully reminded of how tantalisingly slender can the margin be between being champion and runner-up. Lesser men would be haunted by it. Not the phlegmatic Eastwood, even though he had taken on the appearance of an eternal bridesmaid, who was never to kneel at the altar of stardom. Psalms of praise followed Eastwood throughout his career which, to widespread disbelief, was never adorned by a major championship. But no sooner had Eastwood come to the decision to forsake BSA, after his frustration over a lack of engine development led to a row with team boss Brian Martin, than he won his native grand prix on a Swedish-made Husqvarna.

EASTWOOD SADDLES UP

Vic Eastwood was delivered at the same maternity hospital in Colne, Lancashire as Jeff Smith. But Eastwood no more affected to consider himself a Lancastrian than Smith, after Vic senior moved the family to Bexley in Kent and, once the Second World War ended, became a café proprietor and began road racing as a privateer. Young Vic read for a BSc in engineering at Woolwich Polytechnic, but left after a year because there was more money in moto-cross. By 1960 his talent earned him a factory ride for Matchless, after being spotted by Hugh Viney. Vic then went to work in the competitions department at Plumstead Road, where Wally Wyatt saw to it that his young charge was given a solid grounding. Eastwood eagerly absorbed all the knowledge Wyatt wished to impart so, apart from being a fine rider, Vic became a good technician with frames and suspensions, as well as a sound all-round motorcycle engineer.

In just two years the British 500cc Grand Prix had thoroughly established itself at Farleigh Castle. For 1968 it was slap in the middle of the 13-nation world contest for which a rider's best seven scores would count. British hopes rested squarely with the four-stroke BSAs of Banks and Smith who contested most of the series, together with Eastwood, who scored in East Germany and was to win at Farleigh and in Luxembourg.

After the first six rounds, Paul Friedrichs looked in the sort of form which suggested he would retain the title without being presented with much in the way of meaningful opposition. The East German won his home grand prix and also triumphed in Finland and Czechoslovakia – where Banks was runner-up – to head the table by four points from Sweden's Ake Jonsson. Banks was fifth, a further eight points adrift, the better part of his challenge still to come.

Of the seven Englishmen who won the British 500cc Grand Prix in the first 16 years of its running, and all the seasons thereafter, Vic Eastwood was the most diminutive. Alongside him, only John Draper the 1955 European champion would have been outsized; but it would have been a close-run thing, and Draper never won a British GP. However, there were distinct similarities between the two.

Eastwood was only 5ft, 5in (1.65 m) tall and weighed 140lb (63.5kg). Having spent his early years on the massively overweight Matchless which, by Vic's estimation had been trimmed in the post-Curtis years but still weighed 320lb

Opposite **John Banks won both the British 500cc Championship and the Grandstand series on his factory BSA. A splendid double. Though had Banks scored another couple of points in the World 500cc Championship, it could have been an exceptional treble.**

Left **With Derek Rickman retired, younger brother Don concentrated on the lightweight category in 1968, bringing his Bultaco-engined Metisse into second place in the British 250cc Championship.**

Right **Dave Bickers glances across at Roger de Coster during the very wet British 500cc Grand Prix at Farleigh Castle. Both rode CZ machinery. Bickers finished fourth overall, De Coster fifth.**

Centre **The unflappable Vic Eastwood bounces the Husqvarna down one of Farleigh's sodden inclines as he slithers and slides to the biggest victory of his life.**

(145.15kg) – more than twice Eastwood's body-weight – young Vic soon learnt the virtue of balance. In the years since Draper had used that attribute so advantageously, only Don Rickman and Eastwood of the leading English riders had turned it to their gain so assiduously. On Sunday 7 July 1968 Eastwood went into profit big-time.

In a few short weeks after his departure from BSA, Eastwood had taken to the 420cc, two-stroke Husqvarna like a duck to water; which was apposite, for Farleigh Castle was awash. After two grands prix in bright sunshine, the Wiltshire circuit soon became a churning quagmire.

Before practice had ended, Eastwood made adjustments to the rebound damping on the Husqvarna's front forks and had, for the first time, fitted aluminium security bolts designed to hold a tyre to its rim in the event of a puncture. Both decisions were to prove crucial as the weather worsened and Eastwood prepared himself for the biggest day in his young life. Although the Husqvarna may not have been quite as powerful as the factory BSAs of Banks, Smith or Keith Hickman, it was a clear 45–50lb (20.4–22.7kg) lighter than the British four-strokes. On a pudding of a track,

Left Great while it lasted. Malcolm Davis led both heats of the British 250cc Grand Prix at Dodington Park, only for the bark of his AJS to be stilled by ignition problems. Torsten Hallman's Husqvarna is tucked in behind the young Briton, while eventual winner Joel Robert awaits developments in third place, on the factory CZ.

where out-and-out power was hardly a prerequisite, the Swedish bike – especially in Eastwood's gifted hands – was the more manageable.

WET-WEATHER MASTERY

Paul Friedrichs had been detained in East Germany by visa problems, so the CZ challenge came from Belgium's Roger de Coster, the Czech Petr Dobry, and England's Dave Bickers. The Husqvarna threat was headed by two Swedes: Christer Hammargren and Ake Jonsson. Then there were the BSAs, and a posse of England's finest, which included Bryan Wade, Alan Clough, Arthur Lampkin, Andy Roberton, plus the Scot, Vic Allan. Don Rickman appeared with a BSA-engined Metisse.

Eastwood gave them all a wet-weather riding lesson. His mastery of the conditions, and the way he outrode his rivals, had 17,000 drenched spectators applauding what was a remarkable performance. Eastwood led the first 16-lap heat from start to finish. Smith was an early threat, but Bickers, Dobry and Hammargren soon displaced the BSA team-leader, who trailed in sixth behind De Coster,

Above **No leaves on the trees so it must be winter. Scotsman Vic Allan keeps his Greeves ahead of Alan Lampkin's 441cc BSA in the Clifton round of the Grandstand series. By the time the six-round competition ended in March 1969, Allan had finished 10th in the 250cc class and seventh in the up to 750cc category.**

almost a minute adrift of the jubilant Eastwood. Banks was two laps further back and Rickman expired with a stalled motor.

Unexpected, even stunning, as Eastwood's first-race victory had been, it will be the recall of the second heat which will linger longest in the memory of all who witnessed it. Eastwood went off like a hare in a race which had been shortened to 30 minutes plus two laps. Banks and Smith were soon in trouble and, on the seventh lap as the downpour intensified, so was Eastwood. He had deliberately run the Husqvarna's rear tyre at a very low pressure, despite the attendant risk of a concussion blow-out. As he snaked along the finishing straight, it was evident that Eastwood's rear was flat. To mounting excitement it became clear that even if the tyre didn't break free of the rim, it was questionable if Eastwood could

hold off Jonsson and Dobry who were closing fast on the unfortunate Englishman.

The Swede went past on the ninth lap and Dobry did so two laps later. 'I wasn't worried about Jonsson,' said Eastwood afterwards, 'he was nowhere in the first heat. But Dobry was second first time out and, unless I got him back, my chance of victory would also have gone.'

But Dobry was as anxious as Eastwood, and probably as tired. With mistakes inevitable from both riders, Eastwood seized his moment as Dobry slid wide, to re-pass the Czech and put some distance between them on the 13th, and final, lap. Vic's father threw his hat in the air, only for Dobry to run over it as he crossed the line, near to exhaustion. It didn't matter. The cost of a replacement was a small price to pay. His son had won the British 500cc Grand

grand prix. Like Geoff Ward and John Draper before him, Banks was forced to mask his disappointment and get on with the remainder of his career in the search for other prizes. In picking up the pieces, after a dreadfully disheartening day for him and BSA, Banks was realistic, and wonderfully generous in acknowledging Eastwood's *tour de force*.

A BAD DAY AT THE OFFICE

'I could make any amount of excuses,' said Banks, 'but that still wouldn't make it any better for me; I rode like a drain. Yet if I rode badly, Vic had a corker of a day. He hadn't done anything all year. Nobody expected him to win then, when he got away first, it all went right for him. Riding with a flat tyre like that, Vic was terrific.' If there were any doubts about the sincerity of those sentiments, Banks towed Eastwood's car out of the paddock, after it had failed to start. It was typical of the magnanimity which was commonplace between competitors of that era and true-to-type of Banks and Eastwood, who were on the friendliest of terms. Both were blessed with the virtue of utter modesty, and were the most agreeable of men.

Banks, after such a dispiriting afternoon,

Prix. Vic's margin of overall victory, by 19.2 seconds, didn't matter either. It was the quality of his achievement which brought so much pride and pleasure to his family and friends.

The great grand prix performances need time to burnish them with legend. Eastwood's triumph was every bit as worthy as Don Rickman's had been two years previously at the same circuit. Moreover, it had been just as exciting, although it didn't have quite the same significance in the outcome of the championship as did Rickman's defeat of Smith in 1966. Banks might argue differently, for he had been favourite, only to come away from Farleigh without a single point. This, remember, on a day when the title-holder and championship leader, Paul Friedrichs, was unable to compete.

Banks was destined never to win his home

Left **Big John Burton barges his BSA through the mud at a round of the Grandstand TV series, Clifton, December 21.**

165

Right **John Banks has a substantial lead over Arthur Browning (Greeves, 12) in the third round of the 1968-69 Grandstand series, at Clifton. Although Banks was unplaced on that December day, he took his works BSA to victory in the tournament, for the second successive year. Browning was runner-up.**

had a major rehabilitation job on his hands if he was to make anything worthwhile of his world championship season. To his credit, he knuckled down to it admirably. Banks needed victories, and he needed them fast. He began with a fourth in West Germany and followed that with wins in France and Holland to go seven points ahead of Friedrichs, with three rounds still to go.

Bengt Aberg won in Belgium, with Banks runner-up and Friedrichs third. At the penultimate round, in Luxembourg, Eastwood was first, Friedrichs second and Banks third. Thus, with only the Swiss round to conclude the series, Friedrichs had 34 points and Banks 41. However, whereas Banks had amassed his total from eight grands prix, Friedrichs had scored only five times. The arithmetic was blindingly simple. Banks' six best scores gave him 35 points. A tie would be possible if Friedrichs was third and Banks fourth. Similarly, if they were fifth and sixth. Either scenario would put them level on 38 or 36 points. The German would then be declared champion as he had more victories. If both failed to finish in the top six, Banks would win the title. If they each scored, Banks had to be ahead of his rival. Nothing less than that would be good enough to bring the trophy to England.

SHOWDOWN IN SWITZERLAND

The Wholen circuit, for what turned out to be a frenetically exciting winner-take-all showdown, is set in the hills above the River Reuss, just west of Zürich. Being only 13 miles (20km) from the West German border, Friedrichs didn't lack for support. Neither did Switzerland lack for rain that weekend. It never let up in Saturday's practice and showers fell throughout Sunday's racing. The track was a boggy mess. So what should have been a classic head-to-head confrontation on an English-style circuit, which would have suited Banks, had a lottery element to it. Not that this concerned the majority in a mammoth crowd of almost 50,000, so long as Friedrichs won.

Bengt Aberg took the first heat by a narrow margin from Friedrichs, with Banks in third and

Smith fifth. Eastwood's Husqvarna sheared a flywheel key, while Christer Hammargren's similar machine broke its gearbox.

Banks led the second race for the first two laps, but was rapidly relegated to fifth by Ake Jonsson's Husqvarna, Eastwood, Aberg and Smith. Friedrichs quickly forced his way to the front, only to be displaced by Eastwood. Summoning one last effort to save his championship chances, Banks reeled Friedrichs in, until he was at the German's shoulder at the top of the hill above the startline, where the BSA uncooperatively threw its chain. Banks soon got it back on, though not soon enough to deny Friedrichs who became the first rider to win the 500cc title three years in succession. Only Belgium's Roger de Coster has ever repeated the feat.

Since 1968 there have been two 500cc championships decided by two points, but never by less. There was plenty of sympathy for Banks, who was not the first to learn that it's a sentiment of little help in the making of a champion or in a champion's make-up. But the big man grinned, shrugged his shoulders and set about the rest of the season, which still had some way to run.

Not running effectively enough to make much of an impression in the World 250cc Championship, were the AJS two-strokes of Chris Horsfield and Malcolm Davis. Both expired in the British round of the 14-nation contest, held at Dodington on a warm, summer's day, a week before the dramatic Swiss 500cc finale at Wohlen. Dave Bickers was seeking a first British 250cc Grand Prix victory on the CZ to add to the three he won for Greeves. He never looked as if he would make it, being outpaced by Joel Roberts' CZ and the Husqvarna of Torsten Hallman; both of whom were still in contention for the title. With that typically unyielding determination of his, Bickers was third in the first heat and fourth in the second, to claim third overall behind Robert – who won both races – and Hallman. The new men at Greeves who had succeeded Bickers, Bryan Wade and Vic Allan, were fifth and sixth.

The Trophée des Nations returned to Payerne despite the travails of 1965, and though there was joy for Sweden, there was none for Hallman. He had not yet been relieved of his title by Robert in the final round of the 250cc series, in Austria. That painful transfer didn't take place until October. Meanwhile, having won his heat and helped his country into the final of the Trophée, Hallman's chain broke, allowing Aberg, Hammargren and Bengt Arne-Bonn – all on Husqvarnas – to collect the spoils. Belgium were second and Great Britain, with big contributions from Eastwood and Wade, could muster only these two finishers, so were excluded.

POLITICS GET IN THE WAY

Britain's impressive winning sequence in the Moto-Cross des Nations ended not in defeat but muted protest at the Soviet Union's unlawful occupation of Czechoslovakia. Staged at Kishinev, the home country were one of only six who fielded teams; the smallest number since the earliest years. Apart from Britain, Belgium, Sweden, Holland, Denmark and Italy left their riders at home. Only East Germany offered any serious challenge to the Soviets, whose team did not include their grand-prix runners, Victor Arbekov and Gunnar Draugs. For those who make a study of these things

Right **Paul Friedrichs. The first rider to complete a hat-trick of world 500cc titles.**

Below **John Banks had a momentous 1968, but a disastrous day at the British 500cc Grand Prix. His Farleigh no-score on the works BSA, dropped him two places in the World Championship standings.**

(not that it's ever likely to be raised on *A Question of Sport*) the winning members were: Leonid Shinkarenko, Evgeni Petushkov, Vladimir Pogrebynak and Arnis Angers. Their two-leg score totalled 18 points. East Germany were runners-up and France took third place.

ANTI-CLIMAX

Threadneedled into the unbearably congested fixture programme were the national championships and the televised events. Four of the five 250cc rounds were held in the north, while in the 500cc division only one – the final round at Builth Wells – was not on a popular southern track. Although there was no room to allocate more dates for the domestic competitions, the ACU's answer to a call for an expanded series was to have two heats at each event, with no change in scoring values per race; though of course, double the points available for every round.

The 250cc class was the first to be concluded. For a while it looked as if Don Rickman would earn himself a richly-deserved British title. He and Malcolm Davis won a race each at the Cumbrian round which opened the series. Rickman followed this by taking both heats at Chard and, although he missed the Yorkshire round at Carlton Bank, his Bultaco-Metisse still topped the table going into the fourth round, at Cuerden Park. Davis effectively put the title beyond Rickman's reach, by winning both heats in Lancashire where Rickman, due to pressure of work, non-started.

Rickman's unavailability had taken the edge off what could have been a really close series. He appeared for the final round at Nantwich needing to win both heats and hope Davis scored fewer than seven points. In teeming rain, local favourite Alan Clough won both heats on his Husqvarna. Two third places were enough to win Davis the title by a margin of 11 points. It gave AJS their first national championship since Gordon Jackson had won the ACU Trials' Star a decade earlier.

If the 250cc category had been something of an anti-climax, so too was the 500cc division, which was settled a week later in Wales. Banks had accumulated 42 points and Eastwood 35. Not entirely out of it was Dave Nicoll with 31. It was resolved within a couple of laps of the opening heat. Eastwood had taken the lead, but then dropped the Husqvarna into a pool of mud which filled his exhaust pipe. Banks went on to win and though Eastwood won the second heat, Banks was crowned champion.

Jeff Smith, by now very much BSA's elder statesman, finished fifth in the standings; above him were Nicoll and Keith Hickman. With nine British titles to his name, Smith had already announced his retirement from full-time international moto-cross, while remaining with BSA in an advisory and technical capacity. The really serious competing could, from now on, be left to the youngsters.

The advisability of seriously competitive winter moto-cross was soon to be called into question when the first Saturday event to fall foul of inclement weather, was the second round of the ITV World of Sport series, at a frost-bound Hawkstone Park. Vic Eastwood had won both races in November's opening round and also led the BBC Grandstand competition after two meetings. Perhaps he was destined to win a major championship after all. If he was, then it wouldn't be either of the televised tournaments over the winter of 1968/69. After stalling at the start, Eastwood crashed on the third lap of the first heat and broke his right leg. Serious injuries at Hawkstone weren't altogether unknown, though if a rider and his machine were parted the fall was usually broken by deep sand. On that December afternoon the track was bone hard. When Eastwood and his Husqvarna went their separate ways, Vic rebounded off the track like a golf ball from concrete.

It had been an up-and-down year for Eastwood in particular and British moto-cross in general. Few realized it at the time, but thereafter it was to be mostly downhill for the English riders, with only occasional flourishes from the irrepressible John Banks to keep British spirits up.

Above **Alan Clough, once he got a British title under his belt, became a consistently competitive TV performer. Having twice been runner-up to Dave Bickers, Clough at last netted the 250cc class in the popular Grandstand series, when his nearest rival Malcolm Davis no-scored in the final round at Kirkcaldy in March 1969.**

169

1969

JOHN BANKS is once again runner-up in the World 500cc Championship, which goes to Sweden's Bengt Aberg. Banks and Alan Clough win the TV titles. Belgium win the Moto-Cross des Nations at Farleigh; Great Britain are third. Banks and Bryan Wade are the British Champions. Shambles at AJS; Malcolm Davis is sacked.

John Banks seemingly had the moto-cross world at his feet. He had ended Jeff Smith's long reign as British 500cc champion and had come within a whisker of winning the world 500cc title in his first full season of international competition. Surely with that experience behind him, Banks would go one better in 1969. He had the unqualified support of BSA and was the undoubted favourite of the crowd whenever he rode at a British track. Whatever else ensured John Banks his popularity, he was blessed with another attribute which endeared him to the public, and this was the unmistakable depth of his determination.

Ten years Jeff Smith's junior, John Banks was born in Bury St Edmunds, where his father Fred was a prosperous businessman and former mayor. With an unconcealed Suffolk burr and a rolling gait, John could leave one with the impression of being a good looking, amiable country boy of limited ambition. Those who competed alongside John Banks will tell you otherwise.

Banks first became aware of his true potential when he won the previous winter's Grandstand series. From then on he developed a persistently forcing style which earned him the reputation of being a touch untidy at times. It also won him a lot of races. Whether it was good enough to win him a world title is a question most succinctly answered by his record. John's handicap was his size; or so it appeared. Without doubt he was taller and heavier than most of his contemporaries. At 5 foot 11 inches (1.8 m) tall, Banks weighed about 210lbs (95.25kg), which ultimately told against him. Not only was he a mite overweight, he didn't train as diligently as Jeff Smith had in his title-winning seasons. Banks was certainly a very strong man, and had youth on his side. But in the heat of battle, during long races in hot, humid and dusty conditions, the fittest man makes fewer mistakes as tiredness begins to tell. The fit rider has reserves of energy to stay on his chosen line for longer. He can avoid clouting the fences which give rise to those niggling hand injuries. As Smith proved on so many occasions: fitness takes you further, faster.

Vitally important for sure, fitness is only part of the equation. Neither Paul Friedrichs nor Vic Eastwood were noticeably fitter than Banks. The Husqvarnas and the CZs weren't that much quicker or reliable than the BSAs either; certainly not in 1968. But the writing was on the wall, and what eventually undermined Banks' campaign in 1969 was not a lack of athleticism, but BSA's diminishing competitiveness. It didn't help either that Brian Martin attempted too much, with too many riders. Martin's approach appeared to be based on a philosophy which decreed that if you had a big enough team, not all of them would fail at the same time, so you were bound to get some success. Banks and Smith were joined first by Keith Hickman and Dave Nicoll. Later, Andy Roberton and Vic Allan were added to the Armoury Road line-up. The shrinking resources at BSA, and with it their reputation for reliability, were soon stretched to the limit as the factory laboured to provide sufficient support for a six-man team.

Everything becomes clearer with hindsight, and it soon became transparently clear to Banks and BSA that the growing threat of big-bore two-strokes would very soon become unstoppable. By the middle of 1969, the best chance John Banks would have of winning the world 500cc title had already gone. With Paul Friedrichs scoring in only six events the previous year, Banks, with a touch more steadiness, would have been champion. John Banks didn't realise it at the time, but 1968 was the high watermark of his career. By their failure to adopt an enlightened strategy for Banks the following season, BSA must shoulder their share of the blame. As for not ensuring that Banks was physically and mentally well enough prepared for a second tilt at the World 500cc Championship, BSA were negligent in allowing him to compete in the two televised tournaments over the winter. The reason, of course, was the constant need for favourable publicity, whatever the long-term implications for Banks and the other members of the team.

As winter gave way to spring, Banks was involved in a double celebration. He won the ITV World of Sport competition with 30 points in hand over Alan Clough's 420cc Husqvarna, who in turn was five points ahead of Dave Nicoll. In the BBC's Grandstand series, Arthur Browning hauled his 380cc Greeves to within five points of Banks' BSA, by virtue of a last round victory at Kirkcaldy. Clough took the 250cc class by five points from the AJS of Malcolm Davis.

Delighted as Banks was at his latest conquests, so were BSA, who fielded Smith, Nicoll, and Hickman, as well as Banks, in the BBC rounds. Between them they won the manufacturer's prize for the factory. However, Banks now faced the World 500cc Championship after 18 months of relentless competition, with hardly a break. Eager and enthusiastic Banks most surely was; but he was nowhere near his freshest. Be that as it may, Banks rarely gave less than 100% and, if only BSA had produced the same percentage figure in the reliability statistics, it might have been so different.

Below **Dick Clayton hastens his Greeves to fourth place in the fourth round of the 250cc Grandstand Trophy, at Swanley. It was Clayton's best result in the competition in which he finished sixth that winter.**

Right **By 1969 Jeff Smith was nearing the end of his career and restricting himself to some fun in front of the TV cameras. But he was still sufficiently competitive to finish fourth in the big capacity class of the Grandstand series, having won the 250cc category the previous winter.**

Below **Once Jeff Smith departed centre stage, British hopes rested with John Banks. Had BSA not collapsed and development of two-strokes not produced such emphatic results, he might well have followed Smith into the World 500cc Championship record books.**

With Farleigh due to host its first Moto-Cross des Nations in September, there was no British 500cc Grand Prix in the 12-nation World 500cc Championship, for which the best seven finishes would count. New scoring values were introduced in 1969, which enabled the first nine riders to gather points: 15 to the winner, 12 to the runner-up, 10 for third, eight for fourth, six for fifth, then four, three, two, down to a single point for ninth. These values stayed in place until 1984; though from 1977 scores were counted for all heats, with the rider amassing the highest points total being declared champion.

The early threat to British hopes came not from Friedrichs – who was to win only one grand prix – but from the Husqvarnas of the Swedish pair: Arne Kring and Bengt Aberg.

Kring won his home event and in Holland, while Aberg won the opening round, in Austria. Banks had two second places, failed to score in Italy – where Aberg triumphed – though the Englishman took the Czechoslovakian tie at Prerov, and the following round in the USSR. After six grands prix, Banks led on 54 points, with Aberg on 50, Kring with 48, and Friedrichs out of contention with 12. Then the rot set in.

In West Germany, Banks was forced out with ignition failure. At Namur he was runner-up to Roger de Coster. But in the French GP at Albi, electrical problems again frustrated him, after a puncture had sidelined the Banks' BSA in Luxembourg. With two round to go, Aberg had 87 points from seven rounds. Banks had 66 from five. To take the title, Banks needed to win in Switzerland and East Germany to give himself a possible 96. Two second places would leave the Swedish lumberjack Aberg on 95. Having been denied by a single point a year earlier, could Banks now win by the same minuscule margin?

After a depressing sequence in which he had picked up only 12 points in four grands prix, Banks badly needed a breakthrough. Instead there was another breakdown. In Saturday's practice for the Swiss GP at Wohlen, Banks clipped a marker post with his right hand. Dosed with painkillers, Banks competed gamely enough until his rear tyre punctured in the first heat. In the next race the gearbox broke. Aberg rode calmly to victory to win the championship. Banks was fifth overall in the East German round at Schwerin, so concluding a disappointing title offensive, to finish runner-up, 22 points behind the shy Swede.

Nicoll's victory in Luxembourg on 10 August was the last by a four-stroke until Jacky Martens of Belgium, riding a Husqvarna, won the Finnish GP at Salo on 23 May 1993. In 1969 the four-stroke BSAs had reached the end of their development life. As Nicoll, Banks and Hickman travelled home from the final grand prix of the season there were doubts about the life of the company. Rumours were circulating on the London Stock Exchange that the BSA Group was facing unmanageable financial difficulties, and a receiver had been called in. As yet they were only rumours, but it wouldn't be long before BSA's longevity – like the effectiveness of their four-stroke engines – would end. The implications of their failure to win the World 500cc Championship, for Banks and the factory, weren't fully appreciated at the time. Indeed, in some quarters it was hailed as a triumph of sorts. After all, to be runner-up in the sport's most prestigious competition for a second successive year can scarcely be considered unworthy.

There was no time for regrets any more than there had been the previous season. Yet the truth is that Banks and BSA failed to capitalise on the reliability problems experienced by Friedrichs in 1968, when the East German scored in only five grands prix before the final round was reached. This grudging observation takes no account of the fact witnessed by the keenest observers of a lack of fulfilment. They also realised that Banks' popularity masked a paucity of genuine quality among the rest of the British contingent. There were few, if any, who were capable of making it to a grand prix podium; never mind outright victory. With Vic Eastwood obliged to undergo several operations on the leg he broke at Hawkstone, John Banks was, by a country mile, the best Britain had to offer.

Were further substantive proof needed of

Below **Roger de Coster was one of the finest tacticians in world moto-cross. Quick to see the future once the Japanese invasion began, he was the first rider to win a world 500cc title on a Japanese bike, which he did for Suzuki in 1971.**

Right **Torsten Hallman** was on track to lead Sweden to victory in the Trophée des Nations 250cc team contest, at Kester, Belgium, until the engine of his works Husqvarna expired. Great Britain finished sixth.

Opposite **Dave Nicoll** was one of Britain's bright new stars and tipped for major honours. His winter campaign was given a timely lift with victory in the first round of the Grandstand Trophy at Naish Hill. The BSA rider followed that with wins at Caerleon and Hadleigh, and he went on to secure the title with a round remaining.

this assessment, it was provided in full by the Great Britain team at the Moto-Cross des Nations, where Britain's decline as a force in world moto-cross began to accelerate. On the five occasions that the team contest had been staged in England, Great Britain were the victors. At Farleigh Castle in September, the home team slumped to an embarrassing defeat, where almost everything that could go wrong did so. In the first heat, only veterans Jeff Smith – by now into his 35th year – and Dave Bickers made it into the top 10 finishers. Banks was in third place in the 20 lap race, behind the two Swedes, Bengt Aberg and Arne Kring, when the Briton was forced out by ignition trouble. Alan Clough soon followed, so Britains hopes of getting three of their five-man team to the finish, rested with Keith Hickman on the second works BSA. Hickman, who had been troubled by a loose petrol filler cap, limped to the line in 13th place.

Banks gave the 15,000 home supporters something to cheer about when he won the second race from Aberg, with Roger de Coster of the winning Belgium team in third place. Smith was again seventh, Hickman improved to eighth, three places ahead of Bickers. Despite Aberg's splendid individual effort, Sweden were runners-up with 27 points—three more than Belgium—while Great Britain were a distance away in third, with 44 points. It had not been so much that Great Britain had been beaten; it was the nature and size of the defeat which hurt so much.

To some extent, things had looked a shade brighter earlier in the summer, at the British

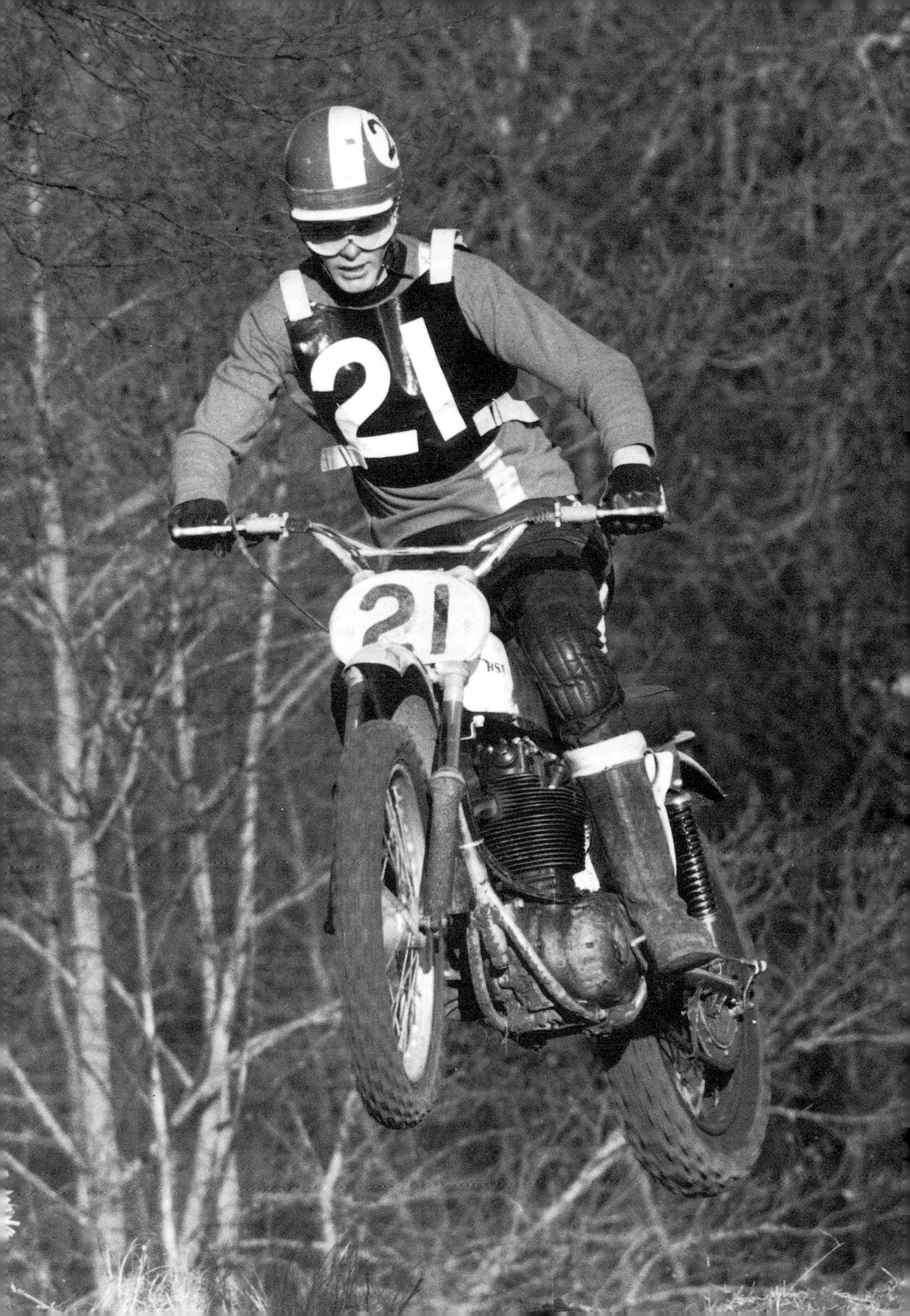
21
21

Right **Dave Nicoll, newly-crowned BBC 750cc Champion,** attends to his blistered hands. Nicoll finished sixth in the World 500cc Championship in 1969.

Below right **Alan Clews' Bolton-based CCM Company** developed the BSA Victor engine for competition after it all began to fall away for BSA.

250cc Grand Prix at Dodington. With Belgium's Joel Robert injured, his compatriot Sylvain Geboers took his CZ to overall victory. But again it was the old hand Bickers who was runner-up. Arthur Browning was a very creditable fourth, riding a Greeves, while Bryan Goss was sixth on his Husqvarna. Elsewhere there was a litany of excuses from the other British riders like Jim Aird and Andy Roberton on the factory AJSs, who both crashed. Fred Mayes, whose CZ was lapped in both races. And Bryan Wade, with a broken gearbox on his Greeves. Malcolm Davis, it is true, could count himself a shade unfortunate. He was in determined mood, and was challenging Geboers for the lead in the first heat, when the front wheel of his CZ punctured. In the second 16-lap race, a jamming front brake put the British 250cc champion out, while he was holding third place.

ANTI-CLIMAX

For Gloucester's Davis, 1969 was not a happy year. He began the new season as the number one rider with the AJS factory. But after two rounds of the national 250cc competition – the first of which, at Tilton, Leicestershire, he won – he was sacked for allegedly not trying. By now AJS were in the hands of Norton Villiers and, two weeks before his dismissal, Davis was talked out of resigning by the group's Managing Director, Dennis Poore. This came after a sequence of mechanical failures had sidelined Davis, as he attempted to retain his British title. In the second round of the domestic series, at Nantwich, the engine of his AJS seized in both races, and Davis no-scored. The eventual parting of the ways came as no surprise to those close to the 24-year-old Davis, or others who were familiar with the frailty of AJS machinery.

The AJS moto-cross campaign, and the running of the team, was in the hands of a former road racer, Peter Inchley. During the time Inchley was at the helm, Bryan Goss, Fred Mayes, Chris Horsfield, Dick Clayton, as well as Davis, fell out with the factory having ridden their unreliable bikes. Jim Aird – on a part-time contract – and Andy Roberton were left. Of Roberton, Inchley said: "I have always admired Andy, and have great hopes that he will become a sort of Jeff Smith of AJS."

Whatever else Andy Roberton was, he most certainly was no Jeff Smith. It was a speculative judgement as flawed as the whole AJS project, which bore all the portents of success, though none of the substance. Davis turned to CZ and quickly regained his place among the leaders in the five-venue chase for the British 250cc Championship. By the time the final round was reached, at Tirley, Gloucestershire, a few miles from Davis's home, Bryan Wade on the works Greeves, Davis, and the Husqvarnas of Alan Clough and Bryan Goss, were locked in a gripping, four-man battle for the title.

Davis won the first 30 minutes, plus two laps, opening race, when Clough's chances of regaining the title were damned by ignition failure. Goss was second and Wade third. Davis and Wade were now tied on 31 points, with Goss on 30., To mounting excitement, Goss overshot a corner on the first lap in the deciding race and dropped to eighth, as Roberton headed the pack, chased by Davis. Wade was fifth. By half distance, Wade had forced his way to the front, passing the new leader Davis. Roberton – without a race win in the series – had his brief moment of glory by retaking Davis, who had to settle for being runner-up in the title stakes behind the jubilant Yorkshireman Wade.

It would be asking a great deal to expect that the drama and excitement of the 250cc class could possibly be repeated in the 500cc category, once John Banks began the business of retaining his title. With his customary zealous commitment, Banks reeled off eight straight race wins at the first four rounds. With the Kidston still to come, Banks was champion. His final points total of 75 was more than twice that of the runner-up, Vic Allan. Quite simply there were no realistic challengers as Banks recovered from the disappointment of missing out on the world title, to reinforce his position as Britain's number one. For the British fans, the uncomfortable reality in 1969 was that the only English rider who imposed his class on all competitions – and who had genuine international ability – was John Banks.

Left **Arne Kring.** Another Swedish tyro set to make his mark in the World 500cc Championship. Kring had a meteoric rise to finish fourth on a factory Husqvarna in 1969. He looked set to win the title the following year, until sidelined by a monster crash in a non-championship event. Kring's enforced absence allowed Bengt Aberg to take the title. Despite missing the final three rounds, Kring had enough points in hand to finish runner-up; and another Swede, Ake Jonsson riding a Maico, was third.

1970

JOHN BANKS wins the ITV World of Sport tournament, but suffers a serious leg injury which puts him out of the World 500cc Championship. Dave Nicoll wins the BBC Grandstand series and Bryan Goss collects British 500cc title. Disaster for home riders at the British 250cc Grand Prix. Great Britain slip to fourth in the Moto-Cross des Nations. Vic Eastwood returns after a 16-month absence.

No sportsmen, especially those racing motorcycles, have been certain of guaranteeing their personal invulnerability, never mind been able to decide their own destiny. So it comes as no surprise when the truth of this maxim impacts on the consciousness of every moto-cross rider at some stage of his career, just as it did for Vic Eastwood, in December 1968 at Hawkstone Park, and was to for John Banks 16 months later.

Before the new season became a turmoil of uncertainty for Banks personally, the sport in general and the British manufacturers in particular, were dealt two body blows. The first was delivered by ITV, who announced without warning that they were slashing their coverage of winter moto-cross by a third, so their six-round series was reduced to a four-venue affair, with programmes cut to 45 minutes each. As all concerned with the well-being of the sport were coming to terms with this unwelcome news, the BBC decided to drop their popular Grandstand series, once the current tournament ended in March. While ITV continued to screen moto-cross into the seventies, it was on an irregular basis, which greatly reduced the casual viewer's awareness of the sport. It was undeniably damaging to the motorcycle makers, who lost the indispensable showcase which television provided. For those who were in the business of making moto-cross machines, there were other damaging setbacks soon to be confronted.

The Grandstand series was the first to be concluded, so ending the BBC's eight years of continuous involvement with the sport; seven

Below right **Although the British motorcycle industry was on the point of total collapse by 1970, there were still some optimistic dealers selling British-made CCM and Rickman products.**

Opposite **Greeves head-to-head, something that would be history soon, both in terms of the machines and of the TV cameras being there to record them. Fred Mayes (8) and John Griffith (12) battle it out in a 1970 Grandstand Trophy race.**

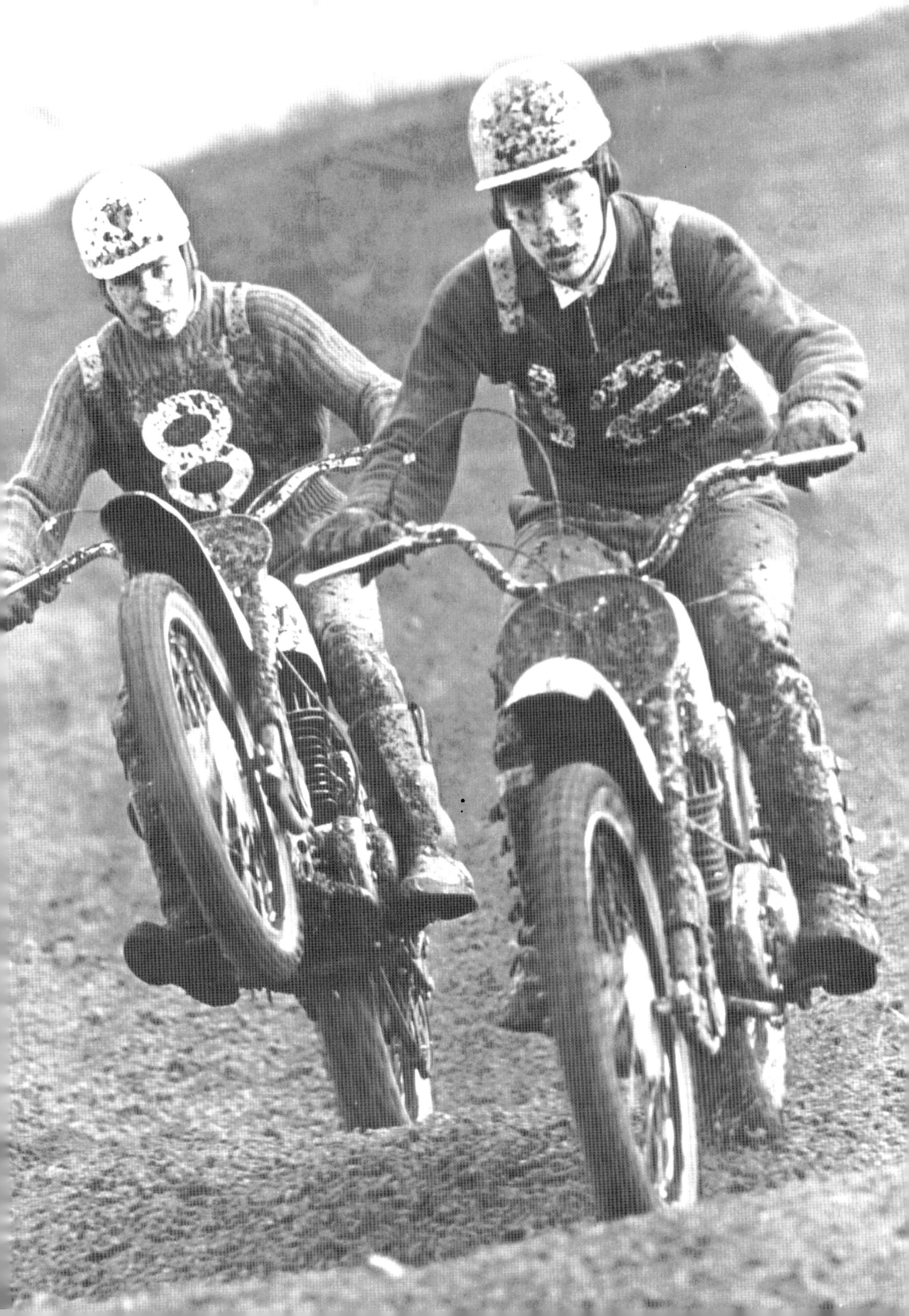

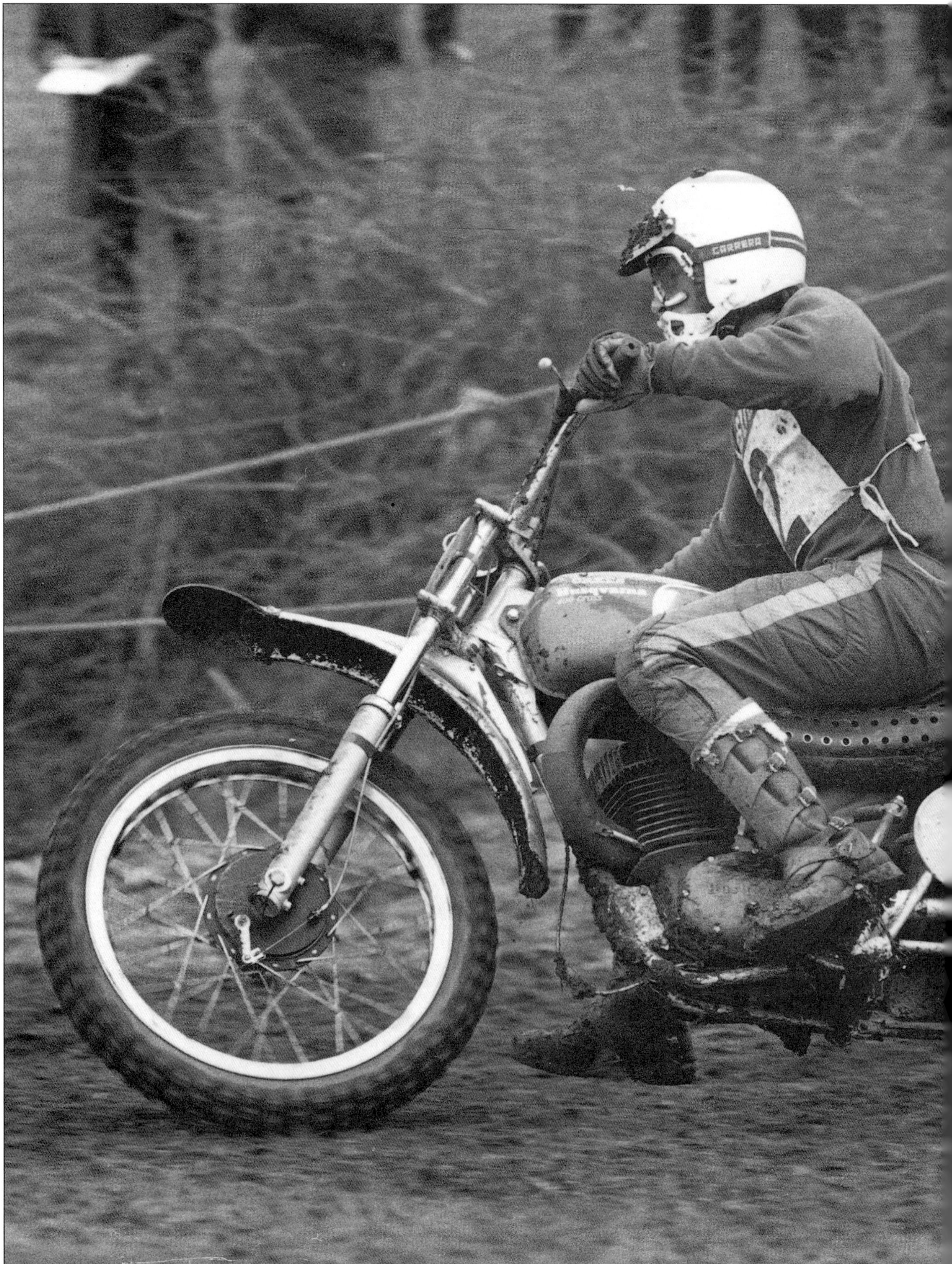
CARRERA

of them with the Grandstand Trophy. In the 250cc class there was a different winner at each of the six rounds. But where Jim Aird, Vic Allan and Arthur Browning scored inconsistently, Malcolm Davis – who had rejoined Andy Roberton at AJS – was in the points at every round. So, too, was Bryan Goss, whose solitary victory was at Canada Heights. With a second place in the penultimate round at Asham Woods, Frome, Goss needed to finish no higher than sixth to take the trophy should Davis win. If Goss failed to score, there would have been a tie. Incredibly, the ACU had made no decision on how this would be broken, if Goss had no-scored. They need not have worried, as Goss wrapped up the series by finishing fifth.

The chase for the 500cc Grandstand title was decided before the final round, at Dodington Park. Dave Nicoll had reeled off three straight wins at Naish Hill, Caerleon and Hadleigh, to give him a healthy eight-point cushion over John Banks, who in turn was five points ahead of Arthur Browning's Greeves. Browning failed to score in the remaining three rounds, where Bryan Goss and Vic Allan shared the victories. But Nicoll, as runner-up to Allan at the penultimate round, was 10 points clear of Banks, so couldn't be beaten.

For once, and for all the wrong reasons, the ITV's World of Sport tournament hogged the headlines in the weeks leading to spring. Eastwood, although he had reappeared in July, was nowhere near ready, so he abandoned riding and concentrated on intensive physiotherapy in an effort to be fully fit for the new season. His recovery complete, Eastwood returned to competitive action in the ITV round at Castleford, in February, where Banks took over the leadership of the series. To BSA's obvious dismay, with their World 500cc Championship campaign commencing in a matter three weeks, Banks' future was thrown into uncertainty by a serious injury to his right leg. Banks sustained this nearing the end of three hectic days of competition at the Cambridgeshire Grand National – the opening round of the British 500cc Championship – on Easter Sunday.

Richard Hughes had his moment of glory when he beat a bevy of established riders to the flag in the Mortimer club's Jackpot Scramble, held as a sideshow to their British Championship round at Beenham Park. The 20-year-old Hughes, sacked by Greeves the previous year, headed Bryan Wade and Chris Horsfield across the line on his Husqvarna to collect the £100 prize.

181

Right **Malcolm Davis saved his best form for the British 250cc Championship, which he won in some style on the factory AJS. In the 250cc Grandstand series, Davis finished runner-up to Bryan Goss on the Husqvarna.**

Banks caught his foot in a rut and dislocated his knee in the second race, having won the first, from Nicoll and Andy Roberton's AJS. The injury immobilised him, though daily treatment had Banks in some sort of limited shape for the deciding leg of the ITV series, the following Saturday at Winchester.

Banks attributed his misfortune to the ACU's grading system for World Championship events. "You've got to go like mad in the British Championship, for which you get nothing more than a star and a travelling clock, to give you the right to even start in the World Championship," said a disgruntled Banks.

But start he did, at the furiously fast Morestead track, in Hampshire, where Banks and Vic Allan were separated by four points before racing began. Allan needed hospital treatment after his lower lip was cut badly by a flying stone during practice. The Scot returned to the circuit just before the opening heat, looking pale and groggy. But if Allan was regretful over this stroke of bad luck, things became worse for both Allan and Banks, before either could be sure which of them would be celebrating.

On a day of wildly fluctuating fortunes, Banks was forced out of the first race after colliding with Rob Taylor's AJS. Allan, with blood oozing from his mouth after the stitches had pulled away, hauled his Greeves from eighth to third. This brought Allan and Banks level on 28 points each. Banks' mounting problems now included his bike. The collision with Taylor had wiped off the contact breaker of his BSA, and the rear tyre of his spare machine was punctured. So after swapping wheels, Banks needed to beat Allan in the last-race decider. Within a lap Allan, had an apparent stranglehold on the outcome, as Banks crashed at the second corner. But the drama didn't end there, as Allan's Greeves stuttered to a halt when the low-tension wire from the flywheel magneto vibrated off the coil, to drop the ITV trophy into Banks' lap. With four wins at the three earlier meetings, where Allan was without a solitary victory, the tie was broken in favour of the BSA rider. In the 250cc class, Bryan Wade beat Dick Clayton and Browning in a Greeves one-two-three.

It was the only piece of luck that came the way of John Banks in 1970. He faced a long lay-off after surgery to repair torn ligament damage to his right knee, which had the added complications of cartilage trouble. He missed the whole of the World 500cc Championship, and by the time he returned in September, his British title was well on the way to a new home. By his own admission, Banks was never quite the force he was, after this damaging and painful setback. Nor for that matter was Vic Eastwood, who took most of the season to readjust to the pace of top-flight moto-cross. In the meantime, the search went on for British riders who were capable of carrying on the tradition of excellence established by the likes of Dave Bickers, John Draper, Brian Stonebridge, Les Archer and the incomparable Jeff Smith.

For the foreseeable future, the quest ended in mid-summer at Dodington Park, where it was replaced by the sort of soul searching at which the British excel. In the aftermath of a quite disastrous afternoon for home competitors in the British 250cc Grand Prix, the inquests began. By any standard – never mind those prevailing at the time the English motorcycle industry was being prepared for liquidation – this was the single most disappointing day in the history of British moto-cross. There were some 17,000 supporters at the hillside, Old Sodbury circuit, to witness the humiliation of the cream of Britain's young riders; it was a painful experience, and one those present are unlikely ever to forget.

Only Dick Clayton scored for the 10-strong British contingent. Riding a Greeves, Clayton was 10th overall, having been 11th in the first heat and lapped in the second race to trail in two from last, in 16th position. Clayton scored a point. It was the symbolism of that single point which gave rise to innumerable post mortems. Joel Robert won on a works Suzuki, after his nearest rival and compatriot, Sylvain Geboers, went out with a puncture on the second factory Suzuki. Those riding British-made machines blamed the indifferent quality and comparative unreliability of their equipment. But the malaise in British moto-cross went far deeper than that. For a start, five of the 10 British runners crashed out of contention. So far as I am aware, no scientific proof existed to explain why it was more likely a rider would

Below **Dave Nicoll (BSA, 14) leads the Suzuki of eventual winner Roger de Coster, and Bengt Aberg (Husqvarna, 2) in the Belgian 500cc Grand Prix at Namur. Aberg finished fifth overall, but Nicoll was forced out with rear brake problems.**

Above **Bryan Goss was the undisputed winner of the British 500cc Championship. Goss wrapped up the series with a round remaining. The third tie in the five-round series was held over the Cotswold course at Nympsfield. Goss took his Husqvarna to victory in both races.**

crash on a bike made in Britain, than on one manufactured in Sweden, Japan or East Germany.

I have already touched on the doomed AJS enterprise, though by now Greeves were matching the Andover-based concern with their mechanical inconstancy. John Ralling, the technical director at Greeves, attempted to define the engine-failure problems with his company's products. But Ralling's apologia contained resonances heard elsewhere in the industry. Greeves were operating like Marcos, the Wiltshire-based car maker, who found their individuality and niche approach was insufficient to save them. Even before 1970, the vulnerability of Greeves to Villiers, and with a product offer not containing any road bikes, but centred solely on the Griffon moto-crosser, made the Essex factory's decline inexorable. What was taxing the minds of those charged with the well-being of British moto-cross, was arresting the decline of the sport.

In his World 500cc Championship campaigns of 1968 and 1969, it was not John Banks' fault that he, like so many others before him, was the unsuspecting victim of motorcycle sport's central inconsistency: the subjugation of talent to technology. Or, as so often happened in his case, technical failure. Equally, there is no ideal moment to confront injury. In an activity like moto-cross, just as in National Hunt racing, injuries are an everyday hazard; the resolute negotiation of which, often being sufficient to determine a rider's career path.

In the arguments and investigations which followed that bleak afternoon at Dodington Park, it was clear that of the two main issues confronting the sport's administrators, only one was partly within their control. The first, concerning the quality of British-made bikes was beyond the orbit of their influence. Though as so many riders were using CZ and Husqvarna equipment, this was the lesser of the two problems. In any case, within a couple of years all the English manufacturers were out of business. The second was more straightforward and concerned the structure and manner of the domestic season. Most agreed it was too long. In essence it contained masses of quantity and far too little quality. British riders were weaned on a diet of sprint races. The televised tournaments were a prime example. Although the TV races were of only 10 or 15 minutes duration – ideal to fit the schedules – it made stars of the participants. Many of them believed in their own star rating. The stardom notion was impossible to sustain, because the grand prix results posted by British competitors told an entirely different story. And the results, as we all know, rarely lie.

Almost a whole decade elapsed between the single grand prix victory of Dave Nicoll's career, and the first of Graham Noyce's 1979 campaign, which ended with the Hampshire youngster lifting the world 500cc title. In between those victories by Nicoll, in Luxembourg, in August 1969, and Noyce at the Austrian GP which was the opening round of the 1979 World Championship, no British rider won a single grand prix in either the 500cc or 250cc classes. Noyce had three third places to his credit in 1978, while John Banks – who was destined to finish no higher than seventh in any of the remaining world title campaigns he undertook – could count on two thirds as his best international performances. The sadness in this desperately barren period for British moto-cross was that until 1976, when Noyce finished fourth in the World 500cc Championship, and Neil Hudson emerged in the 250cc class two years later, no British rider completed a season by finishing in the top 10 of either category.

Moto-cross is only partly a contest of natural ability. Especially in those moments of crisis – when only victory is sufficient to guarantee your place in the title-race – it is won and lost in the mind, the heart, the stomach and the sphincter. By the end of the sixties, only John Banks could be sure that the sum of those particular parts of the anatomy were up to the challenge. Yes, there were brief glimpses of hope engendered by Vic Allan, Keith Hickman, Andy Roberton, Dave Nicoll, and one or two others in the early 1970s, but they were too brief and unsustainable to have any lasting impact.

Below **Rob Taylor was a little-known centre rider until he claimed second overall, behind Bengt Aberg at Farleigh Castle. There being no British 500cc Grand Prix in 1970, the West Wilts club staged an international meeting at their track, with a first prize of £500. Riding his privately-entered Husqvarna, Taylor collected £335 and the scalps of Roger de Coster, Arne Kring and Ake Jonsson, among other famous names, for his afternoon's work.**

The call for fewer and longer races in the domestic championships went largely unheeded. This after all was one problem for which a solution could very easily be found. It was abundantly clear that the sprint ethos which afflicted British moto-cross did nothing to prepare our riders for the more demanding grand prix races.

But so long as there was television to present the riders as stars, and the motorcycle press remained as blithely uncritical as it has been throughout my lifetime, all was apparently well. Or as well as could be expected.

There was no official British 500cc Grand Prix in 1970, only an international meeting at Farleigh Castle which the West Wilts club dubbed a grand prix. Sweden's Bengt Aberg was the winner, just as he was of the World 500cc Championship, once the early leader Arne Kring somersaulted out of contention in a horrific crash at a Belgian national event. Vic Allan was the highest placed Briton in 12th place. Andy Roberton, who raised British spirits with third overall at Payerne in the Swiss GP, was 17th, while Keith Hickman, riding the factory BSA, was two places higher in the final order.

Teams from 10 countries contested the Moto-Cross des Nations in Italy. Vic Allan was the best British performer, being runner-up in the second race, having been sixth in the first. But even a consummate trier like Allan couldn't prevent Great Britain slipping a further rung down the international ladder to fourth. Roberton and Dave Nicoll were Britain's other scorers, as Sweden triumphed for the fifth time in 15 years. Belgium were second.

With no John Banks or Vic Eastwood, the British 500cc Championship promised to be the most open since before Jeff Smith made it his personal fiefdom. As things turned out, it became something of a stroll for Bryan Goss riding his privately-entered Husqvarna, who clinched the only title of his career with a double-race victory in the fourth round, at Tirley. Having four times finished in the top three of the 250cc class, it was a singularly sweet triumph for Goss, once he had seen off the challenge from the BSAs of first-round winner Dave Nicoll, and eventual runner-up Keith Hickman.

Before the season was over, Vic Eastwood endorsed his comeback with victory in the second leg at the final round of the British 250cc Championship, at Beenham Park. It had been a year, 11 months and 21 days since Eastwood had last won a race in the national series, when he took the second heat at the Kidston. Malcolm Davis was the master of the five-round contest, winning both heats at the second, and third rounds on the works AJS. Davis then went on to build an unassailable lead in he fourth round at Cuerden Park, Lancashire, and regain the title he first won in 1968.

The series had opened just a few miles down the M6 motorway, at Nantwich, Cheshire. On a filthy day, at a circuit made treacherous by incessant rain, Jeff Smith stole the show to upstage all the youngsters by finishing second to Bryan Wade in the first heat. Far from being satisfied with that performance, Smith went one better in the next race, to leave Malcolm Davis trailing in his wake. Having dominated the golden years of British moto-cross for so long, this was hardly Jeff Smith's finest hour. But it was the final British Championship victory of his career. In more ways than one it marked the end of an era. The golden era.

		this page
British Championships 1951–1970		this page
European 500cc Championship 1952–1956		188
World 500cc Championship 1957–1970		189
European 250cc Championship 1958–1961		190
World 250cc Championship 1962–1970		191
British 500cc Grand Prix 1952–1970		192
British 250cc Grand Prix 1958–1970		194
Moto-Cross des Nations 1947–1970		195

Results

BRITISH CHAMPIONSHIPS 1951–1970

1951–57

500cc

Posn	Year and Rider	Machine	Points
	1951		
1	Geoff Ward	AJS	28
2	Les Archer	Norton	19
3	Brian Stonebridge	Matchless	16
	1952		
1	John Avery	BSA	32
2	Reg Pilling	AJS	17
3	Les Archer	Norton	15
	1953		
1	Geoff Ward	AJS	34
2	David Tye	BSA	27
3	John Avery	BSA	20
	1954		
1	Geoff Ward	AJS	39
2	Phil Nex	BSA	24
3	David Tye	BSA	21
	1955		
1	Jeff Smith	BSA	35
2	Terry Cheshire	BSA	32

Posn	Year and Rider	Machine	Points
3	Dave Curtis	Matchless	25
	1956		
1	Jeff Smith	BSA	45
2	Dave Curtis	Matchless	35
3	Terry Cheshire	BSA	31
	1957		
	Title Contest cancelled due to Suez Crisis		
	1958		
1	Dave Curtis	Matchless	35
2	Don Rickman	BSA	19
3	Jeff Smith	BSA	17
	Arthur Lampkin	BSA	17
	1959		
1	Arthur Lampkin	BSA	40
2	Don Rickman	BSA or Metisse	33
3	John Draper	BSA	26
	Derek Rickman	BSA or Metisse	26

1960

500cc

Posn	Rider	Machine	Points
1	Jeff Smith	BSA	28
2	Don Rickman	Metisse	20
	John Burton	BSA	20
4	Dave Curtis	Matchless	10

250cc

1	Dave Bickers	Greeves	32
2	Alan Clough	DOT	12
3	Joe Johnson	Greeves	9

1961

500cc

Posn	Rider	Machine	Points
1	Jeff Smith	BSA	30
2	Dave Curtis	Matchless	26
3	Arthur Lampkin	BSA	16

250cc

1	Arthur Lampkin	BSA	32
2	Dave Bickers	Greeves	24
3	Pat Lamper	DOT	13

1962

500cc

Posn	Rider	Machine	Points
1	Jeff Smith	BSA	40
2	John Burton	BSA	16
3	John Harris	BSA	11

250cc

Posn	Rider	Machine	Points
1	Dave Bickers	Greeves	30
2	John Griffiths	DOT	14
3	Alan Clough	DOT	13

1963

500cc

Posn	Rider	Machine	Points
1	Jeff Smith	BSA	27
2	Vic Eastwood	Matchless	25
3	John Burton	BSA	16

250cc

1	Dave Bickers	Greeves/Husqvarna	24
2	Bryan Goss	Greeves	15
3	Norman Crooks	DOT	9

1964

500cc

Posn	Rider	Machine	Points
1	Jeff Smith	BSA	27
2	Vic Eastwood	Matchless	18
3	Chris Horsfield	Matchless	13

250cc

1	Dave Bickers	Greeves	32
2	Alan Clough	Greeves	22
3	Ernie Greer	DOT	15

187

1965

500cc

Posn	Rider	Machine	Points
1	Jeff Smith	BSA	30
2	Vic Eastwood	BSA	24
	Dave Bickers	Greeves	24
4	Jerry Scott	BSA	9

250cc

1	Dave Bickers	Greeves	36
2	Bryan Goss	Husqvarna	22
3	Alan Clough	Greeves	14
	Fred Mayes	Greeves	14

1966

500cc

Posn	Rider	Machine	Points
1	Jeff Smith	BSA	30
2	Vic Eastwood	BSA	24
	Dave Bickers	Greeves	24
4	Jerry Scott	BSA	9

250cc

1	Dave Bickers	Greeves	36
2	Bryan Goss	Husqvarna	22
3	Alan Clough	Greeves	14
	Fred Mayes	Greeves	14

1967

500cc

Posn	Rider	Machine	Points
1	Jeff Smith	BSA	21
2	Alan Clough	Husqvarna	20
	Vic Eastwood	BSA	20
4	Dave Bickers	CZ	14

250cc

1	Alan Clough	Husqvarna	26
2	Dave Bickers	CZ	18
	Fred Mayes	AJS	18
	Bryan Goss	Husqvarna	16

1968

500cc

Posn	Rider	Machine	Points
1	John Banks	BSA	56
2	Vic Eastwood	Husqvarna	43
3	Dave Nicoll	BSA	33

250cc

1	Malcolm Davis	AJS	45
2	Don Rickman	Bultaco	34
3	Andy Roberton	Husqvarna	29

1969

500cc

Posn	Rider	Machine	Points
1	John Banks	BSA	75
2	Vic Allan	Greeves	32
3	Keith Hickman	BSA	18

250cc

1	Bryan Wade	Greeves	39
2	Malcolm Davis	AJS & CZ	35
3	Bryan Goss	Husqvarna	31

1970

500cc

Posn	Rider	Machine	Points
1	Bryan Goss	Husqvarna	52
2	Vic Allan	Greeves	26
3	Keith Hickman	BSA	25

250cc

1	Malcolm Davis	AJS	59
2	Andy Roberton	AJS	41
3	Jeff Smith	BSA	37

EUROPEAN 500CC CHAMPIONSHIP 1952–1956

1952

Posn	Rider	Country	Machine	Points
1	Victor Leloup	Belgium	FN	28
2	Auguste Mingels	Belgium	Matchless	20
3	John Avery	Great Britain	BSA	12
4	Marcel Cox	Belgium	Matchless	12
5	Nic Jansen	Belgium	Saroléa	10
6	Brian Stonebridge	Great Britain	Matchless	8

Six Rounds: *Italy, Belgium, Luxembourg, Sweden, France and Great Britain. Best four Scores to count.*

1953

Posn	Rider	Country	Machine	Points
1	Auguste Mingels	Belgium	Matchless & FN	30
2	René Baeten	Belgium	Saroléa	19
3	Victor Leloup	Belgium	FN	18
4	Basil Hall	Great Britain	BSA	15
5	Les Archer	Great Britain	Norton	12
6	Geoff Ward	Great Britain	AJS	11

Eight Rounds: *Switzerland, Holland, France, Italy, Great Britain, Belgium, Luxembourg, Sweden. Best four scores to count.*

1954

Posn	Rider	Country	Machine	Points
1	Auguste Mingels	Belgium	FN	30
2	René Baeten	Belgium	Saroléa	22
3	Jeff Smith	Great Britain	BSA	20
4	Victor Leloup	Belgium	FN	20
5	Phil Nex	Great Britain	BSA	10
6	Brian Stonebridge	Great Britain	BSA	10

Eight Rounds: *Switzerland, Italy, Holland, Great Britain Luxembourg, Belgium, Sweden, France. Best four scores to count.*

1955

Posn	Rider	Country	Machine	Points
1	John Draper	Great Britain	BSA	23
2	Bill Nilsson	Sweden	BSA	22
3	Sten Lundin	Sweden	BSA	21
4	Victor Leloup	Belgium	FN	21
5	Les Archer	Great Britain	Norton	19
6	Brian Stonebridge	Great Britain	BSA	16

Eight rounds: *Switzerland, France, Italy, Great Britain, Belgium, Luxembourg, Sweden, Holland. Best four scores to count.*

1956

Posn	Rider	Country	Machine	Points
1	Les Archer	Great Britain	Norton	32
2	John Draper	Great Britain	BSA	24
3	Nic Jansen	Belgium	Matchless	19
4	Sten Lundin	Sweden	BSA	17
5	Bill Nilsson	Sweden	BSA	16
6	Geoff Ward	Great Britain	BSA	16

Eight Rounds: *Switzerland, Holland, Italy, France, Great Britain, Belgium, Luxembourg, Sweden, Denmark. Best four scores to count.*

EUROPEAN 500CC CHAMPIONSHIP GRAND PRIX VICTORIES BY WINNER

Year	Rider	Country	Number of GP Victories
1952	Victor Leloup	Belgium	3
1953	August Mingels	Belgium	3
1954	Auguste Mingels	Belgium	3

| 1955 | John Draper | Great Britain | 2 |
| 1956 | Les Archer | Great Britain | 4 |

Les Archer was the only rider to win the European 500 cc Championship with a maximum score.
Archer's gross total of 41 points in 1956 was the highest recorded in the five-year history of the tournament.

The lowest gross score was by John Draper in 1955 with two victories, a second and a sixth place. The only other riders to win two grands prix that season were Archer and Sweden's Sten Lundin.

WORLD 500CC CHAMPIONSHIP 1957–1970

1957

Posn	Rider	Country	Machine	Points
1	Bill Nilsson	Sweden	Crescent AJS	34
2	René Baeten	Belgium	FN	30
3	Sten Lundin	Sweden	Monark	28
4	Jeff Smith	Great Britain	BSA	23
5	Les Archer	Great Britain	Norton	20
6	Auguste Mingels	Belgium	Saroléa	17

Eight Rounds: Switzerland, France, Sweden, Italy, Great Britain, Holland, Belgium Luxembourg and Denmark. Best five scores to count.

1958

Posn	Rider	Country	Machine	Points
1	René Baeten	Belgium	FN	42
2	Bill Nilsson	Sweden	Crescent	34
3	Sten Lundin	Sweden	Monark	33
4	John Draper	Great Britain	BSA	24
5	Hubert Scaillet	Belgium	FN	19
6	Jeff Smith	Great Britain	BSA	18

Ten Rounds: Austria, Denmark, Switzerland, France, Italy, Great Britain, Holland, Belgium,. Luxembourg, Sweden. Best six scores to count.

1959

Posn	Rider	Country	Machine	Points
1	Sten Lundin	Sweden	Monark	44
2	Bill Nilsson	Sweden	Crescent	36
3	Dave Curtis	Great Britain	Matchless	29
4	Broer Dirks	Holland	BSA	26
5	Les Archer	Great Britain	Norton	23
6	Jeff Smith	Great Britain	BSA	21

Eleven Rounds: Austria, Switzerland, Denmark, France, Italy, West Germany, Great Britain, Holland, Belgium,. Luxembourg, Sweden. Best six scores to count.

1960

Posn	Rider	Country	Machine	Points
1	Bill Nilsson	Sweden	Husqvarna	38
2	Sten Lundin	Sweden	Monark	36
3	Rolf Tibblin	Sweden	Husqvarna	26
4	Don Rickman	Great Britain	Metisse	26
5	Gunnar Johansson	Sweden	Lito	21
6	Ove Lundell	Sweden	Monark	10

Nine Rounds: Austria, France, Sweden, Italy, West Germany, Great Britain, Holland Belgium and Luxembourg. Best five scores to count.

1961

Posn	Rider	Country	Machine	Points
1	Sten Lundin	Sweden	Lito	48
2	Bill Nilsson	Sweden	Husqvarna	36
3	Gunnar Johansson	Sweden	Lito	25
4	Miroslav Soucek	Czechoslovakia	Eso	19
5	Rolf Tibblin	Sweden	Husqvarna	15
6	John Burton	Great Britain	BSA	13

Eleven Rounds: Switzerland, Austria, France, Czechoslovakia, Italy, Great Britain, Holland, Belgium, Sweden, Luxembourg, West Germany. Best six scores to count.

1962

Posn	Rider	Country	Machine	Points
1	Rolf Tibblin	Sweden	Husqvarna	46
2	Gunnar Johansson	Sweden	Lito	42
3	Sten Lundin	Sweden	Lito	27
4	Ove Lundell	Sweden	Monark	25
5	Bill Nilsson	Sweden	Lito	23
6	John Burton	Great Britain	BSA	14

Ten Rounds: Austria, France, Switzerland, Italy, Czechoslovakia, Great Britain, Holland Belgium, Luxembourg, Sweden. Best six scores to count.

1963

Posn	Rider	Country	Machine	Points
1	Rolf Tibblin	Sweden	Husqvarna	52
2	Sten Lundin	Sweden	Lito	46
3	Jeff Smith	Great Britain	BSA	44
4	Per-Olaf Persson	Sweden	Monark	20
5	Arthur Lampkin	Great Britain	BSA	18
6	Bill Nilsson	Sweden	Bilsson	17

Twelve Rounds: Austria, Switzerland, Denmark, Holland, France, Italy, Czechoslovakia Soviet Union, Great Britain, Belgium, Luxembourg, East Germany. Best seven scores to count.

1964

Posn	Rider	Country	Machine	Points
1	Jeff Smith	Great Britain	BSA	56
2	Rolf Tibblin	Sweden	Hedland	54
3	Sten Lundin	Sweden	Lito	34
4	Ove Lundell	Sweden	Husqvarna	22
5	Bill Nilsson	Sweden	Metisse	20
6	Per-Olaf Persson	Sweden	Husqvarna	15

Fourteen Rounds: Switzerland, Austria, Denmark, Sweden, Holland, France, Luxembourg, Italy, Czechoslovakia, Soviet Union, West Germany, Belgium, East Germany, Spain. Best six scores to count.

1965

Posn	Rider	Country	Machine	Points
1	Jeff Smith	Great Britain	BSA	54
2	Paul Friedrichs	East Germany	CZ	36
3	Rolf Tibblin	Sweden	CZ	32
4	Vic Eastwood	Great Britain	BSA	32
5	Sten Lundin	Sweden	Metisse	27
6	Per-Olaf Persson	Sweden	Hedlund	13

Thirteen Rounds: Austria, Switzerland, France, Finland, Sweden, East Germany, Czechoslovakia Soviet Union, Italy, Great Britain, West Germany, Holland, Luxembourg. Best seven scores to count.

1966

Posn	Rider	Country	Machine	Points
1	Paul Friedrichs	East Germany	CZ	62
2	Rolf Tibblin	Sweden	CZ	40
3	Jeff Smith	Great Britain	BSA	37
4	Vlastimil Valek	Czechoslovakia	Jawa	34
5	Dave Bickers	Great Britain	CZ	32
6	Jon Johansson	Sweden	Lindstrm	18

Fourteen Rounds: Switzerland, Austria, Italy, Denmark, Sweden, Finland, East Germany, Czechoslovakia, Soviet Union, Great Britain, Holland, Belgium, Luxembourg, West Germany. Best eight scores to count.

1967

Posn	Rider	Country	Machine	Points
1	Paul Friedrichs	East Germany	CZ	56

Posn	Rider	Country	Machine	Points
2	Jeff Smith	Great Britain	BSA	35
3	Dave Bickers	Great Britain	CZ	26
4	Vlastimil Valek	Czechoslovakia	CZ	26
5	Roger de Coster	Belgium	CZ	19
6	Gunnar Draugs	Soviet Union	CZ	16

Eleven Rounds: Austria, Italy, Sweden, Czechoslovakia, Soviet Union, France, West Germany, Great Britain, Belgium, Luxembourg, Switzerland. Best seven scores to count.

1968

Posn	Rider	Country	Machine	Points
1	Paul Friedrichs	East Germany	CZ	42
2	John Banks	Great Britain	BSA	41
3	Ake Jonsson	Sweden	Husqvarna	34
4	Bengt Aberg	Sweden	Husqvarna	29
5	Roger de Coster	Belgium	CZ	21
6	Vic Eastwood	Great Britain	Husqvarna	17

Thirteen Rounds: Austria, Italy, Sweden, Finland, East Germany, Czechoslovakia, Great Britain, West Germany, France, Holland, Belgium, Luxembourg Switzerland. Best seven scores to count.

1969

Posn	Rider	Country	Machine	Points
1	Bengt Aberg	Sweden	Husqvarna	94
2	John Banks	Great Britain	BSA	72
3	Paul Friedrichs	East Germany	CZ	67
4	Arne Kring	Sweden	Husqvarna	66
5	Roger de Coster	Belgium	CZ	65
6	Dave Nicoll	Great Britain	BSA	40

Eleven Rounds: Austria, Sweden, Holland, Italy, Czechoslovakia, Soviet Union, West Germany, Belgium, Luxembourg, France, Switzerland, East Germany. Best seven scores to count.

1970

Posn	Rider	Country	Machine	Points
1	Bengt Aberg	Sweden	Husqvarna	88
2	Arne King	Sweden	Husqvarna	80
3	Ake Jonsson	Sweden	Husqvarna	77
4	Paul Friedrichs	East Germany	CZ	60
5	Christer Hammargren	Sweden	Husqvarna	59
6	Adolf Weil	West Germany	Maico	55

Twelve Rounds: Switzerland, Austria, Holland, France, Finland, Sweden, Czechoslovakia, Soviet Union, West Germany, East Germany, Belgium, Luxembourg. Best seven scores to count.

SCORING VALUES
From 1952 to 1968 in the European and World 500cc Championships, scores were awarded as follows:– First Place 8 points; second 6 points; third 4 points; then 3,2 and 1 for fourth, fifth and sixth places. Similarly for the World and European 250cc Championships, 1958-68.
In 1969 this was changed to:– first 15 points; second 12 points; third 10 points; fourth 8 points; fifth 6 points; sixth 4 points, then 3,2, and 1 for seventh, eighth and ninth places.

WORLD 500CC CHAMPIONSHIP MAXIMUM SCORES

Year	Max	Winner	Score	+ or –
1957	40	Bill Nilsson	34	– 6
1958	48	René Baeten	42	– 6
1959	48	Sten Lundin	44	– 4
1960	40	Bill Nilsson	38	– 2
1961	48	Sten Lundin	48	Max
1962	48	Rolf Tibblin	46	– 2
1963	56	Rolf Tibblin	52	– 4
1964	56	Jeff Smith	56	Max
1965	56	Jeff Smith	54	– 2
1966	64	Paul Friedrichs	62	– 2
1967	56	Paul Friedrichs	56	Max
1968	56	Paul Friedrichs	42	– 14
1969	105	Bengt Aberg	94	– 11
1970	105	Bengt Aberg	88	– 17

WORLD 500 CC CHAMPIONSHIP GRAND PRIX VICTORIES BY WINNER

Year	Rider	Country	Number of GP Victories
1957	Bill Nilsson	Sweden	3
1958	René Baeten	Belgium	3
1959	Sten Lundin	Sweden	4
1960	Bill Bilsson	Sweden	3
1961	Sten Lundin	Sweden	6
1962	Rolf Tibblin	Sweden	5
1963	Rolf Tibblin	Sweden	5
1964	Jeff Smith	Great Britain	7
1965	Jeff Smith	Great Britain	6
1966	Paul Friedrichs	East Germany	7
1967	Paul Friedrichs	East Germany	7
1968	Paul Friedrichs	East Germany	4
1969	Bengt Aberg	Sweden	4
1970	Bengt Aberg	Sweden	4

EUROPEAN 250 CC CHAMPIONSHIP 1958–1961

There has always been some uncertainty about the origins of the European 250 cc Championship. At the 1956 Congress of the FIM in Paris, a competition was proposed for the Medal of the CSI, to be awarded to the winning rider in a series for 250 cc machines. The recommendation was received by delegates with mixed enthusiasm. Races took place in France, East Germany, Belgium, Holland, Austria, Italy and Luxembourg. There was no interest from Great Britain, and no English language records have apparently survived. Though, strictly speaking, the competition was not a formal European Championship, the Maico factory made much of the fact that Fritz Betzelbacher won the silver medal riding one of their machines, and declared him in their publicity as European Champion. Because the Maico factory went into temporary receivership at the end of 1957, their archives – despite much exhaustive research – have revealed little, except that the outcome of what was undoubtedly the forerunner of the European 250 cc Championship proper concluded as follows:–

Posn	Rider	Country	Machine	Points
1	Fritz Betzelbacher	West Germany	Maico	44
2	Willy Oesterle	West Germany	Maico	31
3	Jaromir Cizek	Czechoslovakia	Jawa	29

1958

Posn	Rider	Country	Machine	Points
1	Jaromir Cizek	Czechoslovakia	Jawa	56
2	Rolf Tibblin	Sweden	Husqvarna	27
3	Rolf Müller	West Germany	Maico	26
4	Karl Kamper	West Germany	Maico	20
5	Frantisek Ron	Czechoslovakia	Jawa	20
6	Lennart Dahlen	Sweden	Husqvarna	16

Twelve Rounds: Austria, Switzerland, France, Holland, Belgium, Luxembourg, Sweden, West Germany, Italy, Poland, Czechoslovakia, East Germany. Best Seven Scores to count

1959

Posn	Rider	Country	Machine	Points
1	Rolf Tibblin	Sweden	Husqvarna	51
2	Brian Stonebridge	Great Britain	Greeves	40
3	Jaromir Cizek	Czechoslovakia	Jawa	34
4	Jaroslav Knoch	Czechoslovakia	Jawa	29
5	Stig Rickardsson	Sweden	Husqvarna	23
6	Frantisek Ron	Czechoslovakia	Jawa	22

Thirteen Rounds: Austria, Switzerland, East Germany, Poland, Czechoslovakia, West Germany, Italy, France, Holland, Great Britain, Luxembourg, Sweden and Belgium. Best seven scores to count.

1960

Posn	Rider	Country	Machine	Points
1	Dave Bickers	Great Britain	Greeves	48
2	Jeff Smith	Great Britai	BSA	35
3	Miroslav Soucek	Czechoslovakia	Eso	26
4	Stig Rickardsson	Sweden	Husqvarna	25
5	Arthur Lampkin	Great Britain	BSA	25
6	Lennart Dahlen	Sweden	Husqvarna	25

Twelve Rounds: *Switzerland, Belgium, France, Czechoslovakia, Poland, Italy, East Germany, Finland, Luxembourg, Great Britain, Sweden, West Germany. Best seven scores to count.*

1961

Posn	Rider	Country	Machine	Points
1	Dave Bickers	Great Britain	Greeves	56
2	Arthur Lampkin	Great Britain	BSA	48
3	Jeff Smith	Great Britain	BSA	40
4	Torsten Hallman	Sweden	Husqvarna	33
5	Jaromir Cizek	Czechoslovakia	Jawa	21
6	Aarno Erola	Finland	Husqvarna	16

Thirteen Rounds: *Belgium, France, Holland, Soviet Union, Italy, Great Britain, Poland, Luxembourg, West Germany, Switzerland, Sweden, Finland, East Germany. Best seven scores to count.*

WORLD 250CC CHAMPIONSHIP 1962–1970

1962

Posn	Rider	Country	Machine	Points
1	Torsten Hallman	Sweden	Husqvarna	56
2	Jeff Smith	Great Britain	BSA	48
3	Arthur Lampkin	Great Britain	BSA	39
4	Vlastimil Valek	Czechoslovakia	CZ	31
5	Karel Pilar	Czechoslovakia	CZ	20
6	Aarno Erola	Finland	Husqvarna	11

Fifteen Rounds: *Spain, Switzerland, Belgium, France, Soviet Union, Poland, Holland, Luxembourg, Finland, West Germany, Italy, Great Britain, Sweden, East Germany, and Czechoslovakia. Best seven scores to count.*

1963

Posn	Rider	Country	Machine	Points
1	Torsten Hallman	Sweden	Husqvarna	56
2	Vlastimil Valek	Czechoslovakia	CZ	50
3	Igor Grigoriev	Soviet Union	CZ	32
4	Karel Pilar	Czechoslovakia	CZ	24
5	Jon Johansson	Sweden	Lindstrom	21
6	Cenneth Lööf	Sweden	Greeves/Husqvarna	13

Fourteen Rounds: *Spain, Italy, France, Switzerland, West Germany, Luxembourg, Holland, Great Britain, Sweden, Finland, Soviet Union, Poland, Czechoslovakia, East Germany. Best seven scores to count.*

1964

Posn	Rider	Country	Machine	Points
1	Joel Robert	Belgium	CZ	56
2	Torsten Hallman	Sweden	Husqvarna	50
3	Victor Arbekov	Soviet Union	CZ	31
4	Igor Grigoriev	Soviet Union	CZ	30
5	Dave Bickers	Great Britain	Greeves	23
6	Ake Jonsson	Sweden	Husqvarna	19

Fourteen Rounds: *Spain, Italy, France, Switzerland, West Germany, Belgium, Luxembourg, Great Britain, Sweden, Finland, Soviet Union, Poland, Czechoslovakia, East Germany. Best seven scores to count.*

1965

Posn	Rider	Country	Machine	Points
1	Victor Arbekov	Soviet Union	CZ	52
2	Joel Robert	Belgium	CZ	48
3	Dave Bickers	Great Britain	Greeves	42
4	Torsten Hallman	Sweden	Husqvarna	35
5	Ake Jonsson	Sweden	Husqvarna	30
6	Vlastimil Valek	Czechoslovakia	Jawa	26

Fifteen Rounds: *Spain, Italy, France, Belgium, Czechoslovakia, West Germany, Holland Luxembourg, Poland, Soviet Union, East Germany, Great Britain, Sweden, Finland, Austria. Best seven scores to count.*

1966

Posn	Rider	Country	Machine	Points
1	Torsten Hallman	Sweden	Husqvarna	58
2	Joel Robert	Belgium	CZ	49
3	Petr Dobry	Czechoslovakia	CZ	40
4	Victor Arbekov	Soviet Union	CZ	36
5	Olle Pettersson	Sweden	Husqvarna	29
6	Ake Jonsson	Sweden	Husqvarna	28

Fifteen Rounds: *Spain, France, Belgium, Switzerland, Czechoslovakia, West Germany, Holland, Luxembourg, Italy, Poland, East Germany, Sweden, Finland, Soviet Union, Austria. Best eight scores to count.*

1967

Posn	Rider	Country	Machine	Points
1	Torsten Hallman	Sweden	Husqvarna	52
2	Joel Robert	Belgium	CZ	50
3	Olle Pettersson	Sweden	Husqvarna	44
4	Victor Arbekov	Soviet Union	CZ	25
5	Jyrki Storm	Finland	Husqvarna	20
6	Hakan Andersson	Sweden	Husqvarna	13

Twelve Rounds: *Spain, Switzerland, France, Belgium, West Germany, Holland, Italy, Great Britain, Sweden, Finland, Soviet Union, Poland. Best seven scores to count.*

1968

Posn	Rider	Country	Machine	Points
1	Joel Robert	Belgium	CZ	54
2	Torsten Hallman	Sweden	Husqvarna	52
3	Sylvain Geboers	Belgium	CZ	31
4	Karel Konecny	Czechoslovakia	CZ	29
5	Dave Bickers	Great Britain	CZ	21
6	Hakan Andersson	Sweden	Husqvarna	18

Fourteen Rounds: *Spain, Belgium, Czechoslovakia, France, Holland, West Germany, Luxembourg, Poland, Soviet Union, Yugoslavia, Finland, Sweden, Great Britain, Austria. Best seven scores to count.*

1969

Posn	Rider	Country	Machine	Points
1	Joel Robert	Belgium	CZ	102
2	Sylvain Geboers	Belgium	CZ	96
3	Olle Pettersson	Sweden	Suzuki	71
4	Jiri Stodulka	Czechoslovakia	CZ	44
5	Karel Konecny	Czechoslovakia	CZ	38
6	Torsten Hallman	Sweden	Husqvarna	32

Twelve Rounds: *Spain, Switzerland, Yugoslavia Czechoslovakia, Poland, West Germany, Holland, France, Great Britain, Sweden, Finland, Soviet Union. Best seven scores to count.*

1970

Posn	Rider	Country	Machine	Points
1	Joel Robert	Belgium	Suzuki	96
2	Sylvain Geboers	Belgium	Suzuki	94
3	Roger de Coster	Belgium	CZ	74
4	Heikki Mikkola	Finland	Husqvarna	73
5	Miroslav Halm	Czechoslovakia	CZ	70
6	Uno Palm	Sweden	Husqvarna	43

Fourteen Rounds: *Spain, France, Belgium, Yugoslavia, Italy, Soviet Union, Poland, Great Britain, Finland, East Germany, Switzerland. Austria. Best seven scores to count.*

SCORING VALUES
From 1962 to 1968 in the European and World 250cc Championships, scores were awarded as follows:– First Place 8 points; second 6 points; third 4 points; then 3,2 and 1 for fourth, fifth and sixth places.

In 1969 this was changed to:– First 15 points; second 12 points; third 10 points; fourth 8 points; fifth 6 points; sixth 4 points, then 3,2, and 1 for seventh, eighth and ninth places.

BRITISH 500CC MOTO-CROSS GRAND PRIX 1952–1970

THE FIRST BRITISH 500CC GP NYMPSFIELD, 13 SEPTEMBER 1952

Posn	Rider	Country	Machine
1	Brian Stonebridge	Great Britain	Matchless
2	Phil Nex	Great Britain	BSA
3	Derek Rickman	Great Britain	BSA
4	Victor Leloup	Belgium	FN
5	Bud Ekins	USA	Matchless
6	Bill Barugh	Great Britain	DOT

One 10-lap race

THE SECOND BRITISH 500CC GP BRANDS HATCH, 5 JULY 1953

Posn	Rider	Country	Machine
1	Brian Stonebridge	Great Britain	Matchless
2	Basil Hall	Great Britain	BSA
3	Geoff Ward	Great Britain	AJS
4	Don Rickman	Great Britain	BSA
5	Monty Banks	Great Britain	BSA
6	Bob Manns	Great Britain	BSA

One 15-lap race

THE THIRD BRITISH 500CC GP HAWKSTONE PARK, 4 JULY 1954

Posn	Rider	Country	Machine
1	Phil Nex	Great Britain	BSA
2	Dave Curtis	Great Britain	BSA
3	David Tye	Great Britain	BSA
4	Les Archer	Great Britain	Norton
5	Terry Cheshire	Great Britain	BSA
6	Nic Jansen	Belgium	Saroléa

One 15-lap race

THE FOURTH BRITISH 500CC GP HAWKSTONE PARK, 3 JULY 1955

Posn	Rider	Country	Machine
1	Jeff Smith	Great Britain	BSA
2	John Draper	Great Britain	BSA
3	Brian Stonebridge	Great Britain	BSA
4	Les Archer	Great Britain	Norton
5	David Tye	Great Britain	BSA
6	Geoff Ward	Great Britain	AJS

HEAT ONE (10 Laps) *1, Smith; 2, Draper; 3, Stonebridge; 4, Terry Cheshire (Great Britain, BSA); 5, John Avery (Great Britain, BSA); 6, Archer*

HEAT TWO (10 Laps) *1, Smith; 2, Draper; 3, Ward; 4, Archer; 5, Stonebridge; 6, Basil Hall (Great Britain. Ariel).*

Elapsed time of both heats added together to decide the winner.

THE FIFTH BRITISH 500CC GP HAWKSTONE PARK, 7 JULY 1956

Posn	Rider	Country	Machine
1	Les Archer	Great Britain	Norton
2	John Draper	Great Britain	BSA
3	Nic Jansen	Belgium	Matchless
4	Terry Cheshire	Great Britain	BSA
5	Lars Gustafsson	Sweden	BSA
6	Brian Stonebridge	Great Britain	BSA

HEAT ONE (10 Laps) *1, Archer; 2, Geoff Ward (Great Britain, BSA); 3, Draper; 4, Sten Lundin (Sweden, BSA); 5, Jansen; 6, Stonebridge*

HEAT TWO (10 Laps) *1, Archer; 2, Smith; 3, Jansen; 4, Draper; 5, Cheshire; 6, Gustafsson*

THE SIXTH BRITISH 500CC GP HAWKSTONE PARK, 7 JULY 1957

Posn	Rider	Country	Machine
1	Jeff Smith	Great Britain	BSA
2	Les Archer	Great Britain	Norton
3	Broer Dirks	Holland	BSA
4	Sten Lundin	Sweden	Monark
5	Bill Nilsson	Sweden	AJS
6	Nic Jansen	Belgium	Matchless

HEAT ONE (10 Laps) *1, Smith; 2, Archer; 3, Dirks; 4, Nilsson; 5, Dave Curtis (Great Britain, Matchless); 6, Jansen*

HEAT TWO (10 Laps) *1, Smith; 2, Archer; 3, Lundin; 4, Dirks; 5, René Baeten (Belgium, FN); 6, Gustafsson*

THE SEVENTH BRITISH 500CC GP HAWKSTONE PARK, 6 JULY 1958

Posn	Rider	Country	Machine
1	Lars Gustafsson	Sweden	Monark
2	René Baeten	Belgium	FN
3	Don Rickman	Great Britain	BSA
4	Brian Martin	Great Britain	BSA
5	Mogens Rasmussen	Denmark	Matchless
6	Joep Jansen	Holland	BSA

No other riders were classified as finishers

HEAT ONE (12 Laps) *1, Gustafsson; 2, Don Rickman; 3, B Nilsson (Sweden, Crescent); 4, Broer Dirks (Holland, BSA); 5, Baeten; 6, Hubert Scaillet (Belgium, FN)*
HEAT TWO (12 Laps) *1, Baeten; 2, Gustafsson; 3, Jeff Smith (Great Britain, BSA); 4, Martin; 5, John Draper (Great Britain, BSA); 6, Don Rickman*

THE EIGHTH BRITISH 500CC GP HAWKSTONE PARK, 5 JULY 1959

Posn	Rider	Country	Machine
1	Jeff Smith	Great Britain	BSA
2	Dave Curtis	Great Britain	Matchless
3	Don Rickman	Great Britain	Metisse
4	Broer Dirks	Holland	BSA
5	John Draper	Great Britain	BSA
6	Lars Gustafsson	Sweden	Monark

HEAT ONE (12 Laps) *1, Smith; 2, Curtis; 3, Don Rickman; 4, Dirks; 5, Draper; 6, Ron Langston (Great Britain, Ariel)*

HEAT TWO (12 Laps) *1, Curtis; 2, Smith; 3, Don Rickman; 4, Tibblin; 5, Draper; 6, Dirks*

THE NINTH BRITISH 500CC GP HAWKSTONE PARK, 3 JULY 1960

Posn	Rider	Country	Machine
1	Bill Nilsson	Sweden	Husqvarna
2	Don Rickman	Great Britain	Metisse
3	Gunnar Johansson	Sweden	Lito
4	Arthur Lampkin	Great Britain	BSA
5	Jeff Smith	Great Britain	BSA
6	Rolf Tibblin	Sweden	Husqvarna

HEAT ONE (12 Laps) *1, Nilsson; 2, Don Rickman; 3, Lampkin; 4, Johansson; 5, Lundin; 6, Tibblin. Only the first four finishers completed 12 laps*

HEAT TWO (14 Laps) *1, Nilsson; 2, Smith; 3, Don Rickman; 4, Johansson; 5, Broer Dirks (Holland, BSA); 6, Tibblin. Only the first seven finishers completed 14 laps*

THE TENTH BRITISH 500CC GP HAWKSTONE PARK, 2 JULY 1961

Posn	Rider	Country	Machine
1	Dave Curtis	Great Britain	Matchless
2	Lars Gustafsson	Sweden	Monark
3	Gunnar Johansson	Sweden	Lito
4	John Burton	Great Britain	BSA
5	John Harris	Great Britain	BSA
6	Roger Vanderbecken	Belgium	Triumph

HEAT ONE (12 Laps) *1, Curtis; 2, Gustafsson; 3, Don Rickman (Great Britain Metisse); 4, Johansson; 5, Broer Dirks (Holland BSA); 6, Burton*

HEAT TWO (12 Laps) *1, Curtis; 2, Johansson; 3, Gustafsson; 4, Burton; 5, Les Archer (Great Britain, Norton); 6, Rolf Tibblin (Sweden, Husqvarna)*

THE ELEVENTH BRITISH 500CC GP HAWKSTONE PARK, 1 JULY 1962

Posn	Rider	Country	Machine
1	Rolf Tibblin	Sweden	Husqvarna
2	Gunnar Johansson	Sweden	Lito
3	Don Rickman	Great Britain	Metisse
4	Per-Olaf Persson	Sweden	Monark
5	Dave Bickers	Great Britain	Matchless
6	Gordon Blakeway	Great Britain	Triumph

HEAT ONE (12 Laps) *1, Tibblin; 2, Don Rickman; 3, Johansson; 4, B Nilsson (Sweden, Bilsson); 5, Derek Rickman (Great Britain, Metisse); 6, Persson*
HEAT TWO (12 Laps) *1, Tibblin; 2, Johansson; 3, Don Rickman; 4, Roger Vanderbecken (Belgium, Triumph); 5, Bickers; 6, Persson*

THE TWELFTH BRITISH 500CC GP HAWKSTONE PARK, 7 JULY 1963

Posn	Rider	Country	Machine
1	Jeff Smith	Great Britain	BSA
2	Arthur Lampkin	Great Britain	BSA
3	Derek Rickman	Great Britain	Metisse
4	Mogens Rasmussen	Denmark	Matchless
5	Chris Horsfield	Great Britain	Matchless
6	Walter Baeten	Belgium	Jawa

HEAT ONE (12 Laps) *1, Smith; 2, R Tibblin (Sweden, Husqvarna); 3, Lampkin; 4, Derek Rickman; 5, Vic Eastwood (Great Britain, Matchless); 6, Horsfield*

HEAT TWO (12 Laps) *1, Don Rickman (Great Britain, Metisse); 2, Smith; 3, Lampkin; 4, Derek Rickman; 5, Rasmussen; 6, Baeten*

THE THIRTEENTH BRITISH 500CC GP HAWKSTONE PARK, 4 JULY 1965

Posn	Rider	Country	Machine
1	Jeff Smith	Great Britain	BSA
2	Rolf Tibblin	Sweden	CZ
3	Vic Eastwood	Great Britain	BSA
4	Arthur Lampkin	Great Britain	BSA
5	John Giles	Great Britain	Triumph
6	Jerry Scott	Great Britain	BSA

HEAT ONE (12 Laps) *1, Smith; 2, Eastwood; 3, Tibblin; 4, Lampkin; 5, Giles; 6, Scott.*

HEAT TWO (12 Laps) *1, Tibblin; 2, Smith; 3, Eastwood; 4, Don Rickman (Great Britain, Metisse); 5, Lampkin; 6, Giles.*

THE FOURTEENTH BRITISH 500CC GP FARLEIGH CASTLE, 3 JULY 1966

Posn	Rider	Country	Machine
1	Don Rickman	Great Britain	Metisse
2	Jeff Smith	Great Britain	BSA
3	Chris Horsfield	Great Britain	CZ
4	Dave Bickers	Great Britain	CZ
5	Vic Eastwood	Great Britain	BSA
6	Jan Johansson	Sweden	Lindström

HEAT ONE (16 Laps) *1, Rickman; 2, Smith; 3, Vlastimil Valek (Czechoslovakia, Jawa); 4, Horsfield; 5, Bickers; 6, Johansson*

HEAT TWO (16 Laps) *1, Smith; 2, Rickman; 3, Eastwood; 4, Horsfield; 5, Bickers; 6, Johansson*

THE FIFTEENTH BRITISH 500CC GP FARLEIGH CASTLE, 30 JULY 1967

Posn	Rider	Country	Machine
1	Paul Friedrichs	East Germany	CZ
2	Dave Bickers	Great Britain	CZ
3	Jeff Smith	Great Britain	BSA
4	Vlastimil Valek	Czechoslovakia	Jawa
5	Bill Nilsson	Sweden	Husqvarna
6	Arthur Lampkin	Great Britain	BSA

HEAT ONE (20 Laps) *1, Friedrichs; 2, Vic Eastwood (Great Britain, BSA); 3, Don Rickman (Great Britain, Metisse); 4, Smith; 5, Valek; 6, Bickers*

HEAT TWO (20 Laps) *1, Bickers; 2, Friedrichs; 3, Smith; 4, Valek; 5, Nilsson; 6, Lampkin*

THE SIXTEENTH BRITISH 500CC GP FARLEIGH CASTLE, 7 JULY 1968

Posn	Rider	Country	Machine
1	Vic Eastwood	Great Britain	Husqvarna
2	Petr Dobry	Czechoslovakia	CZ
3	Christer Hammargren	Sweden	Husqvarna
4	Dave Bickers	Great Britain	CZ
5	Roger de Coster	Belgium	CZ
6	Ake Jonsson	Sweden	Husqvarna

HEAT ONE (40 minutes, plus 2 laps) *1, Eastwood; 2, Hammargren; 3, Dobry; 4, Bickers; 5, De Coster; 6, Smith*

HEAT TWO (30 minutes, plus 2 laps) *1, Jonsson; 2, Eastwood; 3, Dobry; 4, Bickers; 5, Hammargren; 6, De Coster*

THE SEVENTEENTH BRITISH 500CC GP FARLEIGH CASTLE, 31 AUGUST 1970

Posn	Rider	Country	Machine
1	Bengt Aberg	Sweden	Husqvarna
2	Rob Taylor	Great Britain	Husqvarna
3	Ake Jonsson	Sweden	Maico
4	Jaak van Velthoven	Belgium	Husqvarna
5	Jan Johansson	Sweden	Husqvarna
6	Roger de Coster	Belgium	CZ

HEAT ONE *1, Aberg; 2, Taylor; 3, Hakan Andersson (Sweden, Husqvarna); 4, Arne King (Sweden, Husqvarna); 5, Keith Hickman (Great Britain, BSA); 6, Jonsson*

HEAT TWO *1, Aberg; 2, Taylor; 3, Johansson; 4, Jonsson; 5, Kring; 6, Van Velthoven*

HEAT THREE *1, Aberg; 2, Bryan Wade (Great Britain, Husqvarna); 3, Hickman; 4, Van Velthoven; 5, Andy Roberton (Great Britain, AJS); 6, Jonsson*

This event did not count towards the World 500cc Championship.

BRITISH 250CC MOTO-CROSS GRAND PRIX 1958–1970

THE FIRST BRITISH 250CC GP
BEENHAM PARK, 15 JUNE 1958

Posn	Rider	Country	Machine
1	Jaromir Cizek	Czechoslovakia	CZ
2	Brian Stonebridge	Great Britain	Greeves
3	Triss Sharp	Great Britain	Francis Barnett
4	Brian Leask	Great Britain	Greeves
5	Frantisek Ron	Czechoslovakia	Jawa
6	Roy King	Great Britain	Greeves

HEAT ONE1 (15 Laps) 1, Stonebridge; 2, Cizek; 3, Ron; 4, Sharp; 5, Pat Lamper (Great Britain, Greeves), 6, Leask.

HEAT TWO(15 Laps) 1, Cizek; 2, Dave Bickers (Great Britain, Greeves); 3, Fritz Betzelbacher (West Germany, Maico); 4, Stonebridge; 5, Sharp; 6, Leask

THE SECOND BRITISH 250CC GP
BEENHAM PARK, 19 JULY 1959

Posn	Rider	Country	Machine
1	Rolf Tibblin	Sweden	Husqvarna
2	Jeff Smith	Great Britain	BSA
3	Frantisek Ron	Czechoslovakia	Jawa
4	Dave Bickers	Great Britain	Greeves
5	John Draper	Great Britain	BSA
6	Brian Stonebridge	Great Britain	Greeves

HEAT ONE (15 Laps) 1, Tibblin; 2, Draper; 3, Stonebridge; 4, Bickers; 5, Ron; 6, Smith.

HEAT TWO (15 Laps)1, Tibblin; 2, Smith; 3, Ron; 4, Bickers; 5, Draper; 6, Lennart Dahlen (Sweden, Husqvarna).

THE THIRD BRITISH 250CC GP
SHRUBLAND PARK, 17 JULY 1960

Posn	Rider	Country	Machine
1	Jeff Smith	Great Britain	BSA
2	Sivert Eriksson	Sweden	Husqvarna
3	Vlastimil Valek	Czechoslovakia	CZ
4	Stig Rickardsson	Sweden	Husqvarna
5	Bryan Sharp	Great Britain	Greeves
6	Arthur Lampkin	Great Britain	BSA

HEAT ONE (15 Laps) 1, Smith; 2, Rickardsson; 3, Lampkin; 4, Lennart Dahlen (Sweden, Husqvarna); 5, Miroslav Souceck (Czechoslovakia, Eso); 6, Eriksson.

HEAT TWO (15 Laps) 1, Dave Bickers (Great Britain, Greeves); 2, Smith; 3, Eriksson; 4, Valek; 5, Triss Sharp (Great Britain, Greeves); 6, Bryan Sharp.

THE FOURTH BRITISH 250CC GP
SHRUBLAND PARK, 16 JULY 1961

Posn	Rider	Country	Machine
1	Dave Bickers	Great Britain	Greeves
2	Arthur Lampkin	Great Britain	BSA
3	Torsten Hallman	Sweden	Husqvarna
4	Aarno Erola	Finland	Husqvarna
5	Jaromir Cizek	Czechoslovakia	Jawa
6	John Draper	Great Britain	Cotton

HEAT ONE (15 Laps) 1, Bickers; 2, Lampkin; 3, Hallman; 4, Don Rickman (Great Britain, Greeves); 5, Erola; 6, Cizek.

HEAT TWO (15 Laps) 1, Bickers; 2, Lampkin; 3, Erola; 4, Hallman; 5, Töre Lundby (Norway, Husqvarna); 6, Cizek.

THE FIFTH BRITISH 250CC GP
WICK, GLASTONBURY, 15 JULY 1962

Posn	Rider	Country	Machine
1	Dave Bickers	Great Britain	Greeves
2	Torsten Hallman	Sweden	Husqvarna
3	Vlastimil Valek	Czechoslovakia	CZ
4	Alan Clough	Great Britain	Greeves
5	Don Rickman	Great Britain	Metisse
6	Jeff Smith	Great Britain	BSA

HEAT ONE (15 Laps) 1, Bickers; 2, Hallman; 3, Rickman; 4, Valek; 5, Clough; 6, Bryan Sharp (Great Britain, Greeves).

HEAT TWO (15 Laps) 1, Bickers; 2, Hallman; 3, Smith; 4, Clough; 5, Valek; 6, Aarno Erola (Finland, Husqvarna).

THE SIXTH BRITISH 250CC GP
SHRUBLAND PARK, 16 JUNE 1963

Posn	Rider	Country	Machine
1	Torsten Hallman	Sweden	Husqvarna
2	Vlastimil Valek	Czechoslovakia	CZ
3	Don Rickman	Great Britain	Metisse
4	Cenneth Lööf	Sweden	Husqvarna
5	Karel Pilar	Czechoslovakia	CZ
6	Jan Johansson	Sweden	Lindström

HEAT ONE (15 Laps) 1, Hallman; 2, Valek; 3, John Banks (Great Britain, DOT); 4, Loof; 5, Johansson; 6, John Griffiths (Great Britain, DOT)

HEAT TWO (15 Laps) 1, Hallman; 2, Rickman; 3, Valek; 4, Pilar; 5, Lööf; 6, Sivert Eriksson (Sweden, Husqvarna)

THE SEVENTH BRITISH 250CC GP
CADWELL PARK, LINCOLNSHIRE, 30 JUNE 1964

Posn	Rider	Country	Machine
1	Joel Robert	Belgium	CZ
2	Dave Bickers	Great Britain	Greeves
3	Malcolm Davis	Great Britain	Greeves
4	Bryan Goss	Great Britain	Greeves
5	Derek Rickman	Great Britain	Metisse
6	Frits Selling	Holland	Greeves

HEAT ONE (18 Laps) 1, Bickers; 2, Robert; 3, Hallman; 4, Goss; 5, Davis; 6, Karel Pilar (Czechoslovakia, CZ)

HEAT TWO (18 Laps) 1, Robert; 2, Bickers; 3, Vlastimil Valek (Czechoslovakia, Jawa); 4, Alan Clough (Great Britain, Greeves); 5, Malcolm Davis (Great Britain, Greeves); 6, Goss.

THE EIGHTH BRITISH 250CC GP
WICK, GLASTONBURY, 18 JULY 1965

Posn	Rider	Country	Machine
1	Dave Bickers	Great Britain	Greeves
2	Don Rickman	Great Britain	Metisse
3	Vlastimil Valek	Czechoslovakia	Jawa
4	Ake Jonsson	Sweden	Husqvarna
5	Karel Pilar	Czechoslovakia	CZ
6	Frits Selling	Holland	Greeves

HEAT ONE (16 Laps) 1, Bickers; 2, Rickman; 3, Valek; 4, Jonsson; 5, Pilar; 6, Malcolm Davis (Great Britain, Greeves)

HEAT TWO (16 Laps) 1, Joel Robert (Belgium, CZ); 2, Bickers; 3, Rickman; 4, Jonsson; 5, Valek; 6, Pilar.

THERE WAS NO BRITISH 250CC GRAND PRIX IN 1966

THE NINTH BRITISH 250CC GP WAKES COLNE, HALSTEAD, ESSEX, 11 JULY 1967

Posn	Rider	Country	Machine
1	Joel Robert	Belgium	CZ
2	Victor Arbekov	Soviet Union	CZ
3	Olle Pettersson	Sweden	Husqvarna
4	Hakan Andersson	Sweden	Husqvarna
5	Jyrki Storm	Finland	Husqvarna
6	Andy Roberton	Great Britain	Cotton

HEAT ONE (20 Laps) *1, Robert; 2, Arbekov; 3, Bryan Wade (Great Britain, Greeves); 4, Pettersson; 5, Andersson; 6, Storm.*

HEAT TWO (20 Laps) *1, Robert; 2, Pettersson; 3, Torsten Hallman (Sweden, Husqvarna); 4, Arbekov; 5, Andersson; 6, Zdenek Strnad (Czechoslovakia, CZ)*

THE TENTH BRITISH 250CC GP DODINGTON PARK, GLOUCESTERSHIRE, 11 AUGUST 1968

Posn	Rider	Country	Machine
1	Joel Robert	Belgium	CZ
2	Torsten Hallman	Sweden	Husqvarna
3	Dave Bickers	Great Britain	CZ
4	Karel Konecny	Czechoslovakia	CZ
5	Bryan Wade	Great Britain	Greeves
6	Vic Allan	Great Britain	Greeves

HEAT ONE – 40 Minutes plus Two Laps (16 Laps) *1, Robert; 2, Hallman; 3, Bickers; 4, Wade; 5, Konecny; 6, Allan.*

HEAT TWO – 40 Minutes plus Two Laps (16 Laps) *1, Robert; 2, Hallman; 3, Konecny; 4, Bickers; 5, Wade; 6, Jyrki Storm (Finland, Husqvarna)*

THE ELEVENTH BRITISH 250CC GP DODINGTON PARK, GLOUCESTERSHIRE, 29 JUNE 1969

Posn	Rider	Country	Machine
1	Sylvain Geboers	Belgium	CZ
2	Dave Bickers	Great Britain	CZ
3	Jiri Stodulka	Czechoslovakia	CZ
4	Arthur Browning	Great Britain	Greeves
5	Zdenek Strnad	Czechoslovakia	CZ
6	Bryan Goss	Great Britain	Husqvarna

HEAT ONE– 40 Minutes plus Two Laps (16 Laps) *1, Geboers; 2, Stodulka; 3, Goss; 4, Bickers; 5, Strnad; 6, Browning*

HEAT TWO– 40 Minutes plus Two Laps (16 Laps) *1, Bickers; 2, Browning; 3, Geboers; 4, Olle Pettersson (Sweden, Suzuki); 5, Chris Horsfield (Great Britain, Bultaco); 6, Stodulka*

THE TWELFTH BRITISH 250 CC GP DODINGTON PARK, GLOUCESTERSHIRE, 28 JUNE 1970

Posn	Rider	Country	Machine
1	Joel Robert	Belgium	Suzuki
2	Roger de Coster	Belgium	CZ
3	Miroslav Halm	Czechoslovakia	CZ
4	Thorleif Hansen	Sweden	Husqvarna
5	Heikki Mikkola	Finland	Husqvarna
6	Torsten Hallman	Sweden	Husqvarna

HEAT ONE – 40 Minutes plus Two Laps (17 Laps) *1, Robert; 2, Sylvain Geboers (Belgium, Suzuki), 3, De Coster; 4, Halm; 5, Mikkola; 6, Olle Pettersson (Sweden, Suzuki)*

HEAT TWO – 40 Minutes plus Two Laps (17 Laps) *1, Robert; 2, De Coster; 3, Hansen; 4, Halm; 5, Hallman; 6, Mikkola*

MOTO-CROSS DES NATIONS

1947 HOLLAND, DUINRELL, 27 JULY

HEAT ONE

Posn	Rider	Country	Machine
1	Bill Nicholson	Great Britain	BSA
2	Jack Stocker	Great Britain	Ariel
3	Auguste Mingels	Belgium	Triumph
4	H Veer Jnr	Holland	Triumph
5	Hugh Viney	Great Britain	AJS
6	J Frenay	Belgium	Gillet

HEAT TWO

Posn	Rider	Country	Machine
1	Mingels		
2	Marcel Meunier	Belgium	Triumph
3	Viney		
4	Nicholson		
5	Eddie Bessant	Great Britain	Matchless
6	Colin Edge	Great Britain	Matchless

FINAL PLACINGS DECIDED ON AGGREGATE TIME FOR BOTH HEATS

1 GREAT BRITAIN A *Nicholson; Fred Rist (BSA); Bob Ray (Ariel)*

2 BELGIUM B *Meunier; Frenay; V Govaerts (Gillet)*

3 BELGIUM A *Mingels; A Van Hove (AJS); L Delhaes (AJS)*

1948 BELGIUM, LA FRAINEUSE, SPA, 8 AUGUST

HEAT ONE

Posn	Rider	Country	Machine
1	Nic Jansen	Belgium	BSA
2	André Milhoux	Belgium	BSA
3	Marcel Spiroux	Belgium	BSA
4	Ted Ogden	Great Britain	Norton
5	Basil Hall	Great Britain	Matchless
6	F Pairiot	Belgium	Gillet

HEAT TWO

Posn	Rider	Country	Machine
1	Marcel Meunier	Belgium	Triumph
2	Bill Nicholson	Great Britain	BSA
3	Marcel Cox	Belgium	Triumph
4	Hugh Viney	Great Britain	AJS
5	Jim Alves	Great Britain	Triumph
6	Geoff Duke	Great Britain	Norton

FINAL
1 Jansen   4 Duke
2 Cox   5 Milhoux
3 Viney   6 Hall

TEAM PLACINGS

1 BELGIUM *Jansen; Cox; Milhoux*

2 GREAT BRITAIN *Viney; Duke; Hall*

No other team finished intact

1949 GREAT BRITAIN, BRANDS HATCH, 28 AUGUST

HEAT ONE (12 Laps)

Posn	Rider	Country	Machine
1	Basil Hall	Great Britain	Matchless
2	Auguste Mingels	Belgium	FN
3	F Pairiot	Belgium	Saroléa
4	Jim Alves	Great Britain	Triumph
5	Marcel Meunier	Belgium	Triumph
6	Ray Scovell	Great Britain	BSA

HEAT TWO (12 Laps)

Posn	Rider	Country	Machine
1	Nic Jansen	Belgium	Saroléa
2	Harold Lines	Great Britain	Ariel
3	Bill Nicholson	Great Britain	BSA

195

4	F Thomas	Belgium	FN
5	André Milhoux	Belgium	BSA
6	S Guilly	Belgium	Saroléa

FINAL (15 Laps)

Posn	Rider	Country	Machine
1	Lines		
2	Jansen		
3	Hendrik Rietman	Holland	BSA
4	Bob Manns	Great Britain	Triumph
5	Scovell		
6	Olle Nygren	Sweden	BSA

TEAM PLACINGS
1. GREAT BRITAIN Lines; Manns; Scovell
2. BELGIUM Jansen; Victor Leloup (FN); R Pickart (BSA)
3. SWEDEN Nygren; L Carlstrom (Ariel); B Hasselrot (AJS)

No other team finished intact

1950 SWEDEN, SKILLINGARYD, VÄRNAMO, 27 AUGUST

HEAT ONE (12 Laps)

Posn	Rider	Country	Machine
1	Basil Hall	Great Britain	BSA
2	John Avery	Great Britain	BSA
3	Bill Nicholson	Great Britain	BSA
4	Auguste Mingels	Belgium	FN
5	John Draper	Great Britain	BSA
6	E Eriksson	Sweden	Triumph

HEAT TWO (12 Laps)

Posn	Rider	Country	Machine
1	Harold Lines	Great Britain	Ariel
2	Brian Stonebridge	Great Britain	Matchless
3	Olle Nygren	Sweden	BSA
4	Geoff Ward	Great Britain	AJS
5	S Guilly	Belgium	Saroléa
6	Don Evans	Great Britain	Ariel

FINAL (17 Laps)

Posn	Rider	Country	Machine
1	Draper		
2	Hall		
3	Hendrik Rietman	Holland	Saroléa
4	Lines		
5	Ward		
6	Nicholson		

TEAM PLACINGS
1. GREAT BRITAIN
   Draper; Hall; Lines
2. SWEDEN
   Nygren; Eriksson; H Brinkeback (Ariel)
3. BELGIUM Marcel Cox (Saroléa); A Meert (Saroléa); Victor Leloup (FN)

No other team finished intact

1951 BELGIUM, NAMUR, 5 AUGUST

HEAT ONE (7 Laps)

Posn	Rider	Country	Machine
1	John Draper	Great Britain	BSA
2	Nic Jansen	Belgium	Saroléa
3	A Meert	Belgium	Saroléa
4	Bill Nicholson	Great Britain	BSA
5	Harold Lines	Great Britain	Ariel
6	S Guilly	Belgium	Saroléa

HEAT TWO (7 Laps)

Posn	Rider	Country	Machine
1	Marcel Meunier	Belgium	Saroléa
2	Phil Nex	Great Britain	BSA
3	Les Archer	Great Britain	Norton
4	A van Heuverswijn	Belgium	Saroléa
5	René Baeten	Belgium	Saroléa
6	Victor Leloup	Belgium	FN

FINAL (11 Laps)

Posn	Rider	Country	Machine
1	Leloup		
2	Jansen		
3	Meunier		
4	Brian Stonebridge	Great Britain	Matchless
5	Geoff Ward	Great Britain	AJS
6	Draper		

TEAM PLACINGS
1. BELGIUM Leloup; Jansen; Meunier
2. GREAT BRITAIN Stonebridge; Ward; Draper
3. FRANCE G Brassine (FN); H Frantz (BSA); J Charrier (BSA)

No other team finished intact

1952 GREAT BRITAIN BRANDS HATCH, 17 AUGUST

ONE RACE (15 Laps)

Posn	Rider	Country	Machine
1	Brian Stonebridge	Great Britain	Matchless
2	Auguste Mingels	Belgium	Matchless
3	Geoff Ward	Great Britain	AJS
4	Phil Nex	Great Britain	BSA
5	Victor Leloup	Belgium	FN
6	John Avery	Great Britain	BSA

TEAM PLACINGS
1. GREAT BRITAIN Stonebridge; Ward; Nex
2. BELGIUM Mingels; Leloup; A van Heuverswijn (Saroléa)
3. SWEDEN E Bergman (Matchless); H Danielson (BSA); K Johansson (BSA)

1953 SWEDEN, SKILLINGARYD, VÄRNAMO, 23 AUGUST

HEAT ONE (12 Laps)

Posn	Rider	Country	Machine
1	K Johansson	Sweden	BSA
2	Lars Gustafsson	Sweden	BSA
3	John Draper	Great Britain	BSA
4	C Carlsson	Sweden	Ariel
5	Les Archer	Great Britain	Norton
6	L Donnay	Belgium	FN

HEAT TWO (12 Laps)

Posn	Rider	Country	Machine
1	René Baeten	Belgium	Saroléa
2	Geoff Ward	Great Britain	AJS
3	Nic Jansen	Belgium	Saroléa
4	Brian Stonebridge	Great Britain	Matchless
5	Phil Nex	Great Britain	BSA
6	Bill Nilsson	Sweden	AJS

FINAL (17 Laps)

Posn	Rider	Country	Machine
1	Archer		
2	Auguste Mingels	Belgium	FN
3	Baeten		
4	Draper		
5	Ward		
6	Gustafsson		

TEAM PLACINGS
1. GREAT BRITAIN Archer; Draper; Ward
2. BELGIUM Mingels; Baeten; Victor Leloup (FN)
3. SWEDEN Gustafsson; Johansson; Nilsson

1954 HOLLAND, NÖRG, NR ASSEN, 29 AUGUST

HEAT ONE (9 Laps)

Posn	Rider	Country	Machine
1	Frans Baudoin	Holland	Matchless
2	Les Archer	Great Britain	Norton
3	Nic Jansen	Belgium	Saroléa
4	Brian Stonebridge	Great Britain	BSA
5	Dave Curtis	Great Britain	Matchless
6	Lars Gustafsson	Sweden	BSA

HEAT TWO (9 Laps)
Posn	Rider	Country	Machine
1	Hendrik Rietman	Holland	BSA
2	René Baeten	Belgium	Saroléa
3	Geoff Ward	Great Britain	AJS
4	Phil Nex	Great Britain	BSA
5	Jean Somja	Belgium	FN
6	K Carlsson	Sweden	BSA

FINAL (14 Laps)
Posn	Rider	Country	Machine
1	Bill Nilsson	Sweden	BSA
2	Ward		
3	Stonebridge		
4	Rietman		
5	Curtis		
6	K Johansson	Sweden	BSA

TEAM PLACINGS
1. GREAT BRITAIN *Ward; Stonebridge; Curtis*
2. SWEDEN *Nilsson; Johansson; G Eriksson (Ariel)*
3. BELGIUM *Victor Leloup (FN); A van Heuverswijn (Saroléa); Jansen*

1955 DENMARK, RANDERS, 28 AUGUST

HEAT ONE (10 Laps)
Posn	Rider	Country	Machine
1	Bill Nilsson	Sweden	BSA
2	Brian Stonebridge	Great Britain	BSA
3	Les Archer	Great Britain	Norton
4	Sten Lundin	Sweden	BSA
5	Hendrik Rietman	Holland	FN
6	Frans Baudoin	Holland	Matchless

HEAT TWO (10 Laps)
Posn	Rider	Country	Machine
1	Jeff Smith	Great Britain	BSA
2	Lars Gustafsson	Sweden	BSA
3	Gunnar Johansson	Sweden	BSA
4	Jan Clynk	Holland	BSA
5	Geoff Ward	Great Britain	AJS
6	René Baeten	Belgium	Matchless

FINAL (20 Laps)
Posn	Rider	Country	Machine
1	Smith		
2	Nilsson		
3	Baeten		
4	Lundin		
5	Gustafsson		
6	Victor Leloup	Belgium	FN

TEAM PLACINGS
1. SWEDEN *Nilsson; Lundin; Gustafsson*

No other team finished intact

1956 BELGIUM, NAMUR, 26 AUGUST

HEAT ONE (7 Laps)
Posn	Rider	Country	Machine
1	Les Archer	Great Britain	Norton
2	Bill Nilsson	Sweden	BSA
3	Lars Gustafsson	Sweden	BSA
4	Hubert Scaillet	Belgium	FN
5	Ove Lundell	Sweden	Monark
6	Auguste Mingels	Belgium	FN

HEAT TWO (7 Laps)
Posn	Rider	Country	Machine
1	Geoff Ward	Great Britain	BSA
2	Jeff Smith	Great Britain	BSA
3	Sten Lundin	Sweden	BSA
4	John Draper	Great Britain	BSA
5	Jan Clynk	Holland	Matchless
6	Gunnar Johansson	Sweden	BSA

FINAL (11 Laps)
Posn	Rider	Country	Machine
1	Smith		
2	Lundin		
3	René Baeten	Belgium	FN
4	Gustafsson		
5	Ward		
6	Draper		

TEAM PLACINGS
1. GREAT BRITAIN *Smith; Ward; Draper*
2. SWEDEN *Lundin; Gustafsson; Johansson*
3. BELGIUM *Baeten; Jean Rombauts (BSA); Nic Jansen (Matchless)*

No other team finished intact

1957 GREAT BRITAIN, BRANDS HATCH, 1 SEPTEMBER

HEAT ONE (8 Laps)
Posn	Rider	Country	Machine
1	Derek Rickman	Great Britain	BSA
2	Dave Curtis	Great Britain	Matchless
3	Brian Martin	Great Britain	BSA
4	Nic Jansen	Belgium	Matchless
5	Hubert Scaillet	Belgium	FN
6	Bill Nilsson	Sweden	AJS

HEAT TWO (8 Laps)
Posn	Rider	Country	Machine
1	John Draper	Great Britain	BSA
2	Jeff Smith	Great Britain	BSA
3	Lucien Donnay	Belgium	FN
4	Jan Rombauts	Belgium	BSA
5	Broer Dirks	Holland	BSA
6	René Baeten	Belgium	FN

FINAL (15 Laps)
Posn	Rider	Country	Machine
1	Smith		
2	Curtis		
3	Baeten		
4	Gunnar Johansson	Sweden	BSA
5	Jansen		
6	Scaillet		

TEAM PLACINGS
1. GREAT BRITAIN *Smith; Curtis; Martin*
2. BELGIUM *Baeten; Jansen; Scaillet*
3. SWEDEN *Johansson; Ove Lundell (Monark); Ray Sigvardsson (AJS)*

No other team finished intact

1958 SWEDEN, KNUTSTORP, 8 SEPTEMBER

HEAT ONE (10 Laps)
Posn	Rider	Country	Machine
1	Bill Nilsson	Sweden	Crescent
2	René Baeten	Belgium	FN
3	John Draper	Great Britain	BSA
4	Lars Gustafsson	Sweden	Monark
5	Ray Sigvardsson	Sweden	AJS
6	Derek Rickman	Great Britain	BSA

HEAT TWO (10 Laps)
Posn	Rider	Country	Machine
1	Ove Lundell	Sweden	Monark
2	Alfons Rombauts	Belgium	BSA
3	Dave Curtis	Great Britain	Matchless
4	Ron Langston	Great Britain	Ariel
5	Sten Lundin	Sweden	Monark
6	Jan Jansen	Holland	BSA

FINAL (16 Laps)
Posn	Rider
1	Nilsson
2	Curtis
3	Gustafsson
4	Baeten
5	Lundell
6	Sigvardsson

TEAM PLACINGS
1. SWEDEN *Nilsson; Gustafsson; Lundell*
2. *GREAT BRITAIN Curtis; Draper; Langston*
3. FRANCE *René Klym (BSA); Robert Klym (BSA); Jean Cros (BSA)*

1959 BELGIUM, NAMUR, 30 AUGUST

HEAT ONE (7 Laps)
Posn	Rider	Country	Machine
1	Bill Nilsson	Sweden	Crescent
2	Hubert Scaillet	Belgium	Matchless
3	Jeff Smith	Great Britain	BSA
4	Gunnar Johansson	Sweden	Crescent
5	Dave Curtis	Great Britain	Matchless
6	Les Archer	Great Britain	Norton

HEAT TWO (7 Laps)
Posn	Rider	Country	Machine
1	Don Rickman	Great Britain	Metisse
2	Ove Lundell	Sweden	Monark
3	Nic Jansen	Belgium	Matchless
4	Broer Birks	Holland	BSA
5	John Draper	Great Britain	BSA
6	René Baeten	Belgium	AJS

FINAL (11 Laps)
Posn	Rider	Country	Machine
1	Don Rickman		
2	Lundell		
3	Sten Lundin	Sweden	Monark
4	Ray Sigvardsson	Sweden	Matchless
5	Smith		
6	Draper		

TEAM PLACINGS
1. GREAT BRITAIN *Don Rickman; Smith; Draper*
2. SWEDEN *Lundell; Sigvardsson; Lundin*
3. BELGIUM *Jansen; Scaillet; Lucien Donnay (FN)*

1960 FRANCE, CASSEL, 4 SEPTEMBER

HEAT ONE (10 Laps)
Posn	Rider	Country	Machine
1	Don Rickman	Great Britain	Metisse
2	Dave Curtis	Great Britain	Matchless
3	Broer Dirks	Holland	BSA
4	Roger Vanderbecken	Belgium	Truimph

All other Finishers were outside the time limit.

HEAT TWO (10 Laps)
Posn	Rider	Country	Machine
1	Ove Lundell	Sweden	Monark
2	Jeff Smith	Great Britain	BSA

All other Finishers were outside the time limit.

No Final was run as only one team, Great Britain, qualified. Thus, Don Rickman, Jeff Smith and Dave Curtis were declared winners.

1961 HOLLAND, SCHIJNDEL, 27 AUGUST

HEAT ONE (14 Laps)
Posn	Rider	Country	Machine
1	Rolf Tibblin	Sweden	Husqvarna
2	Jeff Smith	Great Britain	BSA
3	Roger Vanderbecken	Belgium	Truimph
4	Ove Lundell	Sweden	Monark
5	John Burton	Great Britain	BSA
6	P Andersen	Denmark	BSA

HEAT TWO (14 Laps)
Posn	Rider	Country	Machine
1	Gunnar Johansson	Sweden	Lito
2	Broer Dirks	Holland	BSA
3	Les Archer	Great Britain	Norton
4	Dave Curtis	Great Britain	Matchless
5	Walter Baeten	Belgium	Matchless
6	Bill Nilsson	Sweden	Husqvarna

FINAL (23 Laps)
Posn	Rider	Country	Machine
1	Nilsson		
2	Smith		
3	Tibblin		
4	Curtis		
5	Lundell		
6	Mogens Rasmussen	Denmark	Matchless

TEAM PLACINGS
1. SWEDEN *Nilsson; Tibblin; Lundell*
2. GREAT BRITAIN *Smith; Curtis; Archer*
3. FRANCE *René Klym (BSA); G Ledormeur (BSA); M Beaumard (BSA)*

1962 SWITZERLAND, WOHLEN, NEAR ZURICH, 26 AUGUST

HEAT ONE (15 Laps)
Posn	Rider	Country	Machine
1	Hubert Scaillet	Belgium	BSA
2	Rolf Tibblin	Sweden	Husqvarna
3	Hans-Peter Fischer	Switzerland	Lito
4	Arthur Lampkin	Great Britain	BSA
5	Guy Bertrand	France	BSA
6	Herman de Soete	Belgium	Matchless

HEAT TWO (15 Laps)
Posn	Rider	Country	Machine
1	Don Rickman	Great Britain	Metisse
2	Bill Nilsson	Sweden	Lito
3	Pierre-André Rapin	Switzerland	BSA
4	E Osterero	Italy	Husqvarna
5	Walter Baeten	Belgium	Eso
6	Gunnar Johansson	Sweden	Lito

FINAL (25 Laps)
Posn	Rider	Country	Machine
1	Tibblin, Lundell, Johansson and Nilsson crossed the line together. So no individual winner was declared		
5	Derek Rickman	Great Britain	Metisse
6	Jeff Smith	Great Britain	BSA

TEAM PLACINGS
1. SWEDEN *Tibblin; Johansson; Lundell*
2. GREAT BRITAIN *Derek Rickman; Don Rickman; Smith*
3. BELGIUM *Scaillet; De Soete; Baeten*

1963 SWEDEN, KNUTSTORP, 25 AUGUST

HEAT ONE (15 Laps)
Posn	Rider	Country	Machine
1	Don Rickman	Great Britain	Metisse
2	Sten Lundin	Sweden	Lito
3	Derek Rickman	Great Britain	Metisse
4	Per-Olaf Persson	Sweden	Monark
5	Torsten Hallman	Sweden	Husqvarna
6	John Burton	Great Britain	BSA

HEAT TWO (15 Laps)
Posn	Rider	Country	Machine
1	Lundin		
2	Jeff Smith	Great Britain	BSA
3	Don Rickman		
4	Ove Lundell	Sweden	Monark
5	Derek Rickman		
6	Arthur Lampkin	Great Britain	BSA

SCORING
From 1963 a new method of scoring was adopted. Instead of two heats and a final, with the aggregate time of a team's best three riders deciding the outcome, a points system came into being.

The overall result was calculated by adding together a nation's best three places in each heat. One point was awarded for first place, two to the runner-up, three for third and so on. Three riders from a nation had to finish a heat for their scores to count. Only teams who finished both heats were classified. The team with the lowest overall score were declared winners. Ties were broken in favour of a rider with the fastest time.

TEAM PLACINGS
1   GREAT BRITAIN – 20 POINTS
    Don Rickman; Derek Rickman; Smith; Burton. (NB: Burton and Lampkin each scored 6 points but Burton's time was quicker in the first heat than Lampkin's in the second).
2   SWEDEN – 22 POINTS
    Lundin; Persson; Lundell; Jan Liljedahl (Husqvarna)
3   BELGIUM – 57 POINTS
    Herman de Soete (Eso); Hubert Scaillet (Metisse); F Slechten (AJS); Roger Vanderbecken (Triumph)

1964 GREAT BRITAIN, HAWKSTONE PARK, 26 AUGUST

HEAT ONE (16 Laps)

Posn	Rider	Country	Machine
1	Jeff Smith	Great Britain	BSA
2	Don Rickman	Great Britain	Metisse
3	Derek Rickman	Great Britain	Metisse
4	Hubert Scaillet	Belgium	Metisse
5	Gunnar Johansson	Sweden	Lito
6	Vic Eastwood	Great Britain	Matchless

HEAT TWO (16 Laps)

Posn	Rider	Country	Machine
1	Smith		
2	Sylvain Geboers	Belgium	Metisse
3	Per-Olaf Persson	Sweden	Husqvarna
4	Herman de Soete	Belgium	Metisse
5	Eastwood		
6	Derek Rickman		

TEAM PLACINGS
1   GREAT BRITAIN – 18 POINTS
    Smith; Derek Rickman; Don Rickman; Eastwood
2   BELGIUM – 34 POINTS
    De Soete; Geboers; Scaillet; Roger Vanderbecken (Truimph)
3. HOLLAND – 90 POINTS
    Broer Dirks (Lito); J Heyboer (BSA); B Hartleman (BSA); Peter Dirks (Lito); R Boom (Husqvarna)

1965 BELGIUM, NAMUR, 30 AUGUST

HEAT ONE (12 Laps)

Posn	Rider	Country	Machine
1	Joel Robert	Belgium	CZ
2	Don Rickman	Great Britain	Metisse
3	Jef Teuwissen	Belgium	Metisse
4	Jeff Smith	Great Britain	BSA
5	Herman de Soete	Belgium	Metisse
6	Vic Eastwood	Great Britain	BSA

HEAT TWO (12 Laps)

Posn	Rider	Country	Machine
1	Robert		
2	Smith		
3	Rickman		
4	Arthur Lampkin	Great Britain	BSA
5	Eastwood		
6	De Soete		

TEAM PLACINGS
1   GREAT BRITAIN – 21 POINTS
    Don Rickman; Smith; Eastwood; Lampkin
2   BELGIUM – 25 POINTS
    Robert; De Soete; Teuwissen; Sylvain Geboers (Metisse)
3   SWITZERLAND – 87 POINTS
    Pierre-André Rapin (Monark); H Fischer (Hedlund); M von Arx (Monark); F Thevenaz (Metisse)

1966 FRANCE, REMELARD, 28 AUGUST

HEAT ONE (16 Laps)

Posn	Rider	Country	Machine
1	Victor Arbekov	Soviet Union	CZ
2	Joel Robert	Belgium	CZ
3	Dave Bickers	Great Britain	CZ
4	Don Rickman	Great Britain	Metisse
5	Torsten Hallman	Sweden	Husqvarna
6	Arthur Lampkin	Great Britain	BSA

HEAT TWO (16 Laps)

Posn	Rider	Country	Machine
1	Bickers		
2	Robert		
3	Arbekov		
4	Ake Jonsson	Sweden	Husqvarna
5	Vic Eastwood	Great Britain	BSA
6	Bill Nilsson	Sweden	Husqvarna

TEAM PLACINGS
1   GREAT BRITAIN – 26 POINTS
    Bickers; Don Rickman; Lampkin; Eastwood
2   BELGIUM – 36 POINTS
    Robert; Roger de Coster (CZ); Walter Baeten (CZ); Jef Teuwissen (CZ); Sylvain Geboers (Lindstrom)
3   SWITZERLAND – 54 POINTS
    Hallman; Nilsson; Jonsson; Gunnar Johansson (CZ)

1967 HOLLAND, MARKELO, 2 SEPTEMBER

HEAT ONE (18 Laps)

Posn	Rider	Country	Machine
1	Paul Friedrichs	East Germany	CZ
2	Joel Robert	Belgium	CZ
3	Vic Eastwood	Great Britain	BSA
4	Roger de Coster	Belgium	CZ
5	Dave Bickers	Great Britain	CZ
6	Ake Jonsson	Sweden	Husqvarna

HEAT TWO (18 Laps)

Posn	Rider	Country	Machine
1	Eastwood		
2	De Coster		
3	Jonsson		
4	Torsten Hallman	Sweden	Husqvarna
5	Jeff Smith		
6	Olle Pettersson	Sweden	Husqvarna

TEAM PLACINGS

1   GREAT BRITAIN – 32 POINTS
    Eastwood; Bickers; Smith

2   SWEDEN – 42 POINTS
    Hallman; Jonsson; Pettersson

3   BELGIUM – 59 POINTS
    Robert; De Coster ; F Slechten (CZ); Jef Teuwissen (CZ);

1968 SOVIET UNION, KISHINEV, 14 SEPTEMBER

Most European countries withdrew from the 1968 Moto-Cross des Nations as a protest at the Soviet Union's invasion of Czechoslovakia. No comprehensive results, or an English language eye-witness account of the competition exist. Six nations participated – the lowest number since the early days of the 21-year-old tournament – and the host country were winners. Both races were won by Paul Friedrichs of the second-placed East German team, riding a CZ.

TEAM PLACINGS
1   SOVIET UNION – 18 POINTS
    Evgeni Petushkov; Leonid Shinkarenko; Arnis Angers; Vladimir Pogrebynak and all rode CZ machines
2. EAST GERMANY – 51 POINTS
3. FRANCE – 54 POINTS

No further details of teams are known.

1969 GREAT BRITAIN, FARLEIGH CASTLE, 7 SEPTEMBER

HEAT ONE (2 Laps)

Posn	Rider	Country	Machine
1	Bengt Aberg	Sweden	Husqvarna
2	Roger de Coster	Belgium	CZ

199

3	Arne Kring	Sweden	Husqvarna
4	Jef Teuwissen	Belgium	Husqvarna
5	Joel Robert	Belgium	CZ
6	Torsten Hallman	Sweden	Husqvarna

HEAT TWO (20 Laps)

Posn	Rider	Country	Machine
1	John Banks	Great Britain	BSA
2	Aberg		
3	De Coster		
4	Teuwissen		
5	Kring		
6	Sylvain Geboers	Belgium	CZ

TEAM PLACINGS

1. BELGIUM – 24 POINTS
   De Coster; Robert; Teuwissen; Sylvain Geboers (CZ)
2. SWEDEN – 27 POINTS
   Aberg; Kring; Hallman; Ake Jonsson (Maico)
3. GREAT BRITAIN – 44 POINTS
   Banks; Dave Bickers (CZ); Jeff Smith (BSA); Keith Hickman (BSA)

1970 ITALY, MAGGIORA, 20 SEPTEMBER

HEAT ONE

Posn	Rider	Country	Machine
1	Ake Jonsson	Sweden	Maico
2	Bengt Aberg	Sweden	Husqvarna
3	Jef Teuwissen	Belgium	Husqvarna
4	Jiri Stodulka	Czechoslovakia	Jawa
5	Otakar Toman	Czechoslovakia	CZ
6	Vic Allan	Great Britain	Greeves

HEAT TWO

Posn	Rider	Country	Machine
1	Stodulka		
2	Allan		
3	Arne King	Sweden	Husqvarna
4	Gerrit Wolsink	Holland	Husqvarna
5	Jan Johansson	Sweden	Husqvarna
6	Sylvain Geboers	Belgium	Suzuki

TEAM PLACINGS

1. SWEDEN – 25 POINTS
   Jonsson; Aberg; Kring; Jan Johansson (Husqvarna)
2. BELGIUM – 48 POINTS
   Teuwissen; Roger de Coster (Husqvarna); Sylvain Geboers (Suzuki); Jaak van Velthoven (Husqvarna)
3. CZECHOSLOVAKIA – 60 POINTS
   Stodulka; Toman; Vlastimel Valek (Jawa)
4. GREAT BRITAIN – 105 POINTS
   Allan; Dave Nicoll (BSA); Andy Roberton (AJS)

NOTES:—
1. Until the late 1960s it was the custom for press reports to include only the first initial of foreign riders, unless they were especially successful. Wherever possible, the Christian name of the rider is given. Where not, only the initial of his first name is included.
2. In the 1970 Moto-Cross des Nations, the reports in the Motor Cycle and in Motor Cycle News do not record the length of each heat in laps. What is known is that in each race, the winner's time exceeded 50 minutes.

MOTO-CROSS DES NATIONS BEST INDIVIDUAL PERFORMANCE

Year	Winning Team	Host Nattion	Rider	Representing	Machine
1947	Great Britain	Holland	Auguste Mingels	Belgium	Triumph
1948	Belgium	Belgium	Nic Jansen	Belgium	BSA
1949	Great Britain	Great Britain	Harold Lines	Great Britain	Ariel
1950	Great Britain	Sweden	John Draper	Great Britain	BSA
1951	Belgium	Belgium	Victor Leloup	Belgium	FN
1952	Great Britain	Great Britain	Brian Stonebridge	Great Britain	Matchless
1953	Great Britain	Sweden	Les Archer	Great Britain	Norton
1954	Great Britain	Holland	Bill Nilsson	Sweden	BSA
1955	Sweden	Denmark	Jeff Smith	Great Britain	BSA
1956	Great Britain	Belgium	Jeff Smith	Great Britain	BSA
1957	Great Britain	Great Britain	Jeff Smith	Great Britain	BSA
1958	Sweden	Sweden	Bill Nilsson	Sweden	Crescent
1959	Great Britain	Belgium	Don Rickman	Great Britain	Metisse
1960	Great Britain	France	Don Rickman	Great Britain	Metisse
1961	Sweden	Holland	Bill Nilsson	Sweden	Husqvarna
1962	Sweden	Switzerland	*No individual winner*		
1963	Great Britain	Sweden	Sten Lundin	Sweden	Lito
1964	Great Britain	Great Britain	Jeff Smith	Great Britain	BSA
1965	Great Britain	Belgium	Joel Robert	Belgium	CZ
1966	Great Britain	France	Dave Bickers	Great Britain	CZ
1967	Great Britain	Holland	Vic Eastwood	Great Britain	BSA
1968	Soviet Union	USSR	Paul Friedrichs	East Germany	CZ
1969	Belgium	Great Britain	Bengt Aberg	Sweden	Husqvarna
1970	Sweden	Italy	Jiri Stodulka	Czechoslovakia	Jawa